RODALE'S ANNUAL GARDEN

Flowers, Foliage, Fruits and Grasses
for One Summer Season

Other Gardening Books by Peter Loewer

The Indoor Water Gardener's How-to Handbook
Bringing the Outdoors In
Seeds and Cuttings
Growing and Decorating with Grasses
Growing Plants in Water
Evergreens: A Guide for Landscape, Lawn, and Garden
The Garden Almanac: For Indoor and Outdoor Gardening
Gardens by Design

with Bebe Miles: *Wildflower Perennials for Your Garden*

RODALE'S ANNUAL GARDEN

Flowers, Foliage, Fruits and Grasses
for One Summer Season

Written and Illustrated by
Peter Loewer

WINGS BOOKS
New York • Avenel, New Jersey

Originally published under the title *The Annual Garden*

Copyright © 1988 by Peter Loewer

This 1992 edition is published by Wings Books,
distributed by Outlet Book Company, Inc., a Random House Company,
40 Engelhard Avenue, Avenel, New Jersey 07001, by arrangement with
Rodale Press.

Random House
New York • Toronto • London • Sydney • Auckland

Printed and bound in the United States of America

Library of Congress Cataloging-in-Publication Data
    Loewer, H. Peter.
      [Annual garden]
      Rodale's annual garden / written and illustrated by Peter Loewer.
        p.   cm.
      Originally published as: The annual garden. c1988.
      Includes bibliographical references (p. 233) and index.
      ISBN 0-517-08926-2
      1. Annuals (Plants)   I. Title.
    SB422.L64   1993
    635.9'312—dc20   92-36480
                                                        CIP

8 7 6 5 4 3 2 1

Contents

Preface

Both writing a book on gardening and growing one's own plants, are activities that closely resemble the fashion industry: It's often July in January. And when dealing specifically with annual plants, in order to guarantee a reasonable number of flowers and a goodly display of foliage by summer not only for the garden but for both photographic subjects and line drawings, it's necessary to begin sowing the majority of the seeds by the first of April. In our Zone 5 climate, where Jack Frost can still glaze the garden as late as May 30, we even start a few of the slower species when the green house eaves are coated with ice and the land outside our windows nothing but a dimpled plain of drifting snow.

It's early April as I write this preface. Most of the plant choices for the book have been made and each entry written. Yet it's dull and overcast outdoors, especially in the garden, and even dull in the greenhouse where benches are lined with plastic trays each holding peat or plastic pots and fiber flats, most of them warm and snug on top of heating cables and covered with panes of glass. They are now a sea of brown with only an occasional hint of green from an early riser. But by the beginning of May green will predominate and hopefully by July each plant will bloom, ready to pose for its picture. You see, a great deal of the gardener's world is still based on belief and trust.

Although all the borrowed photos are credited elsewhere in the book, I owe special thanks for help to the National Garden Bureau, Thompson & Morgan, Clyde Robin, Burpee, *Garden* Magazine of the Royal Horticultural Society, and individual gratitude goes to Elvin McDonald and the Brooklyn Botanic Garden for the use of his slide collection and Joe Seals of the Country Garden for checking my list.

And once again there was a great deal of help from my friends: my wife Jean who continues to provide both support and cleans up the dirt left in my wake; Budd Myers, a master gardener and good friend; my agent, Dominick Abel, for his excellent advice; my editor at Rodale, Anne Halpin, for needed and welcomed corrections to prose; Nancy Land for changing computer word to type; and all the garden friends and cronies who are mentioned in the text.

PETER LOEWER,
Cochecton, 1987.

Introduction

The Oxford American dictionary defines annual as: (1) coming or happening once every year, *his annual visit;* (2) reckoned by the year, *her annual income, his annual taxes;* and (3) lasting only one year or season, *annual plants.* This is a book about annual plants and their place in the garden.

For years because of definition two—with a special emphasis on annual taxes—the plants of definition three have been thought of as being at best transient, weak siblings of the perennials, somehow lacking in character because they germinate, grow, bloom, set seed, and die in one season. A slavish belief that the only annuals available to America are the triple threat of petunias, marigolds, and zinnias hasn't helped, either. This, coupled with the continual swing of the garden pendulum, has brought us the present craze for perennials. Perennials are everywhere, touted as magic plants that once set in the ground can be forgotten except for dividing healthy plants every few years and picking an occasional weed. They are, according to the experts, pure beauty without any responsibility. Most gardeners, though, soon find out that just isn't so: Any garden requires a great deal of physical work. And perennials must be clipped, trimmed, divided, fed, and continually cared for. Then once your garden is designed and the beds and borders planted, you might have to wait for years to see the end result. Perennial gardening is a noble pursuit if the design works but not too happy an experience when it fails.

Not so with annuals. Here the experiments of one year can be either utilized or forgotten by the next spring season. The happy combination of cosmos and cleome that charmed your visitors all summer long can be used again, year after year. Or that miserable corner of your herb garden where the castor beans completely took over and hid all else from view need not be repeated, the lesson has been learned: If the plan and planting of 1988 is unsuccessful, then 1989 can see not only a new plan but an entire new garden.

Most gardeners are unaware of the number of annual plants that are available today (this book lists over 368) and that entire gardens can be planned about these energetic flowering plants. If your thinking is on a grand scale, large beds can be filled with annuals yet if you have only a limited area for a garden, annuals once again fill the bill. Using some of the smaller scale plants there is no plot too small for variety of bloom and color, color that will last most of the summer. It's impossible to achieve the same effects with perennials. Not to mention the variety of color and the unlimited range of flower shapes available. With annuals you can be a quick-sketch artist: The garden is your canvas, the blossoms are your paint.

Annuals also adapt readily to pot and container culture. They can withstand the fluctuations of heat and the lack of water common to pot gardening that perennials will not abide.

If you are watching your pocketbook, the annuals will help you economize. Even after the inflation of the past decade, seeds are still a best buy, most packets giving you more than you'll ever need in one season. And there's no waiting for annuals to bloom: most produce flowers 12 weeks after sowing.

And the flowers! Annuals *are* flowers, producing armloads of bloom. In fact, the more you cut the more most of them bloom.

Kinds of Annuals

When grown from seed perennials exhibit little top growth the first year. Since their life expectancy is for many seasons, they put a great deal of energy into growing sturdy root systems. As I mentioned before, annual plants complete their entire life cycle in one year or less. Most of the plant's energy is channeled to the production of flower factories for the express purpose of manufacturing seed. Perennials are in for the long haul while annuals are opportunists, ready to take advantage of even short spans of temperate weather to germinate, grow, flower, and seed, some of them completing the entire cycle in six weeks or less. Thus the systems used for classifying annuals are based on temperatures needed for germination and healthy growth and bloom.

The first systems were formulated in England and are still in use. They divide annuals into three categories: *hardy, half-hardy,* and *tender.* Many gardeners in the warmer sections of the United States think the designation of "half-hardy" is superfluous, but I've found the term is useful to people who, like me, have long, cool, and rainy springs, where temperatures seem to hover between 35 and 40°F for weeks on end, and April showers are more a truism than a cliche. Most seed companies continue to use all three categories.

Hardy annuals (marked in this book as H) are plants that tolerate a reasonable degree of frost,

and even in the colder parts of the country many of their seeds survive a winter outside and germinate in the spring. The alternate freezes and thaws of late February and March will not harm them, and in fact are often necessary to germination.

Half-hardy annuals (HH) are usually damaged, set back, or killed by continued exposure to frost, but most will stand up to an occasional light freeze and are impervious to endless days of cool, wet weather, a common occurrence of the English climate.

Tender annuals (T) come from the warmer parts of the world and need warm soils for germination. They are immediately killed by frost.

There are many perennial plants, either hardy (usually from a temperate climate) or tender (generally from the tropical parts of the world) that will bloom the first year from seed and are also classified as annuals.

Finally there are a few biennial plants, normally taking two years before they bloom, that will flower the first year if the seed is started early enough and they, too, are included in this book as annuals.

About Latin Names

Although many plants can be identified by their common names, many more cannot. There are, for example, fourteen relatively well-known names for the scarlet pimpernel: adder's eyes, red bird's-eye, drops-of-blood, little peeper, old man's glass eye, old man's weatherglass, owl's eye, John-go-to-bed-at-noon, eyebright, ploughman's weatherglass, red chickweed, shepherd's dial, wink-a-peep, and Tom pimpernel. That list does not contain the variations on the above and the local names that change not only from town to town, state to state, but country to country, or countless others never put to paper. And this is only English. Imagine the confusion that could exist when other languages are brought into the scheme of things.

To avoid such confusion, a system of botanical nomenclature was put into use and Latin became the language. All plants known to man have been given these scientific names—each unique—and they are easily understood throughout the world. Whether in Russia, Japan, England, or Cincinnati, Ohio, and regardless of the language spoken by the individual gardener, *Taraxacum officinale* is the common dandelion and *Oenothera fruticosa* is sundrops. And if you are worried about pronunciation, don't be. Very few people today can speak these names aloud with impunity (the English have rules for Latin pronunciation that are at odds with most of the rest of the world) and you will generally be using them in the written sense alone.

Four terms are in general use: *genus, species, variety,* and *cultivar.* All reference books, most good gardening books, and nearly all catalogs and nurseries—even most seed packets—list the scientific name under the common.

In print, the *genus* and *species* are set off from the accompanying text by the use of *italics. Genus* refers to a group of plants that are closely related, while the species suggests an individual plant's unique quality, or color. Either one of the names often honors the person who discovered the plant. For example, the botanical name given to the poinsettia consists of the genus *Euphorbia,* named in honor of Euphorbus, a physician to a king of ancient Mauretania, and containing over 1,600 species that all, like the poinsettia, contain a milky juice. The species name is *pulcherrima,* meaning most beautiful. The *Genus* has an initial capital and the *species* is all in lower case, although one of the major references for botanical names used in this book is *Hortus Third,* and its authors will, on occasion, begin the species with a capital letter when it has been derived from a former generic name, a person's name, or a common name. I have followed that style.

The *variety* is also italicized and usually preceded by the abbreviation "var.", set in roman type. A variety is a plant that develops a noticeable change in characteristics that breeds true from generation to generation. A *cultivar* is a variation that appears on a plant while in cultivation (and thus could be a change either by chance or design). The term was first introduced in 1923 by L. H. Bailey from *cult*ivated *var*iety, and is distinguished in print by being set in roman type inside single quotation marks. (Strangely enough, many garden writers and plant breeders frown upon the term cultivar as being an ugly sounding word but never object to such cultivar names as: 'Baby Darling', 'Little It', or 'Eenie-Weenie'). It is not necessary for a cultivar to breed true from seed but they often do. Most gardeners and nursery catalogs interchange the terms variety and cultivar with ease in general usage and I often have in the descriptions in this book.

Thus the pretty garden annual called flowering tobacco bears the botanical name of *Nicotiana alata* and the variety or cultivar that has green flowers is called 'Lime Green'.

It should be noted here that many flowers listed in catalogs have scientific names that are woefully out of date. This is because the catalog writers know the public recognizes the name *Lisianthus* but are unfamiliar with *Eustoma* although the second name is correct scientifically. To accommodate both the correct and the popular designations many of the entries in the plant descriptions in this book list more than one name.

More about Flowers, Seeds, and Hybrids

One of the major reasons for having a garden—forgetting about the benefits of exercise and communing with nature—is to enjoy the beauty of flowers. Of course, Mother Nature was not really interested in our likes and dislikes when flowering plants were developed: From her point of view the only reason for the existence of flowers is to manufacture seed and guarantee the future survival of each species of plant. Luckily what attracts the bee, moth, or butterfly is also attractive to our eyes.

All flowers are built around one general plan. Many have succeeded in hiding their similarities by evolutionary changes, but if we look closely enough, the basic parts are there. The following illustration shows the floral organs of a typical flower.

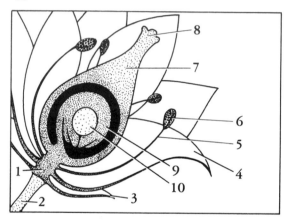

The *receptacle* (1) is attached to the plant stem by a special stalk known as the *pedicel* (2). The receptacle holds the *sepals* (3), which are collectively called the *calyx*. Occasionally sepals are brightly colored, as in tulips and lilies, but usually they are green. Sepals form a protective layer over the *petals* (4), which are usually brightly colored to form the initial attraction for insects, and are collectively called the *corolla*. Inside the corolla there are the *stamens* or male floral organs. The stamens consist of the *filament* (5) and the *anther* (6). The anther is the site of pollen formation. The female floral organ is called the *pistil* and is composed of the *stigma* (7), which receives the pollen and is held by the *style* (8), which in turn is attached to the *ovary* (9), where the *ovules* (10) or seeds develop.

Pollinators, such as the bee by day or the moth at night, are attracted by the color and scent of the flower. Their goal is the nectar produced by the flower. The bee picks up bits of pollen that stick to the hairs on its body, mouth, and legs, and it inadvertently deposits the pollen on flower stigmas. Fertilization occurs and seed production begins. Even grass flowers have the same floral parts, although their petals have all but disappeared because grasses depend on the wind and not on insects for pollination.

Seeds

Seeds for annual plants are usually available as *standards,* where pollination has occurred naturally in the field or as *hybrids,* which are produced by a process of controlling pollination between selected parents, many times by hand. The direct or first generation results of such deliberate crossings are called F1 hybrids by the seed companies and are much more expensive than ordinary seeds simply because of the manual labor required to produce them. The best hybrids take characteristics from both parents and turn out to be more valuable than either. Most of the spectacular annuals are produced by hybridization. Unfortunately, they often will not breed true and must continue to be propagated by asexual means.

The heredity of all living things is controlled by the chromosomes in plant and animal cells. Always busy, plant breeders have found that with applications of a chemical called colchicine, a poison extracted from the autumn crocus *(Colchicum),* they could artificially double the number of chromosomes and raise new plants often superior in the size of the flowers and the vigor of the plants. Such plants are called tetraploids.

Which leads us to the subject of saving seeds for future plantings. Standard seed will breed true, producing new plants just like the parents. Hybrids, however, will not. Each time you cross pollinate hybrids, you step back one generation. After a number of such cross pollinations you arrive back at the beginning with the original parent flower and the new plants lose much of the impressive size and color. After a few summers, the resultant flowers will indeed be unimpressive.

Although found in a mystifying variety of shapes, sizes, and colors, all seeds consist of the *embryo* (1) or baby plant, and the *seed coat* (2) or protective shell.

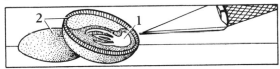

The embryo has a rudimentary stem, one or two seed leaves, or cotyledons, and a tiny root. In addition, the seed stores food in the form of starch, sugars, fats, and proteins. These foods will give the infant plant its start in life.

Germination

In order for the seed to grow, germination must occur and three items are essential: water, a favorable temperature, and oxygen. If any of these things are missing, the seed will not sprout. In addition, after the first three conditions are met, light (or sometimes the lack of it) will play a key role.

Water causes the seed to swell so that it bursts out of the seed coat, and also softens the seed coat making the process a bit easier for the baby plant. Water helps to pass oxygen to the embryo for the life process to begin.

There is also an optimum temperature for seed germination depending on the species. For many crop plants and hardy and half-hardy seeds it is 40 to 50°F while tropical or tender plants usually require 70°F or above.

Finally, many seeds are very small, and if buried too deep in the soil, the seedling will perish before reaching the surface and the sunlight.

These seeds will not germinate without the added stimulation of light.

Seed Dormancy

Many plants that are native to the temperate zone will not germinate until they have passed through a state of dormancy. This procedure protects the plant from sprouting during a January thaw only to expire in a February blizzard. The two most common forms of dormancy are linked to the seed coat, which prevents water from entering, and/or a biological thermostat in the embryo. In some species only one such mechanism exists; others may have both.

If a thick seed coat is the problem, it's easily solved by nicking the seed with a file. Many seed packets will give this advice.

If thermostat dormancy is the problem, it's solved by a process of *stratification*. The seeds are placed in a bed of moist sand or peat moss and exposed to temperatures of 34 to 45°F for several months in an effort to duplicate the temperatures of winter. The family refrigerator works very well and seeds need not be frozen. Commercial seed packets usually note when this process is needed.

Seedlings

The young plant, a seedling, is now emerging from the soil. Before it becomes entirely dependent on food manufactured through its true leaves, the root system develops, and the reserve food supplies in the cotyledons, or seed leaves, is exhausted. At this point, the seedling can exist in a sterile growing medium like sphagnum moss or peat moss, but once the true leaves appear, the plant will require a fertile soil or the application of nutrients through fertilizers.

Chapter One deals with garden design and offers fourteen garden plans to give you a jumping-off point for creating your own annual gardens.

Chapter Two assumes you now have a basic garden plan and are ready to go out into the backyard and prepare the ground.

Chapter Three covers the seed and its progress from germination to seedling and finally to the time plants are set out in the garden. All the equipment needed for successful seed germination is also covered.

Chapters Four through Seven give descriptions of the various annuals including plants for both flowers and foliage.

In the appendixes are lists of suppliers, publications, and seed societies but they are far from complete. If you know of a source not listed—or wish to bring another point to my attention—kindly advise by writing to me in care of Rodale Press, Inc., 33 East Minor Street, Emmaus, Pennsylvania 18098.

CHAPTER 1

Designs for Gardens

There's more to garden design with annual plants than the typical shopping center display of concentric circles of patriotic colors with a flagpole at the center, all surrounded by five acres of steaming asphalt. Pity the poor blue ageratum, the red petunia, and the white begonia, for individually or when used in creative contrast with other flowers, they are attractive plants.

Still, garden design is a personal thing and thank heavens there are unlimited examples of beautiful gardens created by individuals. Inspired gardeners without benefit of any formal training in art or design, have turned many a barren acre of grass into a multi-colored world of grace and beauty. And even the cliche of geometric design can sometimes be successful: at the Shamrock garden at Mount Stewart in Northern Ireland, a giant hand over ten feet long is silhouetted in dwarf red begonias to commemorate the Bloody Hand of Ulster (a tribute to the apparent loser of two Scottish clans, both racing by boat to Ireland, who cut off his hand and threw it ashore to claim the prize) demonstrating that there is always room for the unique.

Basic Guidelines for Good Design

One thing to remember when planning a garden bed, border, or even filling a small concrete container on the back patio, is intensity of color. A flower of gentle blue will be lost when surrounded by dozens of brilliant orange blossoms. Or five red geranium blossoms plunked in the center of a six-foot oval of fiercely yellow marigolds will look more like a dragon's eye than a flower bed.

Color intensity is often tied to climate. The brilliant annuals like marigolds and the tropic vibrancy of the leaves of Joseph's-Coat (*Amaranthus tricolor* 'Illumination') are far more successful under the fiery sun and piercing blue sky of an Arizona desert than in up-state Vermont where they would completely overpower the soft greens of tended lawns and open woodlands. And conversely a shady border of pastel pink Madagascar periwinkles and pale blue Chinese forget-me-nots are more in tune planted with ferns around the fieldstone foundation of a clapboarded farmhouse than a stucco dwelling with a red tile roof.

As for color combinations, I can do no worse than quote from a few of the more successful color combinations worked out by Henry Stuart Ortloff in his 1924 book, *A Garden Bluebook of Annuals and Biennials*:

Use pure deep blues with clear soft yellows, or with scarlet; use creamy white in the combination as a rule.

Clear pale blues with clear pale rose-pink; creamy white or blue-white, or pale yellow, or use all together.

1

With deep red-purple very little is good except paler tints of the same, cream-white, or pale yellow.

Flame pinks with coldest gray-blue, or with cream-white, or both, or alone with a deep green or gray-green foliage.

Pure orange with brown and bronze, and yellow with softest gray-blues or cream white.

Match pure orange with flame orange.

Another color combination to use when gardening in a small area is that of gray, blue-gray, and blue, all of which are colors that when viewed from a bit of a distance increase the apparent extent of the garden by giving the mental suggestion of a blue haze which hides a distant view, acting like atmospheric perspective. Another example of this atmospheric legerdemain is described in Chapter 4, where I varied three colors of different cultivars of cleomes or spider flowers from dark in the rear to light in the front.

In addition to color, always consider final size: a couple of dwarf pink bedding begonias will be overpowered when topped by six sunflowers, each over 3 feet tall. And any discussion of size usually turns to the concept of massing plants in the landscape. Many annual flowers look their best when displayed in the company of others of their kind. While the foliage of a dusty miller (*Senecio Cineraria* 'Silver Dust') is attractive enough in small amounts, the plant really makes a statement when several of them are planted together in the bed or border. The same concept applies to most of the daisies and all of the annual ornamental grasses.

Try to avoid straight lines in your garden: They are never found in nature and (at least to me) are boring to look at—and quite difficult to maintain. A gentle and sweeping curve looks much better and is easier to install and keep up.

Never use garden ornaments that are not in scale with your garden. A small Japanese stone lantern—which can accommodate a candle for evening viewing—would look much better in the average-size garden than a 6-foot marble statue of the Venus de Milo. If you wish to acquire some garden sculpture, keep in mind the specific requirements of your own site. You will find that scaled down ornaments add depth to a garden view rather than overpower it.

Finally, trust your own aesthetic judgment. After all, it is your garden and should reflect your likes and dislikes, not some expert's—and that could include me.

Making a Plan

Before you start any garden—whether from your own design or from suggestions in this or other books—*First, take paper and pencil and sketch a simple map of the area to be developed and planted!* The map need not be complicated or artistic and need not stifle your creativity; it just helps the gardener to arrive at the starting gate with some idea of what's coming down the pike.

Mark the direction of the sun on your plan. One thing that most annual plants want is sun (although some that will do well in partial shade are mentioned in the following chapters). When descriptions call for full sun that means at least eight hours of sunlight; you will not be required to clear an acre of land so the sun can shine from early morning to almost nine o'clock at night. Also many plants that are described as shade tolerant can take full sun in the Northeast. But there are spots even in New England where the summer sun can be deadly if the garden is surrounded by concrete and asphalt and the soil is kept unusually dry. And for gardens in the Deep South or out West, a bit of shade from the afternoon sun can be most beneficial.

Remember as you work on a plan, that annuals are valuable for filling in vacant spaces in the perennial garden, places created when flowering periods have passed or perennials have not yet reached their final size. In the typical perennial garden the first year will see a great deal of open space, the second year the plants start to fill in a bit, and by the third year the plants will reach their highest development. But next comes the fourth year and time to start dividing the plants, and open spaces will be upon us again. So in three of four perennial garden years, the annual plants can be used to great advantage as fillers.

We have a permanent bulb bed that begins to bloom in mid-April and carries through to the middle of May. In order to guarantee future blooming, the leaves must be left to brown and die on their own. But that bed is not left fallow from the start of summer to the end of fall, for it's planted with a wide variety of annuals including a beautiful display of a wild mignonette (*Reseda lutea*) that sparkles next to a group of perennial coral bells (*Heuchera sanguinea*).

Many annuals are easily transplanted and it's often a good idea to keep a separate nursery bed of plants ready to be moved to another location when a dash of color is needed about the yard.

The following fourteen garden designs are presented more for giving you ideas than to be copied exactly (although it's certainly O.K. if you do) and to give some idea of the diversity available when using annuals.

The Corner of Gold Garden

Back in 1922, a little book appeared on the market called appropriately enough, *A Little Book of Annuals* by Alfred C. Hottes. Mr. Hottes, who was with the Department of Horticulture for Ohio State, included a number of garden plans in his book. I am indebted to Mr. Hottes for being one of the few garden writers to embrace the use of

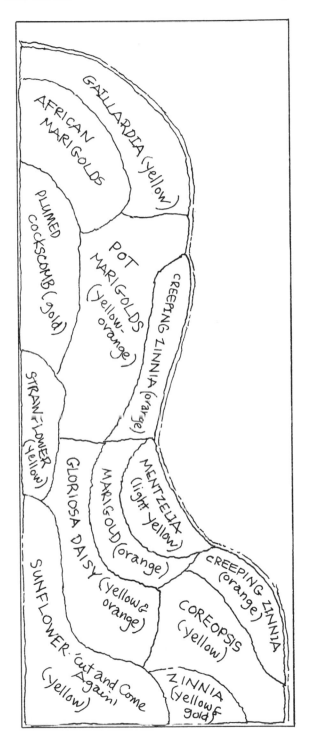

ornamental grasses and for his remark on the use of botanical names: "Do not shun one of these new acquaintances because its name is long—no doubt your name also is long, difficult to pronounce, and with far less meaning."

The following yellow and gold corner was adapted from his plan. The flowers used are common yellow sunflowers (*Helianthus annuus*); yellow or orange gloriosa daisies (*Rudbeckia hirta* 'Gloriosa Daisy'); yellow and gold zinnias (*Zinnia Haageana*); yellow strawflowers (*Helichrysum bracteatum*); yellow coreopsis (*Coreopsis tinctoria*); orange creeping zinneas (*Sanvitalia procum-*

bens); orange marigolds (*Tagetes* spp.); golden plumed cockscomb (*Celosia cristata*); African marigolds (*Tagetes erecta*); yellow-orange pot marigolds (*Calendula officinalis*); yellow gaillardia (*Gaillardia pulchella*); and the light yellow *Mentzelia Linleyi*.

A Border of Six Packets

This annual border is another originally conceived by Mr. Hottes in colors of blue, yellow, and white using only six packets of seed. The design is still valuable but would no doubt require twelve packets today.

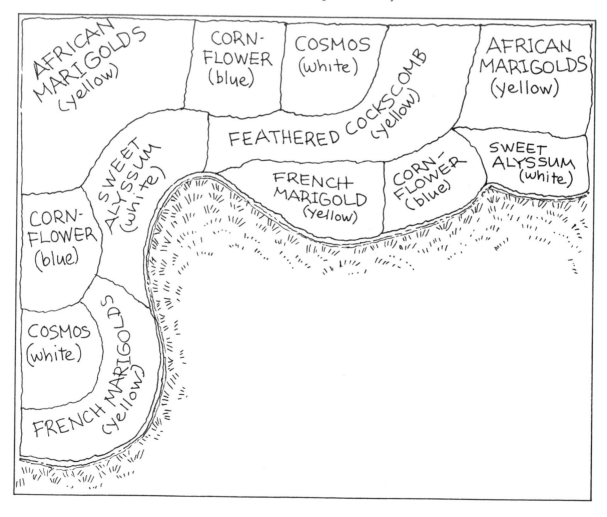

The flowers used are yellow African marigolds (*Tagetes erecta*); blue cornflowers or bachelor's buttons (*Centaurea Cyanus*); white cosmos (*Cosmos bipinnatus*); yellow French marigolds (*T. patula*); white sweet alyssum (*Lobularia maritima*); and yellow plumed cockscomb (*Celosia cristata*).

A Border of Poppies

This free-form border uses a mixture of poppies planted against a hedge or shrub border, and was also inspired by Mr. Hottes. Of the poppy,

Mr. Hottes cut across a torrent of words by simply asking: "Why should we extol the poppy? Why not?"

The flowers used are planted in early spring, late May, and mid-July in order to produce continuous bloom. They are yellow prickly poppies (*Argemone mexicana*); red Shirley poppies (*Papaver Rhoeas*); opium or peony poppies in red, pink, or white (*P. somniferum*); California poppies both golden yellow and white (*Eschscholzia californica*); and yellow Mexican tulip poppies (*Hunnemannia fumariifolia*).

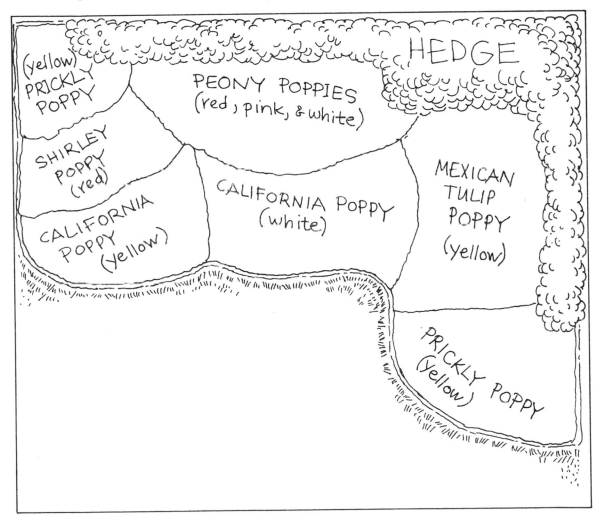

A Blue and Yellow Border

This particular combination of annual plants was originally designed by Mr. Ortloff. It was he who said: "I have read of the so-called 'riots of color' and have always endeavoured to save my gardens from such a calamity, for being a peaceable, law-abiding citizen, I respect law and order even in the gentle art of gardening."

The flowers used are yellow cosmos (*Cosmos sulphureus*); yellow dahlias (*Dahlia* spp.); mignonette (*Reseda odorata*); white nicotiana (*Nicotiana alata*); annual phlox (*Phlox Drummondii*); white sweet alyssum (*Lobularia maritima*); yellow French marigolds (*Tagetes patula*); yellow-orange calendulas (*Calendula officinalis*); yellow coreopsis (*Coreopsis tinctoria*); blue lace flower (*Trachymene coerulea*); blue and white corn flowers or bachelor's-button (*Centaurea Cyanus*); white Cape marigolds (*Dimorphotheca pluvialis* and *D. sinuata*); and white, pink, or blue larkspur (*Consolida ambigua*).

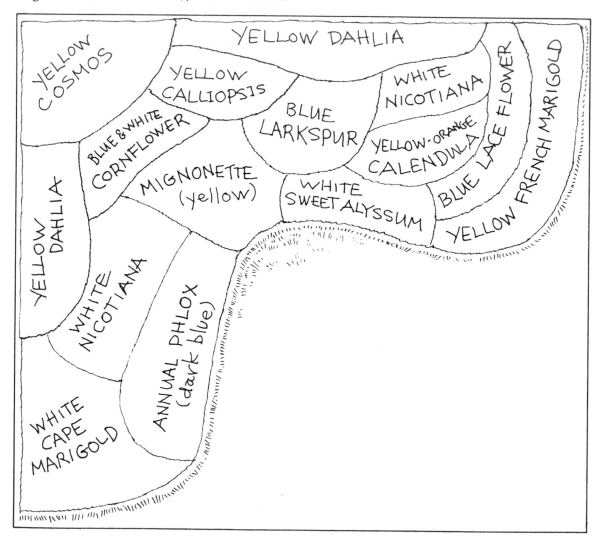

The Fragrant Border

Annuals bring more than color to a garden. The following flowers impart a mixture of sweet fragrance to the summer air. Although the heat of the summer sun at noon will blunt the smell of blossoms, it will once again be drifting upon the air as the afternoon flies by and the sun begins to set.

The flowers are flowering tobacco both pink and white (*Nicotiana sylvestris* and *N. alata*); various colors of sweet alyssum (*Lobularia maritima*); mignoncttc (*Reseda odorata*); blue, rose, or white sweet scabiosus (*Scabiosa atropurpurea*); blue or white floss flower (*Ageratum* spp.); petunias (*Petunia × hybrida*); and for nighttime fragrance, the pink or blue flowers of the evening stock (*Matthiola longipetala*).

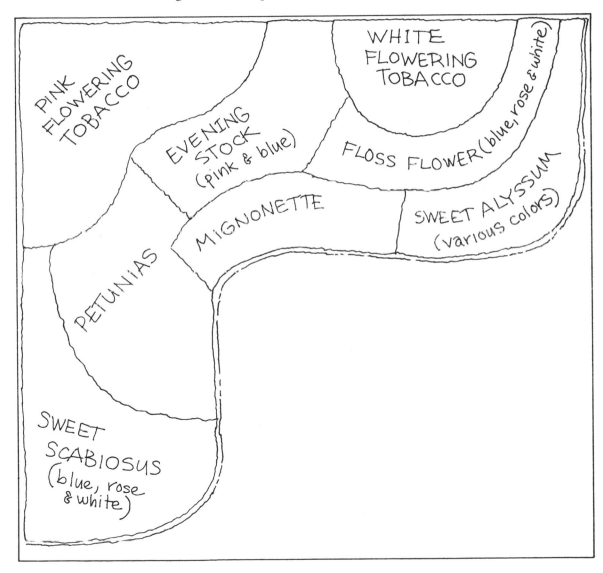

The Night-Blooming Garden

This particular garden is perfect for unwinding at the end of a wearing day. The idea of sitting outdoors, surrounded by plants that have held off blooming for an entire day just to entertain you in the evening is, I think, a fine way to approach the night hours. Two of the plants mentioned are vines and will need a trellis or wires to climb upon.

The flowers are white angel's trumpets (*Datura* spp.); the white flowers of bottle gourd vines (*Lagenaria siceraria*); pastel evening stock (*Matthiola longipetala*); white or pink four-o'clocks (*Mirabilis Jalapa*); white flowering tobaccos (*Nicotiana alata* and *N. sylvestris*); white catchflies (*Silene gallica*); white moonflower vines (*Ipomoea alba*); and white evening primroses (*Oenothera* spp.).

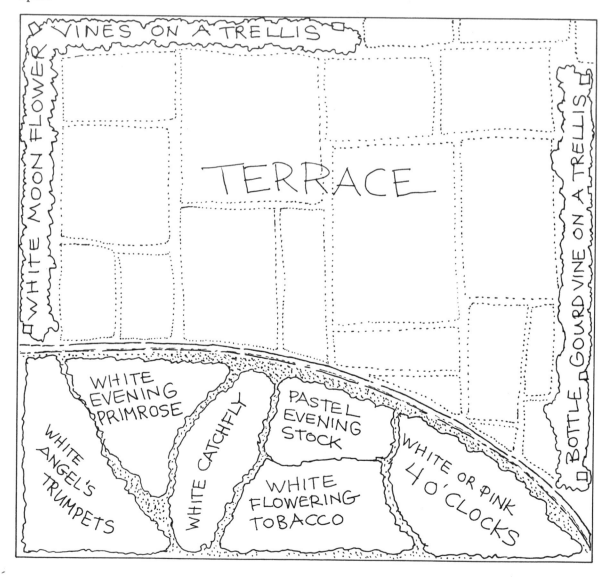

A Garden of Everlastings

What better thing could one do at the end of the garden season than take summer indoors for the winter ahead? Next to digging up plants for the greenhouse or sunporch, a bouquet of everlasting flowers is surely near the top of the list. The following garden plan uses a number of annual plants that bear seedpods or flowers that dry without shattering.

The plants are the yellow-orange safflower (*Carthamus tinctorius*); red, yellow, or pink cockscomb (*Celosia cristata*); purple, rose, lavender, or white globe amaranth (*Gomphrena globosa*); yellow, red, pink, or white strawflowers (*Helichrysum bracteatum*); Swan River daisy (*Helipterum Manglesii*); yellow, blue, pink, or white statice (*Limonium* spp.); green bells-of-Ireland (*Moluccella laevis*); blue, pink, or white love-in-a-mist (*Nigella damascena*); and the tan seedpods of paper moons (*Scabiosa stellata* 'Drumstick').

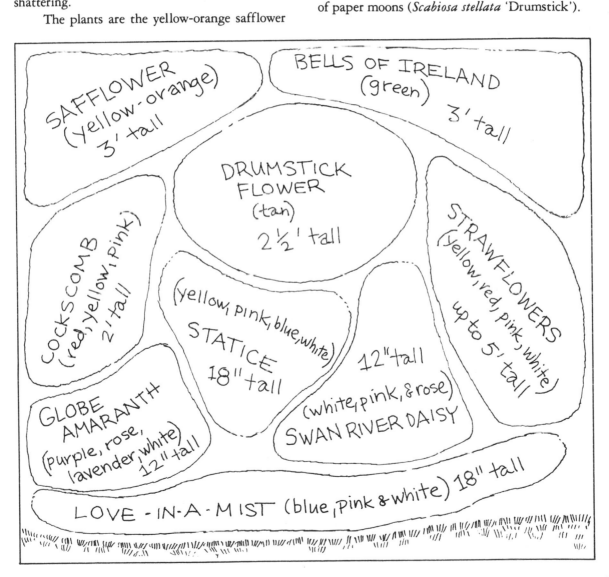

A Garden of Annual Wildflowers

Some of the most beautiful blossoms in the annual garden are wildflowers either in our country or in some other part of the world. The following plan is not formal enough for a place next to a manicured lawn but would be perfect at the edge of a field or wood so the background could be of untrammeled grasses or the entrance to a shady wood.

The flowers are white Bishop's flower (*Ammi majus*); red ribbons (*Clarkia concinna*); orange California poppies (*Eschscholzia californica*); Texas bluebonnet (*Lupinus texensis*); bright yellow blazing star (*Mentzelia Lindleyi*); baby blue eyes (*Nemophila menzeisii*); and scarlet flax (*Linum grandiflorus*).

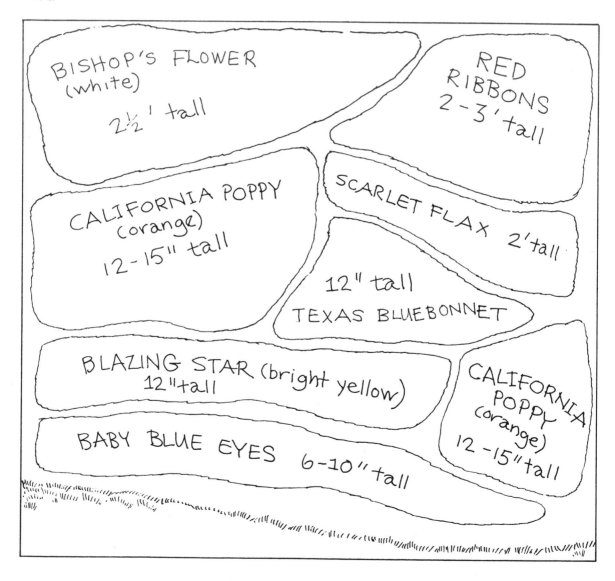

A Garden of Annual Grasses

This planting is to produce cut flowers both fresh and dried. Yes, that's right, use the cut grasses in a bouquet of fresh flowers and you'll be surprised at the charming effect. Like the wildflower garden, it's too unkempt for the formal part of the garden. All the grasses in the plan are annuals and some seeds should be saved for future gardens.

The plants are foxtail millet (*Setaria italica*); quaking grass (*Briza maxima*); brome grass (*Bromus madritensis*); hare's-tail grass (*Lagurus ovatus*); black sorghum (*Sorghum bicolor*); Job's tears (*Coix Lacryma-Jobi*); and broomcorn millet (*Panicum miliaceum*).

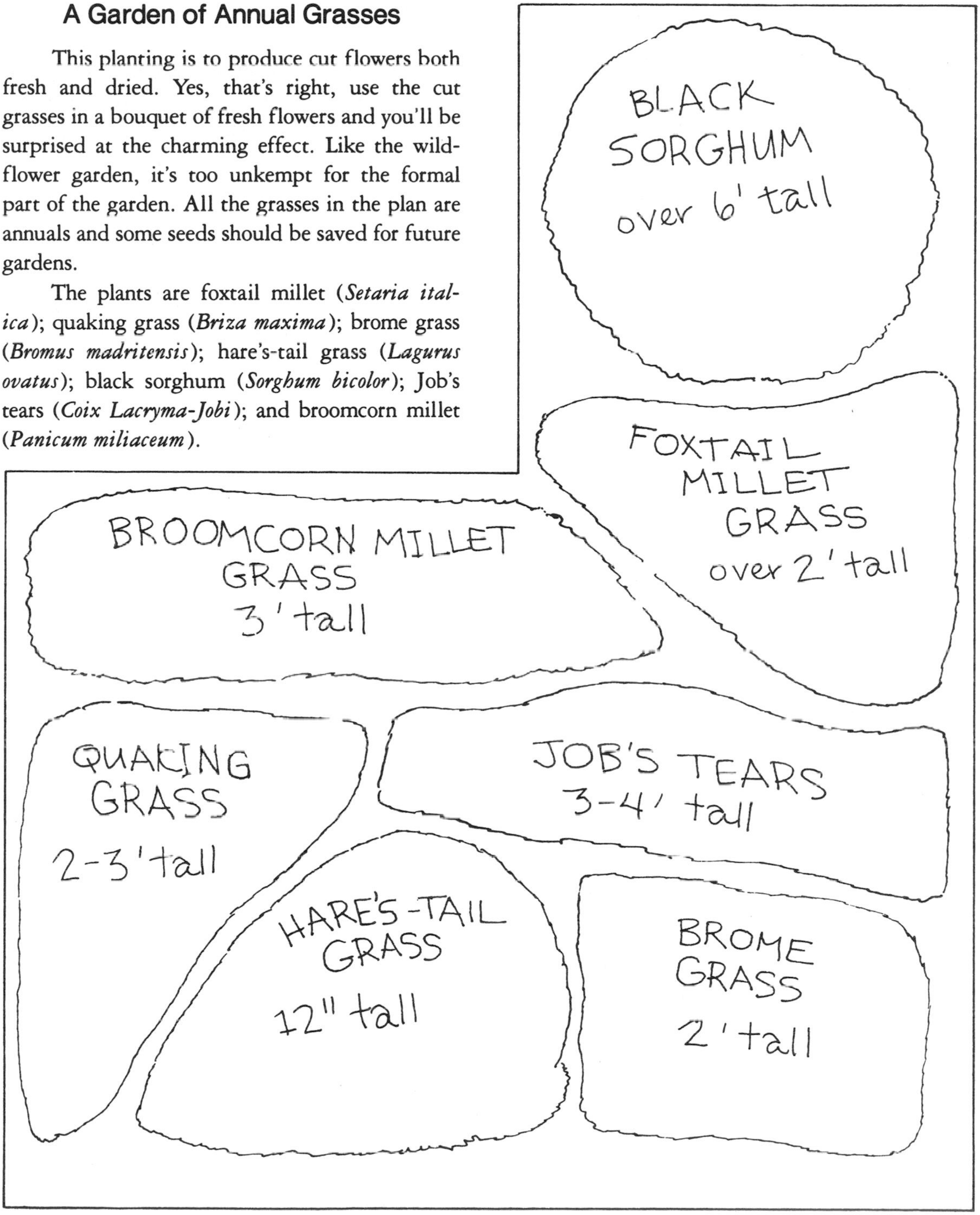

BLACK SORGHUM
over 6' tall

FOXTAIL MILLET GRASS
over 2' tall

BROOMCORN MILLET GRASS
3' tall

QUAKING GRASS
2-3' tall

JOB'S TEARS
3-4' tall

HARE'S-TAIL GRASS
12" tall

BROME GRASS
2' tall

An All-White Garden

A number of all-white gardens have been developed over the years. The first on record was designed in 1833 for the Hon. Ben. Perley Poore, not in England as you might assume, but in Massachusetts. By the beginning of the next century, the great English garden writer, Gertrude Jekyll, had worked in developing such color-theme gardens. But it was Vita Sackville-West who, with her husband, Harold Nicolson, developed the gardens at Sissinghurst in Kent and carried the idea to new heights. Because of the contrast between the white flowers and the green foliage and grass surrounding the beds, an all-white garden is, perhaps, the most successful of the one-color plans.

This garden contains cream-colored pot marigolds (*Calendula officinalis* 'Cream'); white China asters (*Callistephus chinensis*); white cornflowers (*Centaurea Cyanus* 'Snowman'); white spider flower (*Cleome Hasslerana* 'Helen Campbell'); white cosmos (*Cosmos bipinnatus* 'Purity'); white baby's-breath (*Gypsophila elegans* 'Covent Garden'); white candytuft (*Iberis amara* 'Empress'); white rose mallow (*Lavatera trimestris* 'Mont Blanc'); and white zinnias (*Zinnia elegans* 'Purity').

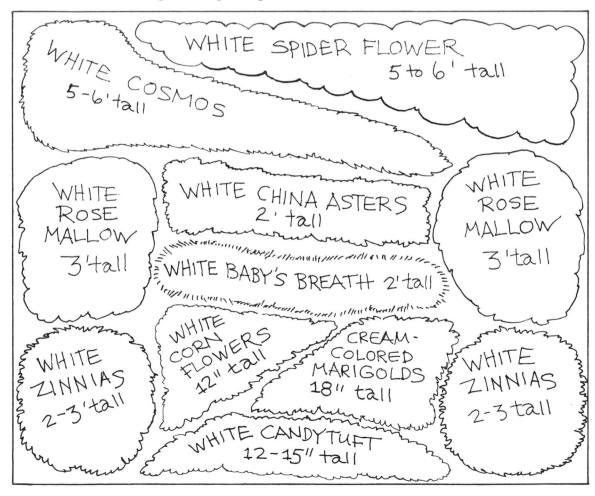

A Garden for Privacy

A garden for privacy has to be flexible to fit a number of different situations so the gardener must adjust the plan below to fit his or her needs. Vines can be grown quite simply on frames made of 2 × 3's using either twine or plastic fishing line for plant supports. Many plants will do quite well in pots so they can be massed together in order to hide a local eyesore from view.

The plants are castor beans (*Ricinus communis*); ornamental corn (*Zea mays* var. *japonica*); Japanese hops (*Humulus japonicus*); Malabar gourd (*Curcurbita ficifolia*); and the white-flowered bottle gourd (*Lagenaria siceraria*).

A Terrace Garden from India

I first thought of designing a terrace garden based on the colors of India after seeing the movie *Ghandi*. The entire garden is grown in pots or tubs so you can move the plants and flowers about, not only to take advantage of the possible move of the sun during the summer, but just to be able to continually change your garden outlook. Thus the flowering plan is easily changed to allow for the idiosyncrasies of your own patio or backyard. To add a bit of dash to the setting, a screen has been built of 2 × 3's and the stretched fabric of an India print.

The plants are castor beans (*Ricinus commu-* *nis* 'Bedding Mix'); two types of scarlet coleus (*Coleus blumei* 'Scarlet Poncho' and 'Salmon Laced Mixed'); red cosmos (*Cosmos bipinnatus* 'Sunny Red'); the silver leaves of dusty miller (*Centaurea Cineraria* 'Silverdust'); bright red or orange canna lilies (*Canna × generalis*); ornamental peppers (*Capsicum annuum* 'Holiday Flame'); the striped and variegated leaves of ornamental corn (*Zea mays* var. *japonica*); scarlet or orange cockscomb (*Celosia plumosa* 'Century Mixed'); brilliant red and yellow Joseph's-coat (*Amaranthus tricolor* 'Illumination'); white angel's trumpet (*Datura Metel*); and hot-colored marigolds (*Tagetes tenuifolia* 'Paprica').

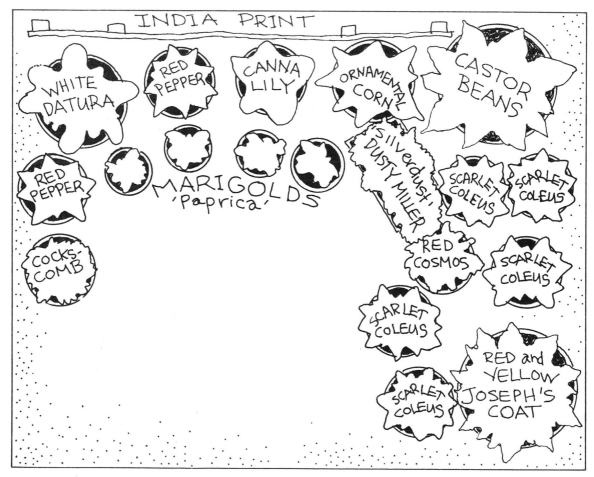

An All-blue Garden

The all-blue flower bed is designed to fit into the corner of a yard. It uses a stand of cleomes in three colors that utilize atmospheric perspective to make the bed look much wider than it is. A few pinks are included to play against the blues. You will be quite amazed to see that a garden border such as this could easily be mistaken for a perennial border.

The plants are spider flowers in three colors (*Cleome Hasslerana* 'Violet Queen', 'Rose Queen', and 'Pink Queen'); champagne grass (*Rhynchelytrum repens*); tree mallows (*Lavatera trimestris* 'Silver Cup'); blue lace flower (*Trachymene coerulea*); cow cockle (*Vaccaria pyramidata* 'Pink Beauty'); butterfly flower (*Schizanthus* 'Morning Mist'); pink baby's-breath (*Gypsophila elegans* 'Shell Pink'); hawk's beard (*Crepis rubra*), Madagascar periwinkle (*Catharanthus roseus* 'Magic Carpet'); and floss flower (*Ageratum* 'Bengali').

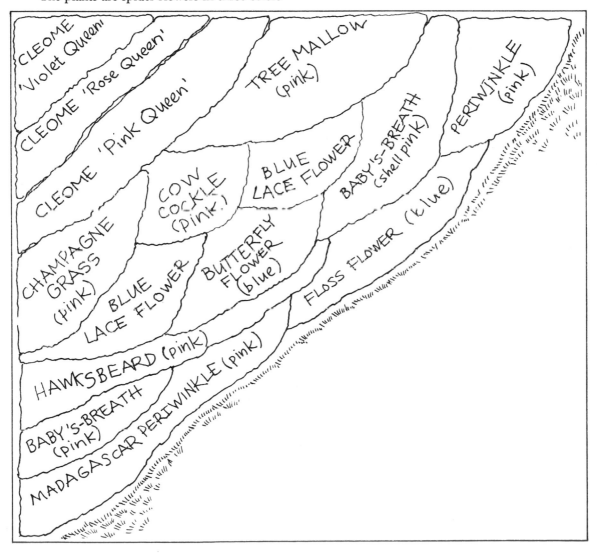

A Garden of Colored Vegetables

A *potager* is a French vegetable garden. For years the French have combined the growing of flowers and vegetables obviously so the people of the house could gather food for both the body and the soul at the same time. I first thought of the following garden design when I saw a picture of summer spinach in the 1987 *Park's Catalog*. The vines were growing up a pole and strings and looked perfect for the centerpiece in a garden of colorful vegetables. In honor of the French, this garden is more structured than the others and follows a strict geometric plan.

The plants used are three of the chards (*Beta vulgaris* 'Ruby Chard', 'Vulcan', and 'Lucullus'); ornamental cabbages (*Brassica oleracea* 'Color-Up'); Malabar spinach (*Basella alba* 'Red Stem'); the cardoon (*Cynara candunculus*); two lettuces (*Latuca* 'Red Sails' and 'Ruby'); two basils (*Ocimum Basilicum* 'Purple Ruffles' and 'Spicy Globe'); and the so-called Easter eggplant (*Solanum Melongena* 'Golden Eggs').

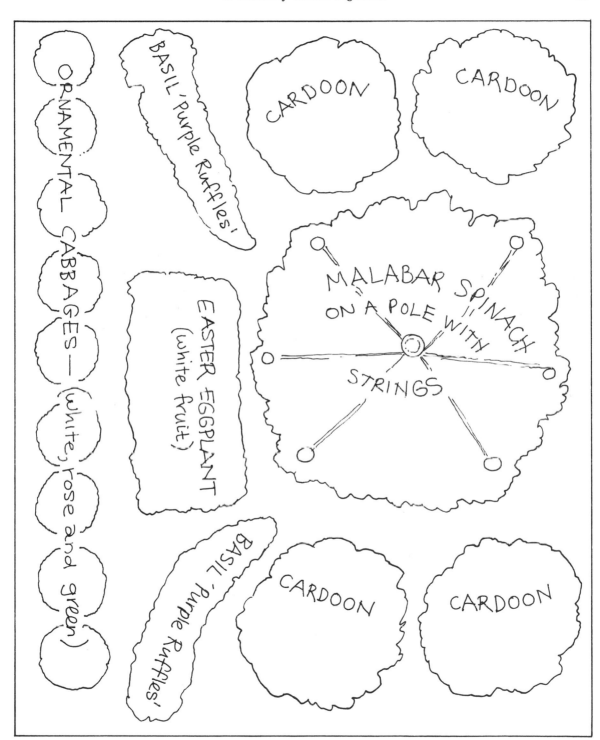

ORNAMENTAL CABBAGES— (white, rose and green)

BASIL 'Purple Ruffles'!

CARDOON

CARDOON

EASTER EGGPLANT (white fruit)

MALABAR SPINACH ON A POLE WITH STRINGS

BASIL 'Purple Ruffles'!

CARDOON

CARDOON

CHAPTER 2

Into the Garden

Just because the plants for the garden are annuals instead of perennials does not mean that site preparation is unimportant. All plants do best when they are settled into the soil of their choice and though it could be considered an anthropomorphic statement, happy with their lot.

Although it's possible to start a new garden from scratch in the early spring, especially when the land has been worked before, the best time is the fall of the previous year. Then the variations of winter temperatures, especially in the areas of Zone 6 and north, can act upon the materials you might add to the existing dirt and help speed up the absorption process.

On Soil and Soil Types

After you have planned your garden and staked out the measurements, it's time to assess the soil. If the area has already been worked and you, the gardener, know its limitations and its values, just skip this part. But if you are new at the garden game, the first thing to do is find out if your soil is solid clay, rich loam, or a combination of both. Is your garden spot well-drained or does water stand in puddles even after a light rain?

Clay soils are sticky, just like modeling clay. If you roll a lump of wet clay soil between your fingers as though rolling a cigarette in a wild west movie and it forms a compact cylinder that does not break up, that's clay. Clay can become rock hard when it is completely dry. Instead of sinking into such soil, water simply rolls to the lowest level and sits. Sandy soils drain immediately; a loamy soil that is rich with organic matter strikes a balance between the other two.

Clay   Sand   Loam

When growing annuals the best thing to do is prepare a garden soil that strikes a balance between all three. It's not that annuals won't grow in poor soil, many will and are noted as such in the plant descriptions. But like any living thing, the better the ambience, the better the performance. And the more organic matter in your soil, the easier it is to water: Instead of sitting on the surface, the bits and pieces of organic matter act as millions of wicks pulling the water down into the depth of the soil.

There are many ways to improve soil. You can add sand, peat moss, or composted manure (fresh manure is too strong for immediate planting so mix it into your soil in late fall or winter or compost it before using). Peat moss is usually available in 4 cubic foot bales, wrapped in plastic at most garden centers. Mix about 10 cubic feet into an area of 100 square feet. When in a hurry I've been known to buy a few 40 pound bags of prepared topsoil and work that into a bed.

Double-Digging

If you've decided where to garden and the area you've picked has never been worked before, read on.

First clear the ground of all existing weeds or grass with a mower or—if you have the strength—a scythe. Rake the result into piles for later use at the bottom of the trenches that you will be digging. The following figure gives the general idea.

Don't use a Rototiller at this point: The idea of double-digging is to replace the subsoil with a better quality of fill, not just to work the surface soil about.

Checking the pH of the Soil

pH is a method of measuring the relative acidity, or sourness, and alkalinity, or sweetness, of the soil. Most plants grow in pH ranges between 5.0 and 7.0. Swamps and bogs that have high percentages of peat are extremely acidic; in humid regions, and most woods and forests, the soil is moderately acidic to slightly alkaline; arid regions go up from a moderate to a strong alkaline content; and desert areas in the Southwest have vast alkali flats.

Most garden centers now stock an inexpensive paper pH tape that can be held against a moist soil sample and will turn colors to indicate

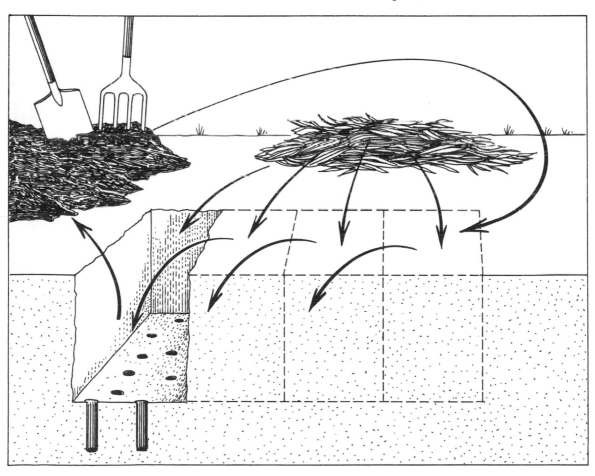

the degree of acidity. Acid soils are usually corrected by the addition of lime. Ground limestone is best to use but it's slow to act and should be added to the soil in the fall before gardening begins. To raise the pH about one unit, add five pounds of ground limestone for every 100 square feet of average soil. If in doubt, call your county extension agent about the quality and character of your local soils. And don't add lime and manure to the soil at the same time. Start the lime first, then wait a few weeks before adding the manure.

Raised Beds

If your soil is truly bad and not worth the effort to improve, try the concept of raised bed gardening. Instead of digging down, mark your area and build it up about 2 feet above the existing ground with railroad ties from the lumber yard—try to stay away from those that have been treated with creosote—or build a wall of concrete blocks or fieldstone, or the first topped by the second. Then fill with purchased topsoil.

If you live on the side of a hill, this idea can be used to build terraces and prevent the rain from washing down the slopes.

Much of our garden is on a hill composed of granite with an overlay of red shale an a sprinkling of larger rocks, with a new crop of rocks appearing after every winter. By building retaining walls of concrete blocks, topped with a finishing layer of fieldstones—hauled back from old stone walls—we've been able to have good soil and perfect drainage, and we don't have to stoop over all the time for cultivation jobs.

Weeding and Mulching the Garden

A week counts out to be 168 hours and a lot can happen in the garden in that much time: Weed seedlings germinate and grow inches high; flowers open, bloom, then die; entire plants can wither or be chewed to smithereens by bugs; and if the gardener doesn't check it all out, disaster can be around the bend. Buy yourself a lightweight gooseneck hoe (not a regular hoe as that's too big for comfortable weeding) and scuffle up the soil around your plants so water can drain through to the roots. Remove the weeds as they appear. If you do it every week you'll keep ahead and you won't miss anything, either.

Next, when the hot sun beats down on your garden, especially during the dog days of August, soils bake and what water there is quickly evaporates. Putting down a garden mulch will both help to conserve water and cut down on your crop of weeds. And a neatly applied layer of mulch looks better between the plants than parched and dusty dirt.

A number of mulches are available about the country, including buckwheat hulls, cocoa husks, corn cobs, garden compost, hay, leaf mold, marble chips, oak leaves (soft leaves like maple will mat), pea gravel, peat moss, pecan hulls, pine bark chips, pine needles, and wood chips.

There is also black plastic film that can be made somewhat more acceptable by covering it with another, more pleasing material from the list above but I always view this item as something created by the oil companies to get even with the organic movement.

Be careful with peat moss because once it packs down it really repels water with a vengeance, so remember to keep it fluffed up.

Watering the Garden

Water does more than slake the thirst of plants. It actually carries oxygen down into the soil and, at the same time, picks up and dissolves nutrients and trace elements from the tiny particles of dirt and organic matter, transporting them in solution to the cells of plants, arriving through tiny hairs that cover the surface of every root. If you live in an area where there is one good soaking rain every week, you will probably never have to water. But most of us live in climates that fluctuate wildly from year to year and if the rains refuse to fall, the hose must make up the difference. And that means watering well, not just sprinkling for a few minutes until only the surface of the soil is wet, but soaking the ground. Light waterings quickly evaporate and stimulate the roots of plants to turn about and reach for the surface, there to dry and die. Deep waterings force roots to grow down where there is always more water to absorb.

Pinching and Dead-Heading

An active thumb and forefinger can be a great gift to a garden by effectively pinching back young plants to encourage bushiness and removing spent flowers before they can go to seed.

When the main stem is pinched back on plants now about 4 inches tall, it stimulates the development of hormones that encourage side shoots to grow, eventually leading to a fuller plant with more blossoms. Although everyone wants flowers as soon as possible, you should remove the first buds on most annuals, especially early in the season. This allows the plants to produce more shoots and leaves thus producing more blossoms down the line.

The same applies to older plants that become tall and straggly as the season wears on. Coleus immediately springs to mind. By cutting them back you will have more attractive specimens and often the cuttings can be used to produce new plants.

Dead-heading by removing dead flowers before they can go to seed also involves hormone production. In this case every time you remove a potential or burgeoning seedpod the plant gets a chemical message to produce more flowers and it will, generally for weeks on end.

Pests and Diseases

There is a dark side to the garden that has little to do with available light: All those creatures who live to feed and wreak havoc on our favorite plants. But there are ways to defend flowers against attack without resorting to those brown plastic bottles with colorful labels and small type warning you to wear rubber gloves when handling.

Pest control begins with good housekeeping: Never allow diseased or decaying plant material to lie about. When weeding, carry your pickings away with you to the compost bin and never leave them in heaps along the border.

Plants in good condition, with enough water, and growing in good soil will resist much that the enemy can do. And don't get overly upset when an occasional leaf is nibbled. Relax, and enjoy the rest.

In our garden Japanese beetles are becoming a bigger trial than they ever were. I pick them off individually and drop them in a can of soapy water, the resulting mix to be buried deeply when the can is full. I also use milky spore disease to infect the grubs and that's cut down a lot on our problems.

Insects like flea beetles and aphids are controlled by spraying with an insecticide derived from the dried flower heads of the pyrethrum daisy (*Chrysanthemum cinerariifolium*), a plant that resembles the common field daisy. The active ingredients are removed from the plants with solvents and the result is a powdered concentrate that is used to formulate the spray. Pyrethrum has one drawback: It is rapidly broken down chemically by the action of light, often in a matter of hours, so it should be applied in late afternoon.

Rotenone is another plant-based insecticide, manufactured from the roots of the tuba root (*Derris elliptica*) and the lancepod (*Lonchocarpus* spp.), but it can cause severe irritation to humans if inhaled. It is sold as a dust and is an extremely potent control for many insect species but the killing action is slow and like pyrethrum, it breaks down in the environment, although not as quickly.

Spider mites bite the dust when confronted with the new insecticidal soaps.

For those gardeners who have the inclination to carry the war directly to the enemy there are firms which now supply the eggs of ladybugs (*Hippodamia* spp.), praying mantis (*Mantis* spp.), and green lacewings (*Chrysopa* spp.), for troops that will wage the war for you.

Holding Up the Garden

Many annuals will grow tall and the upper leaves and large blossoms become too heavy and topple over, especially during summer storms. So it becomes necessary to prop them up. Here are three methods:

1. *Pea-staking* was originally an English method that involves placing branches pruned from trees, upright in an annual bed early in the season. The plants will grow up through the sticks and eventually cover them with foliage. They should be at least 6 inches shorter than the plants. We use birch, wild cherry, and maple from our neighboring woods but even branches from trimmed shrubs can work. The name originated in the vegetable garden where the stakes were used to hold up pea vines.

2. *Cat's-cradle* is the result of putting in four short corner stakes and winding green garden twine across and between.

3. *Bamboo or reed stakes* can be used to support single-stemmed plants, chiefly delphiniums. I gather all the stems of my eulalia grasses in late fall and use them with twistems or plastic clips.

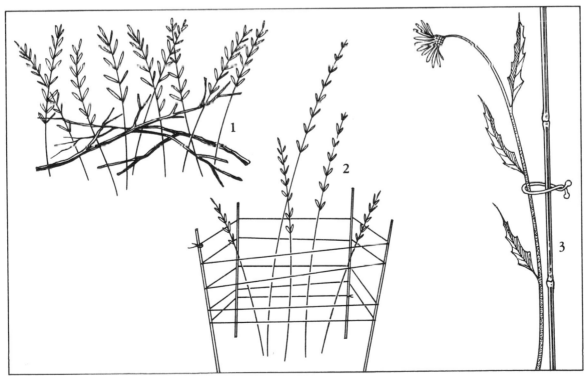

CHAPTER 3

Starting from Seed

When winter winds blow across city streets and country lanes, there is one entertainment I know of—shy of a fully-paid vacation in a tropical part of the world—that will quickly gladden a snow-weary heart: Looking at seed catalogs from both America and England. Page after page of colored pictures will stun your eyes, pictures of flowers either rampant on elegant grounds or flagrantly sprawled about manicured gardens. The specter of greed then takes control and a bedazzled mind wills a weakened hand to order far more seed packets than any gardener could possibly need. But considering the many ways of wasting money in this world, surely ordering excess amounts of seeds is basically harmless.

And ordering early is the thing to do if disappointments are to be avoided for companies quite often run out of seeds. When you imagine the sheer volume of seeds that must be gathered in one year to supply the needs of gardeners in the next, it's a wonder that most nurseries can ever plan ahead. Then take into account crop failures due to weather or insects and disease or all three, and you should begin to marvel that your uncle in Nebraska gets a new cultivar of corn cockle and you get a new poppy from England and a new gardener down the road, a fascinating wax gourd from China.

When the seeds arrive it will usually be a bit too early to plant them, so store the packets in a glass jar on a refrigerator shelf. Do NOT put them in the freezer—4°F below zero is too cold for most seeds. If the shelves are full the next best bet is a cool and dry place. Most of the bigger seed companies use new foil packets that are sealed with a vacuum but many of the smaller firms—and they usually have the most interesting new varieties—cannot afford the packing process.

While most seeds will grow after their second year of storage (and beyond), some lose vitality, especially when left to lie about in the open air. Instead of getting up to 80 or 90 percent germination, you'll wind up with 20 percent or less. It's also a good idea to mark each packet with the date of receipt, since it's very easy to forget.

Check to see if any seeds, whether purchased or collected, need stratification. If indicated, now's the time to start that procedure. Put a slightly moist mixture of sand and/or sphagnum moss in a plastic bag, then open the seed packets and add the seed to the mix. Next tightly close the bag and label as to date and variety. Store in the refrigerator (not the freezer) for six to eight weeks. When the right amount of time has passed, the seeds and medium can be sown as a unit.

Keep Records

It's wise to make a growing chart and individual plastic labels marked in permanent ink with the day of planting, the popular and scientific name, and the projected time of germination, if available. To avoid identification and transplanting problems later on, never put more than one type of seed in a container. If possible, keep some seeds from the package for later sowings in case an unplanned-for emergency arises.

New Products

In order to introduce a new generation of gardeners to growing plants from seed and endeavor to prevent them from making the mistakes that lead to gaining true knowledge, a number of gimmicks have been devised, such as seed tapes where the paper tape is planted and the grower need not pay attention to seed count or proper planting depth, and pelleted seeds where smaller seeds have been coated with clay to make them easier to handle. Both these special "packages" cost more than standard seed packs and to my mind are not worth the additional money when measured against the time and trouble saved in using them.

Saving Seed

When saving your own seeds for the following seasons remember that F1 hybrids are not worth the effort. And very often nurseries have gone to a great deal of trouble to isolate many species to ensure a high quality of seeds. In your garden it will be easier for the standards to slip so don't be disappointed if after a few years, the quality of some species of saved seed falls. But if you do save, always keep your seeds in a cool, dry place. Remember, too, that the longevity of seeds varies with each crop and some seeds like heliotrope or lantana will last no longer than a year in storage. Most good catalogs will point out the short-lived species.

Growing Mixes

I first wrote about growing mixes fourteen years ago and began that particular essay with the line from Marshall McLuhan, "The medium is the message," thinking it clever beyond belief to use such a quote in a book on gardening. Well over the years three things have happened: growing mixes haven't changed, I certainly have, and not many people ever think of Marshall McLuhan anymore.

So the following list of materials that can be used alone or in combinations with each other, has not changed.

1. *Aquarium gravel and bird gravel,* found in pet supply stores and supermarkets, are useful for providing drainage to a mix and easy to find if sand or vermiculite are unavailable. They contain no nutrients.

2. *Humus* is the residue of the compost heap. It is well-decomposed vegetation that is black, sweet-smelling, loose in texture, but must be sterilized to prevent the worst threat to emergent seedlings: Damping-off.

3. *Loam* is the catchall word for good garden soil. It can be used to start seeds but must first be screened or pulverized and sterilized.

4. *Perlite* is made from volcanic rock, commercially cooked in giant pressure cookers. It is sterile. While performing the same function as sand, it's just too light and has no nutrients.

5. *Peat,* sold by bale or bag, is the organic residue of many different kinds of plants that have decomposed in water. Slightly on the acid side, it's very difficult to get wet, and can easily pack down too tightly. It has some nutrient value but should never be used alone as a growing medium.

6. *Peat moss* is partially decomposed sphagnum moss and, like peat and sphagnum, a chore to

moisten if completely dry (use warm water). It will eventually form a surface crust that's quite impervious to water and should never be used alone as a growing medium.

7. *Sand* is one of the main constituents for a good mix. Use builder's or sharp sand, being sure to wash it well. "Sharp" simply means that the sand grains are rough to the touch, as opposed to soft sand, which is too fine to be useful. Beach sand is soft and contains salt.

8. *Sphagnum moss* identifies several different mosses found in bogs and swamps. They grow very slowly, the lower parts gradually packing together to form a compact mass that is sold as peat. Sphagnum leaves are made of long, hollow cells with a fantastic ability to absorb water, and, coupled with their natural sterility caused by a slight antiseptic quality—pads of these mosses have been used for battlefield dressings—they make an exceptional medium for seed germination. Like all peats, they are initially difficult to get wet and if not kept continually moist, will form a tough, surface crust that seems to repel water. Sphagnum is sold both milled and unmilled. Either will work for germination purposes but the milled sphagnum is easier to handle. Note: the dust from dried sphagnums can be very irritating to nasal passages.

9. *Store-bought mixes,* available under many trade names, are generally very good but much more expensive than making your own. But if your time is valuable they can be a good investment. Many have some nutrients added.

10. *Vermiculite* is the lightweight material made from expanded mica and often used for seed mixes. It is sterile, does not pack down, but has a tendency to hold a little more water than the seeds demand. It has no nutritive value.

Any of the materials listed above could be used to germinate seeds; after all, seeds fall in the most unlikely places and manage to survive. Nature, however, can afford to waste thousands of seeds, but obviously we can't.

Damping-off

Damping-off is a disease of seedlings caused by fungus often associated with unsterilized earth and encouraged by the moisture in seed germination mediums. As the seedlings emerge and stretch their stems to the light, the fungus injures the plant tissues at soil level and seedlings then fall over as though chopped through with a microscopic ax; there is no recovery. Chemicals are available to kill the fungus spores but I've found over the years that if your mix and potting materials are clean to begin with, there are no problems. I've lost seedlings three times and each calamity could be traced to unclean mediums.

My Favorite Mixes

Of all the possible combinations for mixes, I've settled on the following two:

1. The first contains 1/3 sterilized potting soil (commercial potting soil can be used), 1/3 milled sphagnum moss, and 1/3 sand. I like this particular combination because I don't have to bother with feeding seedlings with liquid fertilizer before setting them out in the garden.

2. The second mix uses: 1/3 milled sphagnum moss, 1/3 vermiculite, and 1/3 sand. With this mix feeding is necessary after the true leaves appear. Since I've never been up to making manure tea, I use one of the fish emulsions available commercially. Note: Even though fish emulsion is sold as being deodorized, it still has a potent aroma. If mixing a solution, open windows, or preferably move everything outside. Never mix it in the kitchen on a day you are planning to entertain family or friends.

If you plan on using garden compost or soil in your mixes either buy, rent, or borrow a soil sterilizer or—after warning the family of what's up—bake in a 250°F oven for at least two hours. I underline warning because while the smell is not that unpleasant, it is piercing.

Equipment

One of the problems in today's world revolves around affluence: We have too many cars, too many can openers, and often, it seems, too many types of equipment for growing seeds. Some, I admit, are a bit more aesthetic than old margarine cups, coffee cans, foil pans from TV dinners, and cut-down milk cartons, all of which make excellent seed flats (make sure drainage holes are punched in the bottoms), although they cost a bit more than using food packaging left over from last night's dinner.

So for those readers with a thirst for the new, the following containers are available on the commercial market, either as individual items or components of kits:

(1) Flats made of compressed peat, wood fibers, or plastic. They generally come in two sizes, $7\frac{1}{2} \times 5\frac{1}{2} \times 2\frac{1}{4}$ inches or $10 \times 12 \times 2\frac{1}{2}$ inches and stack for storage. Only use these for large sowings of one kind of annual like a flat of petunias. (2) Peat pots both square and round are good for starting those seeds that resent transplanting later on. Often plastic trays are available made to specifically hold a number of these containers. Remember when using peat pots to cut slits in the walls when planting because some roots won't force their way through the peat walls, and never leave any of the top edge uncovered since it acts like a wick taking water from the soil and evaporating it into the open air. (3) Peat pot strips are a series of smaller pots, molded together for ease of handling. (4) Jiffy-7's are small pieces of

compressed peat encased in a thin plastic net. When water is added, the discs expand to 2 inches high and $1\frac{3}{4}$ inches in diameter. Roots penetrate the open sides with ease. They're very handy to have around to start one or two plants. (5) Fertl-Cubes are 1-inch square blocks of compressed sphagnum moss, perlite, and vermiculite with the addition of nutrients. (6) Honeycombed paper pots fit in their own trays and have open bottoms for roots to grow through with ease.

In addition, there are various other combinations of the previous systems, some with self-watering trays and wicks, marketed as complete kits for seed propagation.

Heating Cables

The most important reason that gardeners often have trouble germinating seeds is simply that the seed bed is too cool. While there are many crop plants that refuse to sprout unless subjected to temperatures below 50°F, most annuals will respond to a gentle warmth. Lack of heat works in combination with too much moisture, rotting the seeds before they can sprout. The majority of seeds prefer temperatures between 65 and 80°F.

Far and away the best solution is a waterproof, insulated heating cable. They're sold with or without thermostats. Pay a bit more for the thermostat—it's usually preset to 74°F—just to be on the safe side. Cables vary in length from 12 to 120 feet. A 12-foot cable uses the power of a 40-watt light bulb and at the time of this writing, costs $9.00. This will heat an area of four square feet.

Germination Frame

The following drawing shows a simply constructed seed bed made from locally obtained materials.

(1) ¾ x 4-inch planking. (2) ½ or ¾-inch waterproof plywood. (3) Aluminum nails. (4) Heating cable. (5) Thermostat. (6) Heavy plastic liner. (7) Staples. (8) Sand or gravel filler (even kitty litter could be used).

The cable can be held in place with staples, just be careful not to pierce the plastic insulation on the electric wires. Place the outside rows of the cable 2 inches from the edge of the box. Leave about 3 inches between the adjacent rows. Don't let the cable touch the thermostat, or it will shut off before the soil is properly heated, and don't overlap or cross pieces of cable, since it will prevent even distribution of heat.

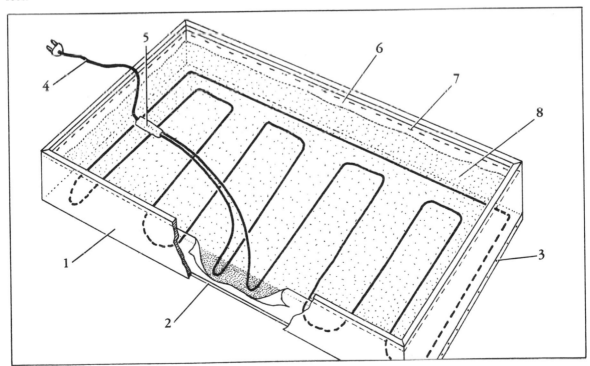

Ready to Sow

It's time to put the mix into your containers. Before starting, measure out the amount of mix you think you'll need and wet it thoroughly. Put it into a large plastic bag and add water—four cups of medium to one cup of warm water should be about right—then knead until the water is absorbed. The medium should be very damp but not so wet that excess water can be squeezed out. Another way is to take the filled containers and stand them in a tray of warm water until enough is absorbed to thoroughly wet the medium.

Let the mix sit for a bit and take the time to write all your labels with clean hands.

Now fill the containers, leaving 1/4 inch of space at the top to allow for free circulation of air. Pat down the mix.

We know that seeds need water for germination, but they also need oxygen from the air for the life processes to begin. If we are too heavy-handed, the mix will be so wet that the seeds will be completely surrounded by water, and no oxygen will be readily available to the embryo plants and they will die. This is the reason why control of watering is so important.

If you are worried about how deep to plant the seeds or if the seed package neglected to give the information, use the following rule to determine the depth at which seeds should be planted: Seeds 1/16 inch or larger should be covered by the thickness of one seed; tiny seeds, like begonias and calceolarias, need not be covered at all but just settled in with a light spray of water from a hand mister. If the seeds need light for germination, do not cover.

Use a pencil to mark off rows, spacing them about 2 inches apart. Now sow the seeds. Gently fold back the mix over the seeds. When sowing smaller seeds, cut the top off the seed packet, squeeze the sides together, and tap with your finger or empty seeds into a folded piece of paper,

tapping it gently as you move it across the surface. Large flat seeds should be placed in the mix vertically so any excess water will not sit on their tops.

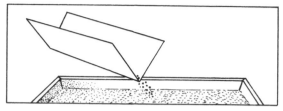

Once the seeds are planted, cover the containers with sheets of glass, plastic, or a plastic food wrap. Be careful to keep plastic wrap away from the surface; a plant label or small stick can act as a tent pole. Drops of moisture will condense (especially if you are using a heating cable) and could form small swamps that will drown the seeds. Or place the containers in one of the new plastic trays that come with an 8-inch high clear plastic cover with vent holes on the top.

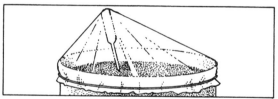

These miniature greenhouses will prevent the medium from drying out—an event to be avoided at all costs. Once germination begins, seeds must never be allowed to dry out or they will quickly die.

Place the containers in your propagation box, or in a warm spot away from the direct rays of the sun. Soon they will want all the sun available, but not until they germinate.

After an initial wait of about five days, check your flats every morning. When the first green shoots appear, note the date on your label and move the container into the direct sunlight (unless you are raising seeds in midsummer, when caution should be taken with the very hot rays of the midday sun; some protection like screening should then be used). Turn the plants daily to keep them from bending to the light. Remove the plastic or glass covering and check on the water needed twice a day at least. When the mix starts to dry, either water from the bottom through the drainage holes or from the top with a mister.

You might ask at this point, why all the fuss about being careful? After all the plants survive in nature. Right, but as noted before, one in a thousand or more survives, not twenty in one flat.

After the true leaves appear above the seed leaves, it's time to add a liquid fertilizer if you are using a medium without nutrients. As mentioned before I use fish emulsion.

You can now transplant to small peat pots or, if leaving the plants in their original flats or container for a while longer, thin them out to at least 1 inch between each plant. Small plants will have to remain in the original containers until large enough to handle.

The pointed end of a knife or a plastic plant label makes an excellent tool for transplanting. Just be gentle! Pick up the plant and lightly cover the roots with soil that is damp, but not mucky.

Five Rules for Proper Germination

1. Don't overwater, since you deprive the seed of needed oxygen.

2. Never let the mix dry out.

3. Use a mister for watering tiny seedlings.

4. Never sow seeds too deeply.

5. Keep seeds out of the sunlight until germination is complete.

Moving Up and Out

Unless you are lucky enough to have a large greenhouse or sunporch to house your seedlings, you'll soon find yourself both running out of

room and needing increased light to prevent the seedlings from becoming too tall and spindly. The answer is an outdoor coldframe, a place to keep the annuals safe from frosts and heavy spring rains.

Nothing fancy is needed, just a few old storm windows or sheets of plastic that will rest on a frame high enough that the seedlings have room to grow. Find a spot where the soil is well drained and in full sun. If you can build a wooden frame, make it about 18 inches in the rear and 12 inches in the front and face it to the south.

Transplanting Out to the Garden

As spring advances the seedlings will once again crowd each other and will again be ready for transplanting either to the garden bed or into pots and containers. Water the soil a few hours before you begin so that small soil particles will adhere to the plant's root system. Try for a dull and cloudy day either in the early morning or, second best, later afternoon.

If the seedlings have been grown in fiber flats the medium can be cut with a knife or carefully torn apart with your hands and set out in its permanent spot. Make a decent planting hole with a trowel or with your hands, and put water in the bottom of the hole.

Hardening-off

The young seedlings have been pampered while in your hands. They have been protected from the sun, wind, and the rain of the real world. As a result, the surface cells of each leaf are tender, much like your skin on that first day at the beach. In order to allow time for these surface cells to become stronger, the young plants will need some protection for the first four or five days in the garden. You can easily make portable lath frames to cover plants, set old screens on a few corner stones, make paper tents, or use one of the new spun polyester shade cloths for protection. This last item is notable because it admits maximum light and water but is so lightweight it won't harm the plants; and it still gives some shade and protection from late spring frosts and chill winds.

Starting Annuals from Cuttings

Many plants considered annuals in the garden are really perennials. Coleus, begonias, impatiens, and garden geraniums immediately come to mind. In addition to starting from seed, these and many more plants will easily grow from cuttings.

If just a few plants are needed, I've found the best method involves a combination of 3-inch peat pots and small plastic food bags. First, choose a plant that needs pruning. Cut healthy stems, about 3 to 5 inches long, with a clean sharp knife or razor blade slightly below the point where a leaf stalk (or petiole) joins the stem. Remove any damaged leaves and flowers and neatly slice off any bottom leaves close to the stem. Fill the pot with moist seed medium and make a hole with a pencil or similar object, to 3/4 of the pot's depth. Insert the cutting, making sure the base of the stem touches the bottom of the hole. Firm the medium back into place around the stem. Now put the whole affair in a plastic bag with the opening at the top.

Now seal the bag with a twist. The bag holds the moisture that the leaves throw off, but cannot replace until new roots form. The medium should be moist at all times, but never soggy. In about two weeks, give the cutting a slight tug to check if rooting has commenced. If not, pull out the cutting and see if the end has started to rot. If all looks well, try again. Make doubly sure that the base of the cutting is touching the rooting medium; it needs the stimulus of this contact to start new roots.

When you wish to root many new plants, use a 6-inch clay pot filled with one of the mixes. Cuttings are inserted and the whole pot is placed in a plastic bag. Check every few days for mold and if found, open the bag's top to allow fresh air within.

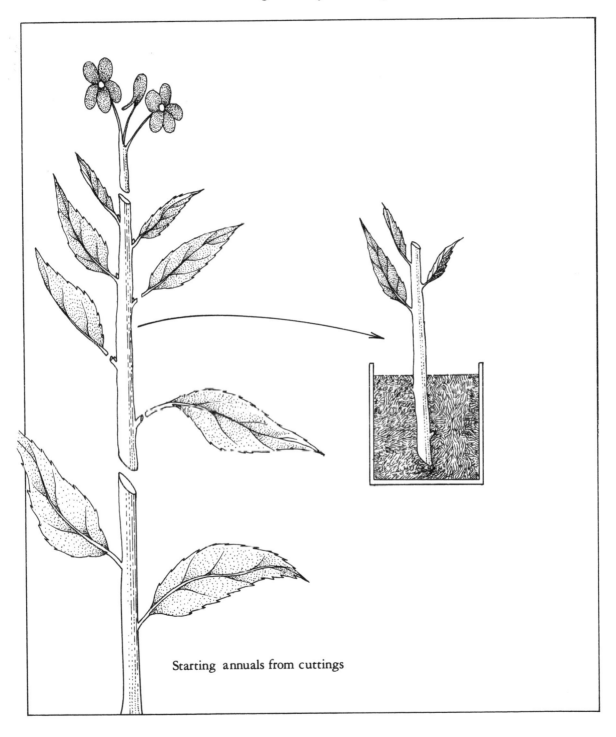

Starting annuals from cuttings

CHAPTER 4

Annual Flowers from A to Z

This and the following three chapters list over 368 annuals in encyclopedia form. The plants have been classified according to their use as flowers, ornamental grasses, vines, and a final chapter devoted to the producers of foliage, fruits, or vegetables.

The entries begin by giving the pronunciation and then the derivation of each of the genuses. Growing instructions are provided along with generalized information about raising the plants from seed and individual specifications if needed. A number of cultivars are also named if they are generally available, and finally the necessary spacing is given for each plant in the garden. These cultivars were taken from catalogs published for the 1987 growing season and should be carried in stock for a number of years. Where available the time needed for germination is also listed. Each entry is accompanied by a line drawing showing the mature flower.

A number of seed companies and seed exchanges are listed in the Appendix. With so many plants, no one seed company is going to carry all of them so you, the gardener, might have to search among the different suppliers and on to the exchanges to find every flower that might pique your interest. But then, that's part of the fun of gardening.

And don't think there are only this many annuals to choose from. In reality there are over 700 more. Richardson Wright, the editor of *House & Garden* for many years during the 1920s and 30s, wrote the following in his book *Truly Rural*:

"Before starting in to raise annuals one should consult an actuary's chart to determine approximately how long he or she has to live. He may strike an average on the longevity of his family. Figuring on this basis, I calculate that there remain forty years to me, barring automobile accidents, plague, and canned salmon. I could raise annuals for forty years. And since there are about ten hundred and eighty-two different varieties of annuals that I would like to try, I could plan to devote my time

35

to twenty-seven of them a year. When I finished the entire ten hundred and eighty-two I would know something about annuals. This would bring me past eighty, after which I could raise my favorites until the summons came.

"Then, when I had climbed up to the Pearly Gates and was being interviewed, I might answer the questions after this fashion:

"St. Peter: Well, old fellow, what have you done to get into heaven?

"I (anxious to play my trump card): Well, I—ah—raised flowers.

"St. Peter: That's good. What kind?

"I (Proudly): Annuals, sir. One thousand and eighty-two different varieties of them.

"St. Peter (reflecting): Ah, yes, annuals! They are a great trouble. You have to plant 'em every year. Well, old fellow, go on inside. You'll find Linnaeus and La Notre and Johnnie Appleseed and the rest of the boys over there planting Asphodels."

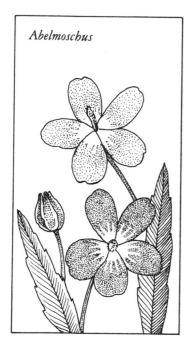

Abelmoschus

Abelmoschus (ab-el-mos'kus) Arabic referring to musky-smelling seeds.

A genus of annual and perennial plants, that include the vegetable, okra (which see). All are from the tropics, boast large flowers and so closely related to *Hibiscus* they are often listed under that name. The first garden flower under this genus is *A. moschatus* 'Mischief' (HH), a new introduction for 1987 with blossoms of red or pink petals fading to a white center, that average 3 inches across on 15-inch high plants. In colder climates start seeds indoors with heat, eight weeks before the last frost. The plants need some 15 days to germinate and will bloom in 100 days of germination. Space plants about 1 foot apart. The correct botanical name for this species has yet to be established.

A. manihot (HH) is a perennial hibiscus that has produced an annual cultivar called the sunset hibiscus 'Golden Bowl', producing 6-inch yellow flowers with a maroon center on plants about 5 feet high. The attractive seed pods covered with silvery bristles are excellent in dried flower bouquets. Start seeds indoors six weeks before the last frost.

Abronia (a-bro'ni-a) from the Greek for graceful.

The sand verbenas include some 25 native American wildflowers of which one *A. umbellata* (HH), is a perennial in its native California but usually grown as an annual elsewhere. Many dealers still call it *Tripterocalyx*. Prostrate, trailing plants bear half-inch pink flowers in 2-inch clusters. They are excellent for rock gardens, for soil must be well-drained. Before starting seeds given them a cold treatment of about six weeks in the refrigerator, not the freezer. Start seeds indoors six weeks before the last frost. Temperatures should range between 25° and 55°F. If you do not purchase acid-scarified seeds, then remove the husk before sowing or soak the seed for 24 hours in warm water. Not all seeds will germinate in 20 days seedlings when small to individual peat pots as they do not move well when mature. Or start seeds outdoors in early spring as soon as the ground can be worked. Set plants 6 inches apart.

Abronia umbellata

Abutilon (a-bu′ti-lon) Arabic name for a mallow-type flower.

Flowering maples—the name is from the maple-like leaf—or Chinese lanterns are only hardy in Zone 9, but make excellent house plants (dig them up before frost, cutting back about half the growth) becoming 6 or 7 feet in height. In the garden they grow about 1 foot high. The usual plant in cultivation is *A. hybridum* (HH) with bell-shaped flowers, about 2 inches across, which come in many colors including yellow, pink, red, and white. Start the seeds ten weeks before the last frost, potting them individually when the true leaves appear. Germination takes about 20 days. Plants will adapt to some shade in the summer months. Depending on the size achieved in your garden, start plants about 1 foot apart.

Abutilon hybridum

Adonis (a-don′is) named for the Greek youth who, when slain by a wild boar spilled blood upon the earth, each drop becoming a crimson flower.

Pheasant's eye is the other name for *A. aestivalis* (H), an annual wildflower from Central Europe, with lacy leaves resembling long green feathers some 15 inches high but easily bending to the ground. The flowers have black centers and are such an intense shade of red that they do look like drops of blood. Plants will take some summer shade and resent very hot summers. Adonis does not transplant well so sow seeds in drifts directly in the garden in early spring after the ground can be worked. Seeds take about two weeks for germination. Stand plants 1 foot apart.

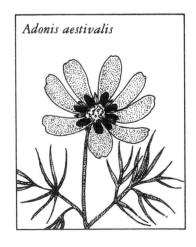

Adonis aestivalis

Aethionema saxatile

Aethionema (e-thi-o-nee′ma) from the Greek *aitho*, to scorch, and *nema*, filaments, referring perhaps to the appearance of the stamens.

Burnt candytuft is the common name for *A. saxatile* (H), a little annual usually found growing in the mountains of southern Europe. Plants are 8 inches high with small pointed leaves on branches arising from a common base and terminal clusters of white, violet, or rose-pink flowers each about ¼ inch wide. The only source for these dainty plants is in a seed list from one of the various rock garden societies but it's worth searching for. They are perfect for growing between rocks or in a scree bed where they will often self-sow. Sow seeds directly outdoors in early spring. Space 3 or 4 inches apart.

Ageratum Houstonianum

Ageratum (a-jur-a′tum) from the Greek for not growing old and probably referring to both the long period of flowering and the flower's ability to keep its color for a long time.

The flossflowers or pussy-foots come from a genus of annual plants known as *A. Houstonianum* (T), originally found in Mexico and Central America. The ¼- to ½-inch flowers are packed in small balls of fluff, forming carpets of color and tolerating light shade in summer. They are very tender, turning black with the first touch of frost. For bedding plants set out as drifts of color they are superb. The colors available now include a number of shades of blue from the palest of soft blues to a deep blue like a twilight sky, many pinks, and of course white. The white however can look a bit fusty because of the contrast between the fresh and the dying flowers. Most cultivars form dwarf mounds but a few can reach 15 inches in height. Flowers are excellent cut for bouquets and small plants may be dug up in fall for houseplants. Start seeds eight weeks before the last frost. They will germinate in five days and bloom in about 65 days. Set plants 6 to 8 inches apart.

Agrostemma Githago

Agrostemma (a-gro-stem′ma) from the Greek meaning garland of the fields.

The corn cockles are annuals native to the Mediterranean region and tossed off by farmers there and in England as a noxious invader of grain fields. In addition its seeds are said to be poisonous. Thus it would seem a back-of-the-border plant at best, especially as the wild form, *A. Githago*, (H) produces stems up to 3 feet high. But the flowers of a soft magenta-rose with overtones of satin deserve better press. Each petal is marked with three dotted-to-solid lines that serve as an insect's guide to the flower center. A cultivar called 'Milas' (named after a small town in Turkey where it was discovered) bears soft lilac-pink flowers often more than 2 inches in diameter and has shorter stems. Corn cockles are excellent cut flowers.

A new cultivar called 'Milas Cerise' with flowers of that color persuasion is now on the market. Sow seeds when the ground can be worked in early spring. Germination is in 12 days. Set plants 1 foot apart.

Ajuga (aj'oo-ga) from the Latin for not yoked and referring to a characteristic of the flower.

Ajuga Chia

The bugleweeds are usually thought of as perennial groundcovers but one species, *A. Chia* (sometimes called *A. chamaepitys* ssp. *chia*) (HH), is an annual from the mountains of southern Europe and is often called European ground pine. It's a leafy, branched plant growing about a foot high with a strong pine-like smell when crushed. Leaves are light green, about 1 inch long. Bright yellow flowers, also about 1 inch long, arise from nodes along the stems. This is a perfect plant for a groundcover in a small rock garden. Start seeds indoors 6 weeks before the last frost. Space plants 6 inches apart.

Alcea (al-see'a) an ancient name for a mallow.

Alcea rosea

Hollyhocks are the beloved members of this genus of flowers and bring to mind cunning cottage doors with picket fences and cherubic children making dolls out of the 4-inch wide blossoms and toothpicks. Hollyhocks are usually biennial in habit but a few cultivars of *A. rosea* (HH) will reach up to 6 feet in height and bloom the first year—and often the second—if started indoors eight weeks before the last frost. These special cultivars are: 'Summer Carnival' and 'Pinafore'. Seeds germinate in 10 days. When the first true leaves appear transplant to 3-inch peat pots. Set plants at least 18 inches apart in the garden.

Alonsoa (a-lon-zo'a) named after Alonza Zanoni, Colonial Secretary for Spain in Bogota, Columbia.

There are some seven species of mask flowers but the one generally found in cultivation is *A. Warscewiczii* (T) a perennial in the

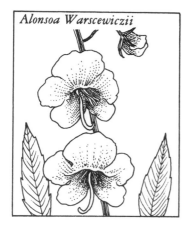

Alonsoa Warscewiczii

Amaranthus caudatus

Amethystea caerulea

mountains of its native Peru but usually treated as an annual elsewhere. Half-inch flowers of reddish orange turn themselves upside down on the twisting flower stalks, a habit perhaps leading to their common name. Because of their original mountain home mask flowers prefer cooler nights and dislike intense heat. Stems are up to 2 feet high. Seeds should be started at least eight weeks before the last frost. Plants may be dug up in the fall and will continue to flower indoors. Set plants 1 foot apart.

Amaranthus (am-a-ran'thus) from the Greek meaning not to wither, referring to the everlasting quality of some species.

Most botanical references list this genus of annual plants as being coarse and weedy, which they are. Some species are also used as food-stuffs both for vegetables and for seeds. Most are grown for their color-ful foliage (see page 152) but two species are known for their colorful flowers. *A. caudatus* (T) is known by the quaint and poetic name of love-lies-bleeding and produces drooping beaded ropes of tiny blood-red flowers often 2 feet long that hang from stems usually 4 feet high. The flowers may be cut and dried but don't hang them upside down. Instead stand the stems upright in a weighted bottle. They also make excellent container plants on a sunny patio or porch. A cultivar 'Viridis' produces flowers of a vibrant green while 'Pigmy Torch' exhibits flow-ers of deep maroon but growing in an upright manner.

The other amaranthus grown for the striking flowers is *A. cruen-tus,* the Prince's feather, which can reach 5 feet. It produces red or purple spikes resembling upright caterpillars of a large dimension. Both amaranths are for the rear of the garden. Start seeds indoors six weeks before the last frost, or plant them directly in the garden but only when nights are warm. Seeds will germinate in ten days. Set plants at least 2 feet apart.

Out of the Old West comes the tumbleweed, *A. albus* (H), occa-sionally listed in seed catalogs as a curiosity, and to quote Chiltern Seeds: "How many plants are there, when dead, will roll themselves up in a ball, detach themselves from the soil, and—at the first suitable wind—bid you a fond farewell?"

Amethystea (a-me-thiss'ti-a) named for the color of the amethyst.

There is but one member in this genus, *A. caerulea* (H), an annual originally from Asia in an area stretching from Turkey to Japan. Square stems up to 18 inches high bear oval leaves with three to five lobes and small flowers about ⅛ inch long which form dense heads of bright blue blossoms. Use this plant in the bed or border. The botanical name is a tautology, that is, it says the same thing twice, since *caerulea* is another word for blue. Plant seeds outdoors in early spring. Germination is in 10 days. Thin plants to stand 6 inches apart.

Ammi (am'mi) an ancient Greek name.

Bishop's weed or white lace flower are the common name for *A. majus* (H), a plant that belongs to the same family as Queen Anne's lace but is a true annual and far more attractive in the garden. The stems are up to 2½ feet tall and bear 5- to 6-inch round flowerheads made up of tiny white individual flowers. They make a beautiful garden picture when massed in the border. Originally from northeast Africa, bishop's weed is now naturalized in parts of North America where it is often used in the cut flower trade. Start seeds indoors in a cool place (55–60°F.) six weeks before the last frost, or sow directly outdoors in early spring when the ground can be worked. Seeds germinate in 15 days. When four leaves develop move the plant to a 3-inch pot. Set plants at least 1 foot apart.

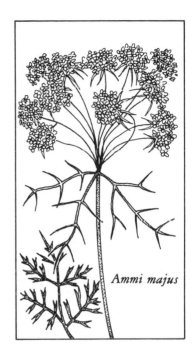

Ammi majus

Ammobium (am-moe'bi-um) from Greek meaning to grow in sand.

Winged everlastings are perennial natives of Australia but one species, *A. alatum* (HH), is treated as an annual. The popular name refers to the form of the stem which looks like a 3-foot-long paper covered wire or "twistem" from a giant plastic trash bag. Look for the cultivar 'Grandiflora', as the flowers are up to 2 inches wide, white with yellow centers, and larger than the common species. Seeds should be started six weeks before the last frost or may be planted outdoors in late April. Set plants 9 inches apart.

To keep as everlasting flowers cut the stems just before the flowers open and hang them upside down in a dry room.

Anagallis (a-na-gal'lis) means delightful in Greek.

Known as The Scarlet Pimpernel (capitalized because of the flower's identification with Sir Percy Blakeney, dandy by day but rescuer of innocents from the French Reign of Terror by night, in the novel of Baroness Orczy) is an annual wildflower native to Europe and

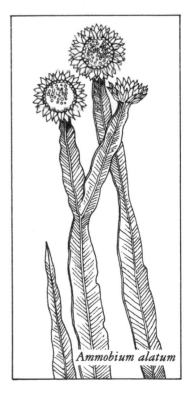

Ammobium alatum

Anagallis arvensis

properly known as *A. arvensis* (H). Other common names of the poor-man's-weather-glass or shepherd's-clock refer to the flower's use as a barometer. The small flowers will close as clouds approach and temperatures drop. They also close at night and you can set your watch (or at least your sundial) as they usually open about 8:00 A.M. and petals fold over for the night by 3:00 P.M. The plants creep along the ground, an excellent choice in an informal rock garden. While not spectacular, they are certainly charming. A blue form (forma *caerulea*) is a species variation and occasionally available. Sophisticated gardeners consider the pimpernel a weed but I, for one, do not agree. Start seeds indoors six weeks before the last frost or plant directly outdoors in early spring. They will reseed.

A perennial species from Zone 8 and south is *A. Monelli* (HH), which is best treated as an annual in most of the country. The flowers are larger than the wild type and of a particularly beautiful shade of gentian blue. Start this species indoors as above. Set 6 inches apart.

Anchusa (an-koo′sa) named for the chemical *anchusin,* used as a red coloring in pigments and dyeing wool.

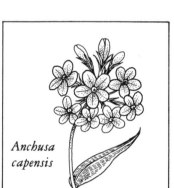

Anchusa capensis

A. capensis (HH) or the summer forget-me-not is a true biennial but is usually treated as an annual. The original plants come from Africa with flowers of a lovely blue, about 1/4 inch wide, growing in clusters on plants 16 inches high. Best used in masses so the color really shines, they will tolerate some shade. They are also excellent in pots. 'Blue Bird' flowers are a deep indigo blue; 'Pink Bird' is, of course, pink, and 'Alba' is white. Start seeds indoors six weeks before the last frost or directly outdoors when frost is past. Cut them back after the first blooming for a second floral show. Germination is in 10 days. Set plants 1 foot apart.

Anethum (a-nee′-thum) from the Latin word for dill.

One of the two species in the genus is *A. graveolens,* the common dill, sometimes living as a biennial but usually acting as an annual. Both the feathery leaves and the seeds are used for seasonings. Although purists would probably disagree, I find that dill makes an attractive addition to the annual garden when its 3-foot high stems are massed at the back of the border. The flat-topped clusters of tiny yellow flowers are also attractive. Start seeds indoors, six weeks before the last frost, using individual peat pots as the plants resent root disturbance. Or plant seeds directly outdoors after frost danger is past. Seeds need light to germinate. Set plants 10 inches apart.

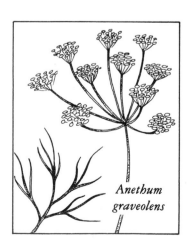

Anethum graveolens

Antirrhinum (an-tir-ry'-num) from the Greek meaning like a snout, referring to the flower's shape.

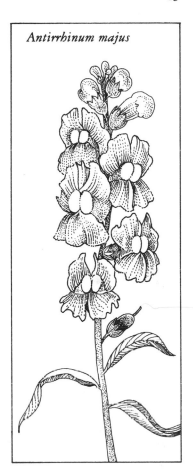

Antirrhinum majus

The common garden snapdragon is so popular it almost ranks with petunias, marigolds, and zinnias. Known as *A. majus* (HH), it is especially valuable because the flowers open from the bottom up, making them excellent cut flowers. Although plants will act as perennials in all but the coldest climates, living through temperatures of 10°F. and above, because of disease problems it's best to start with new plants each year. Snapdragons can be host to a fungus disease that causes rust or orange-colored spots on the leaves, so be sure and buy rust-resistant seeds. The number of cultivars is legion: Colors are many with single and double blossoms, and plants are now available in three heights: dwarf, to 1-foot; intermediate, to 24 inches; and large, growing up to 4 feet depending on the climate conditions in your garden. Because it takes a while for plants to reach blooming size, snapdragons are often purchased at garden centers for a head start. If growing from seeds, start at least eight weeks before the last frost, moving the young plants outside to cold frames as soon as the weather is settled. Seeds sprout in 10 to 14 days and require light for germination. Pinch young plants to make them bushy. Unlike most annuals, snapdragons do not like heavy soils as their roots are very fine, so be sure to add additional compost if your soil is mostly clay. Set plants, depending on final size at least 6 inches apart.

Among the most attractive snapdragon cultivars are: 'Double Madam Butterfly', an F1 hybrid of double blooms in orange, pink, red, and yellow (it has won awards in both England and America); 'White Wonder' with snow-white blossoms on 18-inch stems; and the very beautiful 'Black Prince', with deep crimson blossoms on 18-inch stems.

Aphanostephus (aff-an-os'-tef-us) from the Greek for inconspicuous crown, referring to the moderate size of the flower heads.

The prairie or lazy daisy, *A. skirrhobasis* (HH), is an annual flower and American native from Kansas to Texas and New Mexico. Flower centers are yellow and surrounded by petals that are usually white but can vary to violet or purple, each on a 16-inch stem and about 1 inch in diameter. While not spectacular they will do well in a hot, dry climate and poor soil. Start seeds indoors eight weeks before the last frost. Space plants 8 inches apart.

Aphanostephus skirrhobasis

Arachis hypogaea

Arachis (a′ra-kis) from the Greek for a pea-like plant.

You will need a four month growing season to have any luck with peanuts, *A. hypogaea* (T), a true annual that loves heat. But by starting them indoors even northern gardeners will at least see the yellow flowers, which are quite charming, even if they do not have the chance to make peanut butter in the blender. Either buy seed or use fresh unroasted "nuts," shelled or unshelled, starting them in individual 3-inch peat pots, covering peanuts with one inch of soil. Germination takes 18 to 21 days. Plant them out after frost danger is past, in full sun and a well drained and deeply worked soil. The "nuts" are formed by spent flowers bending down and forcing themselves into the soil where they will grow into peanuts. The plants need a lot of room to develop.

Arctotis stoechadifolia

Arctotis (ark-toe′tis) from the Greek for bear's ear, referring to the shape of minute bristles on the floral head.

The African daisy or *A. stoechadifolia* (HH), is a native perennial of South Africa that is usually grown as an annual. Blossoms are often 3 inches in diameter on 2 1/2-foot stems. Cultivars are available in shades of white, cream, orange, red, yellow, and purple, all with dark centers. Although the blossoms close at night they are excellent as cut flowers. Start seeds indoors six weeks before the last frost. Seeds germinate in 10 days. Space plants 1 foot apart.

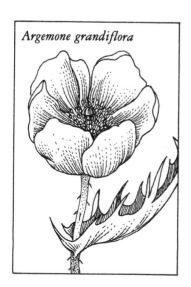

Argemone grandiflora

Argemone (are-jem′o-nee) from the Greek *argema,* a cataract of the eye, for which this plant was thought to be a remedy.

The prickly poppy is one of a number of annuals in this genus from Mexico and the West Indies. *A. mexicana* (HH) grows up to 2 feet with spiny-tipped sea green leaves, producing glorious lemon yellow flowers 2 1/2 inches across. *A. grandiflora* (HH) is a short-lived perennial, taller, to 3 feet, and bears silky textured, white blossoms fully 4 inches across. Individual flowers will not last long but plants produce many over the summer. Since they are originally desert plants they prefer poor but well-drained soil and stand up well to heat. Like all poppies, they develop taproots and do not transplant well. Start plants indoors six weeks before the last frost in individual 3-inch peat pots, or start them directly outdoors after all danger of frost is past. Seeds germinate in 14 days. Space plants 9 inches apart.

Asclepias (as-klee′pi-as) named for Aesculapius, the Greek god of medicine, referring to the supposed curative powers of the poisonous milky juice or latex.

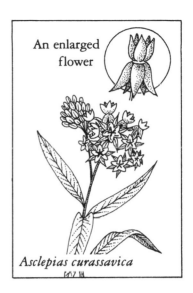

An enlarged flower

Asclepias curassavica

The bloodflower, *A. curassavica* (T), is a perennial in its native South America and is often called a weed over much of the tropics. The individual red and orange blossoms each less than an inch across form umbels—the flowers all begin from a common point—about 6 inches wide. They are far more attractive than the common milkweed of the fields, which is a close relative. The leaves are about 5 inches long, dark green on top and a pale blue-green on the bottom. Plants grow up to 4 feet high and are especially suited for the back of a bed or border. Bloodflowers need full sun but will adapt to dry soil and are excellent plants for hot summer areas. It is only hardy in Zone 8 and south so do not be misled by conflicting claims in seed catalogs. Start seeds indoors in February; they often take a month to germinate. Seeds might need stratification—a process of exposing them to cold for a few weeks—so follow the instructions on the packet. Use individual 3-inch peat pots and move outdoors after all frost danger is past. Space plants 18 inches apart.

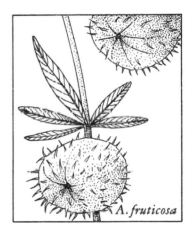

A. fruticosa

Gomphocarpus, *A. fruticosa* (T), is another perennial member of this family that is treated as an annual. It bears small, white flowers that are attractive but not as valuable in the garden as the species listed above. This plant is grown for the pods, each taking the form of yellow to greenish brown balls, and covered with soft, green spikes. Years ago the 3-inch oval pods were very popular in dried flower arrangements and were called Caracas balls. Gomphocarpus are large, spreading plants and best kept in the cutting garden. Start seeds indoors about eight weeks before the last frost. Plant outside after frost danger is past. Although tender in the spring, mature plants will survive fall temperatures of −26°F. Space plants 1 foot apart.

Wild kapok, *A. physocarpa* (HH), is much like gomphocarpus except the pods are spherical in shape and silvery green in color. Grow as above.

Asperula (as-per′-u-la) from the Latin for rough, referring to the leaf surface.

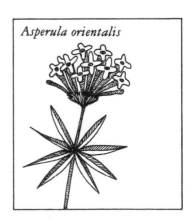

Asperula orientalis

Woodruff, or *A. orientalis* (H), is a branched annual growing to about 1 foot but often tumbling over to creep along the ground. The old name is *A. azurea*. Plants bear small, 3/8-inch long lavender-blue flowers with a sweet fragrance that pop up from a whorl of eight

Baileya multiradiata

Begonia × semperflorens-cultorum

leaves. Woodruff does well in light shade and prefers a moist spot, even by stream or pond. Start plants outdoors as soon as the soil may be worked. Germination takes about 20 days. Space plants 6 inches apart.

Baileya (bay-lay′a) named after American biologists Vernon and Florence Bailey.

The desert marigolds make up a small genus of three species including one, *B. multiradiata* (HH), a perennial wildflower from southern California to Texas that is grown as an annual and is very attractive in a garden setting. Two-inch wide daisy-like blossoms are yellow with yellow centers on 20-inch stems. The petals become papery with age and can be used in dried arrangements. Start seeds indoors six weeks before the last frost. This plant needs well-drained soil and withstands heat. Sheep and cattle are said to be poisoned from eating this plant. Space plants 6 inches apart.

Begonia (bee-go′ni-a) named for Michel Begon, French patron of Botany and once Governor of Canada.

Among the hundreds of species of *Begonia* there is one that is invaluable as a bedding annual and that is called, naturally, the bedding or wax begonia, *B. × semperflorens-cultorum* (T), a hybrid with a confused nomenclature. But the resulting plant is a natural as an edge to a border, massed in garden beds, filling windowboxes or hanging baskets and happy to continue as a houseplant after a season in the garden. These plants usually grow about 6 to 9 inches tall, and have foliage that runs the gamut from a shiny green to maroon and on to chocolate brown. Flowers, either single or double, come in pink, white, or red, and even include a new white with a soft pink edge called 'Red and White Picotee'. They will grow in sun (with plenty of moisture) or shade but need good soil with plenty of organic matter to maintain their fibrous root systems.

In order to have reasonable sized plants for the garden either start seed in January and February or buy plants from a garden center. Seeds are very small and sprout in 15 days; they need light for germination. Many growers mix the seeds with fine sand in order to evenly cast them on the soil's surface. Don't set the plants outside until you are sure the nights will not go below 50°F. Once you have bedding begonias, you can dig up a few in the fall for houseplants and then take cuttings the following spring to provide more plants for the garden. They will bloom almost continually. Space plants 6 to 8 inches apart.

Recent reports from the Royal Botanical Gardens at Hamilton, Ontario, give high marks to 'Othello Improved' as a variety that will withstand summers that are wetter and cooler than normal.

Biscutella (bis-cu-tel'-la) from the Latin bis, double, and scutella, shield, referring to the shape of the fruits.

Biscutella laevigata

Of the 40 some species in the genus, one called buckler mustard, *B. laevigata* (HH), is a short-lived perennial used as an annual in the rock garden. The common name comes from the word buckler, meaning a shield, and refers to the seed pods. The flowers are small, with four yellow petals growing on foot high stems. The interest in the plant rests with the large, double seedpods. Start plants indoors six weeks before the last frost. Space plants 4 to 6 inches apart.

Borago (bore-ray'go) from Old French and Middle English borage meaning hairy, and referring to the leaves.

Borago officinalis

Borage is usually considered an herb and overlooked as the beautiful border plant that it can be. *B. officinalis* (H), also known as talewort and cool-tankard, reaches a height of 2 feet with silvery gray, downy leaves and large drooping sprays of violet-blue five-petalled flowers. A single blossom lasts only a day but is quickly replaced by more. The common name refers to the use of both leaves and flowers to flavor and cool drinks with the taste of cucumber. Bees, too, love this plant. Start the seeds outdoors in early spring where plants are to grow. Seeds sprout in seven to ten days and must be covered because they need darkness to germinate. Borage does not transplant well. Thin the plants to 10 inches apart.

Brachycome (bra-kick'o-me) where brachys means short and kome, hair, in allusion to short bristles on the flowers.

Brachycome iheridifolia

The Swan River daisy or *B. iheridifolia* (HH), is an Australian annual with sweet-smelling daisylike blossoms of white, rose, pink, or lilac about 1 inch wide on foot-high stems. Plants are excellent as edging in the border and bloom throughout the summer. Start seeds indoors six weeks before the last frost or plant directly outdoors when frost danger is over. Plants will bloom in about 80 days germination. Space plants 6 inches apart.

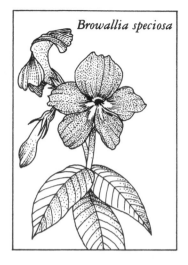

Browallia speciosa

Calandrinia ciliata

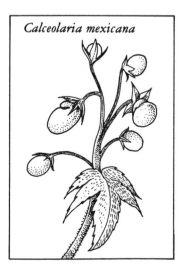

Calceolaria mexicana

Browallia (brow-wall'ee-a) named for Bishop John Browall, a Swedish botanist.

Two species of *Browallia* are generally offered by seed houses: *B. speciosa* (T) and *B. viscosa* (T), both perennials in tropical America. Flowers up to 2 inches wide come in many shades of blue and pure white. These plants are perfect for bedding, where they grow about 14 inches tall, in hanging baskets, and in pots as houseplants. Start seeds indoors 8 weeks before the last frost. Seeds sprout in 15 days and need light for germination. Never overfeed and overwater these plants or you will get leaves instead of flowers. Set plants about 10 inches apart.

Calandrinia (kal-an-drin'i-a) named in honor of J. L. Calandrini, a botanist from Geneva.

The rock purslanes are fine plants for the rock garden or the border. The flowers will close at night and under cloudy skies, but the satiny bright magenta and purple blossoms more than make up for that fault when open. Three species are generally available from seed houses and exchanges. *C. ciliata* (HH), also called redmaids, is a true annual from western North America. Crimson flowers about $5/16$ inch long are borne erect on stems up to 1 foot high. The other two species are really perennials in their native Chile, flowering the first year from seed, and will overwinter in the Deep South.

C. grandiflora (HH) bears light purple flowers 2 inches across on stems up to 2 feet tall, with thin, elliptical leaves. *C. umbellata* (HH) is a much smaller plant only 6 inches high. Start seeds of all three plants indoors six weeks before the last frost. Seeds germinate in about two weeks. Space plants about 6 inches apart.

Calceolaria (kal-see-o-lay'ri-a) from the Latin word *calceolus,* for slipper.

Pocketbook plants or slipperworts are well known flowers for the greenhouse and sold for Easter and Mother's Day, but are generally hard to manage in the garden. However there is one species that is perfect for the garden, a true annual from Mexico and Central America called *C. mexicana* (HH). Pale yellow pouch-like flowers about $1/2$ inch long will cover plants about $1 1/2$ feet high with somewhat sticky foliage from midsummer until frost. Plants look good when bunched and look especially fine when planted next to pastel pinks and blues. They will also take some shade and are beautiful in a woodland garden.

Your first seeds must be sought out from the seed exchanges (see appendix) because I've never seen it available at a commercial seed house. But once you have a plant, you'll never be without because each blossom produces hundreds of tiny seeds. South of Philadelphia the seeds are hardy and will self sow but in our area the seeds should be gathered when the 1/4-inch pods turn a dark tan color. Although seeds can be sown directly outdoors after the last frost, you can get a head start by starting indoors about four weeks earlier. Space plants about 1 foot apart.

Calendula (ka-len′dew-la) has a name from the Italian *calendae*, the first day of the month and when interest was paid at the bank, referring to the plant's long blooming period.

The pot marigold, *C. officinalis* (H), is a true annual once thought to possess wondrous medical virtues and grown in every medieval garden, where plants bloomed from spring to snow fall. It is still used by herbalists. Flowers are up to 4 inches wide and come in a wide variety of colors usually revolving around orange, apricot, cream, and bright yellow. The leaves are long and narrow and slightly clammy to the touch but not unpleasant. Plants reach 18 inches in height and resent overly hot summers, happy for some shade in warm climates. They are beautiful when massed in the garden, cut for bouquets, or grown in pots. Make sure you pick off dead blossoms to ensure continued bloom. Start calendulas indoors six weeks before the last frost, or sow seeds directly outdoors as soon as the ground can be worked. Seeds germinate in ten days and will generally bloom two months after sprouting. Space dwarf varieties 8 inches apart and the tall varieties to 12 inches apart.

Callistephus (kal-lis′tee-fuss) from Greek meaning beautiful crown, and applies to the fruit rather than the flower.

China asters, *C. chinensis* (HH), make a wonderful show in the garden as well as lovely cut flowers, although once cut, the plant will not rebloom. Originally from China, this one known species has been endlessly cajoled by breeders into producing many cultivars. They need good soil and prefer full sun but will do well even in partial shade. The particular cultivar in our garden is 'Giant Princess', which produces a number of mum-like flowers up to 4 inches across on 2-foot stems in colors of amethyst, ruby-red, deep purple, deep pink, pale rose, and creamy white. Start seeds indoors six weeks before the last frost. Plant

Calendula officinalis

Callistephus chinensis

Campanula isophylla

on to 3-inch peat pots when the first true leaves appear. Seeds germinate in 12 days. Make successive sowings over the summer and space plants 10 inches apart. Never plant China asters in the same soil twice, as they are subject to fungal diseases that might overwinter in the soil.

Campanula (kam-pan'you-la) from the Latin for little bell.

Star-of-Bethlehem or falling-stars, *C. isophylla* (HH), are very popular perennial plants for hanging baskets that will bloom the first year. Gardeners before the 1980s had many problems raising this plant from seed and usually resorted to wintering over a few specimens in the greenhouse in order to produce a new crop with cuttings. But now the new 'Krystal White' and 'Krystal Blue' will produce flowering plants. every year from seed and are as easy to grow as geraniums. Flowers are 1 to 1½ inches across and stand above attractive foliage that will spill out and over the sides of containers. Start seed indoors 16 weeks before the last frost and plant out after all frost danger is past. They will start blooming in mid-June.

The spiked bellflower, *C. spicata* (H), is a wildflower of the alps that is an annual or biennial. Stems are up to 20 inches high and bordered with blue flowers along at least two-thirds of the stem. Flowers are especially effective when massed. The oblong, hairy leaves form dense rosettes about 1 foot wide. Start seeds outdoors in early spring. Space plants 8 to 10 inches apart.

Carthamus (kar'tha-mus) from the Arabic word meaning to paint, referring to the excellent color dyes taken from the safflower.

Carthamus tinctorius

The safflower, *C. tinctorius* (H), is a true annual and has many uses including the use of the seeds as the source of low cholesterol cooking oil. Introduced from Egypt over 400 years ago—where it was then extensively used to produce a bright yellow dye—its spiny leaves and 1-inch flower heads of an intense orange are excellent for dried bouquets and in the border or wild garden. Plants are 3 feet high with 2½-inch thistle-like leaves. Start seeds four weeks before the last frost and use individual 3-inch peat pots as these plants resent transplanting. Or start directly outdoors after frost danger is past. Germination is in 12 days. Space plants 1 foot apart. Save seeds for flavoring; their taste resembles saffron.

There is a new cultivar 'Goldtuft' that produces golden-orange flowers.

Cassia (kash'ah) from the old Greek and Hebrew word for this plant.

Cassia fasciculata

The partridge-pea or golden senna, *C. fasciculata* (H), is an American annual wildflower growing about 1½ feet high, bearing leaves reminiscent of a sensitive plant—senna's leaves fold at night—and yellow flowers a little over an inch wide. Although it's now a roadside weed from Maine to Florida having escaped from its original home in the midwest, this is a fine plant for a hot and dry place in the border or the same type of slope in a wild garden. Start seeds directly outdoors as soon as soil can be worked. Space plants 8 inches apart.

Catananche (kat-a-nan'ke) from the Greek word for incentive referring to this plant's ancient use in love potions.

Cupid's dart, *C. caerulea* (H), is a perennial in southern Europe that blooms the first year from seed with 2-inch-wide blue blossoms on 2-foot-high stems with grey-green leaves. With their tall stems they are perfect as cut flowers and will dry beautifully in winter bouquets keeping the lovely color. Start seeds indoors six weeks before the last frost. Seeds will germinate in 20 days. Space plants 9 inches apart.

Catananche caerulea

Cultivars available are: 'Alba', white; 'Major' with flowers of deep violet-blue; and 'Bicolor' with blue flowers edged with white.

Catharanthus (kat-a-ran'thus) from the Greek for a pure, unblemished flower.

The Madagascar periwinkle, *C. roseus* ('T'), for years listed under the name *Vinca,* is a perennial in Zone 9 and above, flowering in the first year from seed. Five-petalled pink, lavender, or white flowers resembling phlox, bloom on plants up to 10 inches high but often prostrate. Periwinkles are perfect for hanging baskets and make a fine groundcover. Plants will take full sun or partial shade. Start seeds twelve weeks before the last frost. Germination takes 15 to 20 days. Seeds need complete darkness for germination. Space plants 1 foot apart.

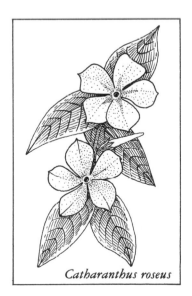

Catharanthus roseus

Celosia (sell-o'si-a) from the Greek *kelos* for burnt, alluding to the flame-like color of some flowers.

The woolflowers are among the most artificial looking of any blossom in the garden. The colors of red, orange, yellow, and purple are truly vibrant, and some of the forms are quite bizarre. One, commonly

Centaurea americana

C. Cyanus

C. moschata

called cockscomb, looks exactly like an alien brain from outer space as imagined in the science fiction movies of the 1950s. Except for winter bouquets and in pots, I find celosias an acquired taste for planting directly in the garden. *C. cristata* (HH) is the usual species offered and comes in three groups: Childsii, with ball-like knobs at the branch ends; Plumosa, where the flowers look like feathers; and Spicata, with flowers in slender spikes. Depending on the cultivar, the height ranges between 8 and 24 inches. All do well growing in pots on a terrace in any good garden soil, and dry beautifully for winter bouquets. Start seeds indoors four weeks before the last frost, using individual peat pots as plants will not transplant well. They also resent being pot-bound so keep potting up if the weather prevents outdoor planting. If planting directly outside, start the plants after frost danger is past. Flowers should appear about 90 days from sprouting. Seeds germinate in 10 days. Space plants 1 to 2 feet apart depending on type.

Centaurea (sen-tor′ree-a) a Greek name in honor of the biennial flower centaury being used to cure a wound in the foot of the centaur Chiron.

Four species of this genus are usually grown for the flower garden: four with flowers and one for foliage (see page 157). For all the following sow seeds directly outdoors. Most germinate in 10 days and bloom eight weeks from seed. Thin to 6 inches apart and make successive sowings during the summer. All are excellent cut flowers.

C. americana (H), the basket flower is one of my favorite annuals and it's hard to understand why more gardeners don't fuss over it. This American wildflower is interesting both in bud and in bloom. Each flower sits atop a 4-foot stem and opens to 4 inches across. The color is light rose and the flower resembles an open thistle without thorns. The common name refers to the unopened head, which is surrounded by soft, spiny, strawcolored fingers that overlap and give the distinctive appearance of tiny woven baskets. They are best at the back of the border because of their height and the fact that blossoms close at night.

C. Cyanus (H) is the beloved cornflower or bachelor's button and comes in colors of white, pink, rose, purple, red and blue. Plants are, except for dwarf varieties, about 1 foot high. Look for the new cultivar 'Frosty Mixed' where blossoms are blue, maroon, pink, or crimson, with contrasting white or pastel tints at the petal tips. Be sure to keep removing the dead flowers to keep plants blooming.

C. moschata (H), called sweet-sultan, comes from the Orient and bears sweet-scented thistle-like flowers about 2 inches across, on 2-foot stems. They resemble cornflowers with fringed petals. Colors are white, yellow, carmine, plum, and pink.

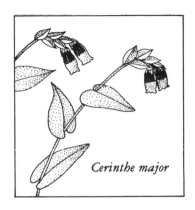

Cerinthe major

Cerinthe (sir-rin'the) from the Greek for wax flower, as bees were thought to gather wax from them.

One species, an annual called *C. major* (H), or honeywort is in cultivation. It's a wildflower from southern Europe and bears 3/4-inch-long, nodding flowers of yellow with a purple rim on 1- to 2-foot stems with light green clasping leaves. Plant seeds directly outdoors in early spring or start indoors six weeks before the last frost. Space plants 6 inches apart.

Charieis (kar-ree'is) from the Greek word for elegant.

C. heterophylla (H) is an annual daisy from South Africa whose flowers are a rich blue with yellow centers. Blossoms are about 1 inch wide on 8-inch stems, and they close at night. Plants need well-drained soil and bright sunlight and are perfect in a rock garden. Start seeds indoors six weeks before the last frost, or plant them outside when the soil can be worked. Space plants 6 inches apart.

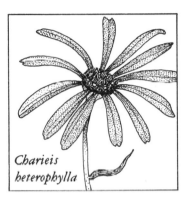

Charieis heterophylla

Chrysanthemum (kris-san'the-mum) from the Greek for golden flower.

Chrysanthemum carinatum

This is a large genus of plants and includes the beautiful bedding plants that favor fall temperatures. The annual chrysanthemums are mostly from the Mediterranean region and for unknown reasons have never been too popular in America. They are beautiful in the garden border alone or mixed with other annuals, bloom most of the summer, are excellent cut flowers, and do well grown in pots for the cool greenhouse. *C. carinatum* (HH), or the tricolor chrysanthemum, grows about 2 feet high with flower heads about 2 1/2 inches across. They are white with a zone of yellow at the base of the "petals" all surrounding a dark chocolate center. Look for the cultivar 'Court Jesters' in colors of red, pink, orange, yellow, maroon, and white.

C. coronarium (HH) is the crown daisy with blossoms 1 1/2 inches across on stems up to 3 feet high. Colors are variations of yellow and white. Crown daisies are used as salad greens in Japan. There are many cultivars available with different color combinations for each of the above species. For both species start seeds indoors six weeks before

Cirsium japonica

Cladanthus arabicus

Clarkia concinna

the last frost, or plant directly outdoors when ground can be easily worked. Seeds germinate in 10 to 14 days. Plants will bloom in about 100 days from seed. Space plants about 1 foot apart depending on the variety.

Feverfew, *C. Parthenium* (H), is a perennial from Southern Europe, now naturalized in America but not always permanently hardy. It can become weedy. Plants grow to 30 inches and bear many white, button-like flower heads ¼ inch wide. The foliage has a strong scent and was used medicinally to reduce fever. Plants will bloom the first year from seed. Start as for *C. coronarium,* but feverfew needs light for germination. Space plants 6 to 12 inches apart.

Cirsium (sir'si-um) from a Greek word for a type of thistle.

C. japonica (H) is a perennial thistle with rose-red flowers about 1½ inches across on 2-foot stems. They are excellent when massed at the back of a border. While not overly fussy about soil, they dislike heavy clay so if that's the condition of your garden, lighten it up with compost for this plant. Start seeds directly outdoors when the ground can be worked for plants that will bloom by late summer.

Cladanthus (kla-dan'thus) from the Greek for branch and flower, referring to the flowers at the ends of the branches.

There is one species in this genus, *C. arabicus* (H), from Morocco and Spain, with yellow daisy-like flowers some 2 inches across blooming from the tip of each branch. This plant is sometimes called, for no reason I can fathom, the Palm Springs daisy. The lacy leaves have a strong but not unpleasant smell. Plants may grow to 2½ feet and are quite attractive when massed. These flowers need good drainage and full sun. Sow seeds directly outdoors as soon as the ground can be worked. They will germinate in four weeks and bloom twelve weeks later. Space the plants 1 foot apart.

Clarkia (clark'i-a) named after Captain Lewis Clark of the Lewis and Clark expedition.

Satin flower, *C. amoena* (H), is a most beautiful American annual from the Rocky Mountains. It is generally a free bloomer in cooler climates but is quite unhappy where the weather is hot. Satin flowers do beautifully in our Catskill Mountain home. The ruffled flowers, up to 2 inches long, are borne on wiry stems up to 3 feet tall. They are perfect for cutting. Cultivars of many colors are now available including white, cream, yellow, rose, pink, and salmon. Plants will become topheavy and might need staking. Start seeds directly outdoors when the soil can be worked, thinning to 9 inches apart. Will flower in 90 days from seed. Seeds germinate in five days. Satin flowers are said to make excellent pot plants in a cool greenhouse.

    C. concinna (H) or red-ribbons is another beautiful wildflower in this family from California. Treat as above.

Cleome (klee-o'me) is a name of uncertain origin but used by the Greek, Theophrastus, who wrote about plants c. 250 B.C..

    Spider flower, *C. Hasslerana* (H), gets its name from the spider-like flowers with long, waving stamens. Later in the season the seed pods are also attractive. Planted in large masses, cleomes look like blooming shrubbery with 8-inch balls of blossoms. Plants like full sun but will take partial shade. They can reach 6 feet in a good growing season and make a striking statement when massed in large groupings and will also do quite well in dry soil. Start seeds indoors four weeks before the last frost or plant them directly outdoors in spring although frost can damage them. They will often seed themselves. Seeds germinate in 10 days. Space plants at least 1 foot apart.

    In our annual border I used the following cultivars with the darkest color to the rear: 'Violet Queen' is a vivid purple; it was followed by 'Cherry Queen', a bright carmine rose; next came 'Pink Queen'; and in the front went 'Helen Campbell', a glistening white. The result was a study in atmospheric perspective that made the border look twice as deep as it really was.

    C. lutea (H) or the yellow bee plant is a native American annual from California and Colorado, reaching 3 ½ feet with yellow flowers.

Cnicus (ny'kus) From the Latin for a thistle-like plant.

    There is but one member of this genus, *C. benedictus* (H), an annual plant from the Mediterranean region, known as the blessed thistle, Our Lady's thistle, or sometimes incorrectly as sweet sultan (which see) as the flowers are remotely similar. Plants are about 2 feet high with leaves toothed and wavy and sporting spiny margins. Blessed thistle is not meant for a garden with children. Both stems and leaves are covered with silvery hairs. Spiny buds open to thistle-like flowers of yellow, not beautiful but interesting. Once used as a tonic and a cure for gout, this plant is best in a hot, dry, area, and looks good in front of a stone wall preferably facing to the south. Start seeds outdoors in late spring. Space plants 10 inches apart.

Cleome Hasslerana

Cnicus benedictus

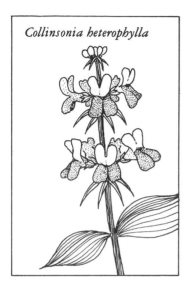

Collinsonia heterophylla

Collinsonia (kol-lin-so′ni-a) in honor of Zaccheus Collins, Vice President of the Philadelphia Academy of Natural Sciences during the 1800s.

The one annual usually found in catalogs from this genus is *C. heterophylla* (H), or Chinese houses. The popular name is rather far fetched, but there is a resemblance between the whorls of flowers blooming on the stem and the shape of a pagoda. Each flower is about 1 inch long with two deeply cleft lips, the upper white and the lower lavender or pink. They occur on stems about 2 feet high. Chinese houses are very attractive plants for both the border and grouping in beds. Like Clarkias, these flowers resent heat so don't bother with them if your climate is hot. Plant directly outdoors when the soil can be worked. They are said to be excellent pot plants in a cool greenhouse. They prefer a well-drained soil and a little shade from hot summer sun. Germination takes 14 days. Thin to 6 inches apart.

Collomia grandiflora

Collomia (kol-lo′mi-a) from the Greek for glue, alluding to the seeds which are sticky when wet.

C. grandiflora (H) is an American annual from Southern California east to the Rocky Mountains. I first found out about it from the Royal Horticultural Society in their annual seed exchange. A bunch of light apricot-colored flowers, each less than an inch long, sit atop strong stems up to 2 feet high. They are an effective plant in the border but dislike hot weather. Start seeds indoors four weeks before the last frost. Germination is in ten days. Space the plants 6 inches apart.

Consolida ambigua

Consolida (kon-sol′i-da) from the Latin to make solid, referring to healing properties originally associated with this genus.

The larkspurs were once lumped in with the delphiniums but now have a genus of their own. *C. ambigua* (H) is a beautiful plant looking more like a perennial than an annual. They grow up to 5 feet tall with many blossoms usually an inch long, covering the stems. Cultivars now offer single and double flowers in colors of pink, light blue, dark blue, lilac, violet, and white. Grow them in the mixed border and at the back of the border. They make excellent cut flowers. Both seeds and leaves of larkspur are said to be poisonous. Start seeds indoors six weeks before the last frost but use small peat pots because these plants resent transplanting; soil should never fall away from the roots. Best is to plant directly outdoors in early spring. Seeds need complete darkness to germinate taking about 20 days. They will bloom about 100 days from seed. Space plants 10 to 12 inches apart depending on the type. Taller varieties may become topheavy with blossoms and may need staking.

Convolvulus (kon-voll′view-lus) from the Latin meaning to entwine.

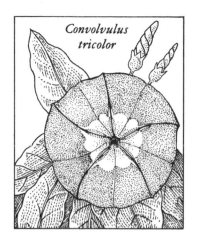

Convolvulus tricolor

The bush morning glory, *C. tricolor* (HH), doesn't climb like the typical morning glory or *Ipomoea* (which see) but merely gets about 1 foot tall and then spreads, making it perfect for a hanging basket or the edge of a wall. The plants are constantly in bloom with flowers like their climbing brethren but smaller, about 1½ inches wide. Each flower comes in three colors: the outside edge and most of the petal is blue, pink, or purple, then comes a white area descending to a yellow center. The flowers are usually open all day. They resent transplanting so start the seeds in individual 3-inch peat pots, nicking the seed with a file to hasten germination. Put two to a pot, discarding the weaker seedling later. Space plants 12 inches apart.

Coreopsis (ko-ree-op′sis) from the Greek for bug, referring to the shape of the fruit.

Coreopsis tinctoria

C. tinctoria (H) is perfect for bedding, or edging the border, and it makes a great cut flower. Daisy-like flowers about 1¼ inches wide bloom most of the summer. Cultivars available now provide colors of yellow, mahogany, red, pink, or purple, either solid or banded. Plants need good drainage and will tolerate poor soil. Start seeds indoors six weeks before the last frost or plant directly outdoors in early spring. Germination takes five to ten days. Space plants 8 inches apart.

Cosmos (kos′mus) from a Greek word for beauty.

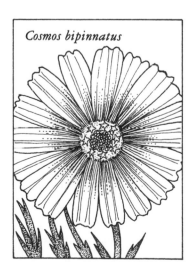

Cosmos bipinnatus

Cosmos daisies, *C. bipinnatus* (T), have been in every garden we've ever had both for show and for cutting. Plants produce all summer long and even the lacy foliage looks good in the border. Blossoms are between 3 and 4 inches wide on top of stems that grow up to 6 feet in a good growing season. Yellow centers are surrounded by pink, red, crimson, or white petals. Plants tolerate poor and dry soil but need excellent drainage. Too much nitrogen in the soil produces rank foliage and holds flowering back until early fall, so don't use fertilizers with these plants. Taller types will need staking. Start seeds

Cotula barbata

Crepis rubra

Cuphea ignea

indoors four weeks before the last frost or plant directly outdoors when frost danger is past. Germination usually takes six days. Space plants about 1 foot apart depending on the variety.

For something new in the cosmos line, look for 'Sea Shells' with petals that curve in on themselves like delicate denizens of the deep or 'Candystripe' with white petals edged with crimson.

C. sulphureus (T) is the yellow cosmos and is also available in many cultivars including both single and double flowers but doesn't grow as high as the type.

Cotula (kot'you-la) from the Greek word for cup, describing the clasping leaves at the flower base.

The pincushion flower, *C. barbata* (HH), comes from South Africa. This is another charming annual perfect for edging the garden bed or border and perfect in the rock garden. Plants grow about 9 inches high bearing little yellow tufted flowers about ¹/₃ inch across. Start seeds indoors six weeks before the last frost or plant directly outdoors when frost danger is past. Space plants 4 inches apart.

Crepis (creep'is) from the Greek word for slipper, but no one apparently knows its application with this plant.

Hawk's beard or *C. rubra* (H) is an annual that looks somewhat like a pink dandelion with flowers about 1¹/₂ inches across on foot high stems. I planted it last year in a tight mass in front of a dwarf willow tree and behind an edging of pale blue lobelia (which see), making a lovely combination. The plants will do well in poor and dry soil. Start seeds indoors six weeks before the last frost or plant directly outdoors in early spring. Germination takes five to seven days. Space plants 6 inches apart.

Cuphea (kew'fee-a) from the Greek word for curved, referring to the curved calyx of some plants in the genus.

C. ignea (HH) is a perennial from Mexico called the firecracker plant or the cigar flower, and is a very popular houseplant. Few gardeners realize what a great plant it is either for the edge of the border and a summer pot plant, hanging or on the patio. Red tubular flowers about ³/₄ inch long have a black and white tip that is supposed to resemble cigar ash, but one wonders just how much tequila was imbibed to inspire that description. Start seeds indoors 8 weeks before the last frost. Seeds germinate in 10 days and require light. Since they are really an everblooming shrub, they make an excellent border but need a good and well-drained soil. Space plants 9 inches apart.

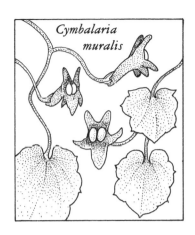

Cymbalaria muralis

Cymbalaria (sim-ba-lay′ri-a) from the Greek for cymbal, alluding to the rounded leaf shape.

Kenilworth ivy, *C. muralis* (H), is a perennial plant that will bloom the first year from seed. It is a creeping plant, with small scalloped leaves and lilac-blue flowers ³/₈ inch long and resembling tiny snapdragons with two little yellow eyes. Although it can become weedy that is never a real problem in colder climates, although it often reseeds itself. This is a wonderful plant for growing in and along walls where the stems grow in and out of crevices, rooting at the nodes. This plant is not generally available commercially. The best source is a friend who owns a greenhouse where Kenilworth ivy does become a weed, or the seed exchanges. A number of cultivars have been developed. Start seeds indoors six to eight weeks before the last frost. Space plants 8 inches apart; they will quickly fill in.

Cynoglossum amabile

Cynoglossum (sin-o-gloss′um) from the Greek for dog's tongue, alluding to the shape of the leaves.

The Chinese forget-me-not, *C. amabile* (H), is a biennial that blooms the first year from seed. Blossoms of a fine blue, ¹/₄ inch wide are borne on 2-foot branches. Plants are especially fine when grouped and the myriad flowers really show up and will tolerate some shade. They can self-sow and become weedy but are easy to remove. Start seeds indoors six weeks before the last frost or plant directly outdoors as soon as the soil can be worked. Germination is in five to ten days and seeds need darkness to germinate. Space plants 9 inches apart.

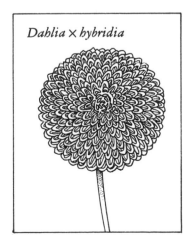

Dahlia × hybridia

Dahlia (dahl′ya) in honor of Andreas Dahl, a Swedish pupil of Linneaus.

Dahlias are tender perennials originally from Mexico. The plants grow from tubers and outside of Zone 10, must be dug up in the fall or treated like other annuals and allowed to die with the frosts. *D.× hybridia* (T) is the botanical name and refers to the fact that so many cultivars are now in existence that the original plant has long faded from view. Growing dahlias is a job in itself and the American

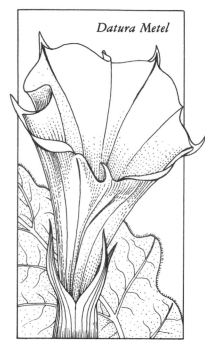

Datura Metel

Dahlia Society now recognizes twelve different groups based on the structure of the flower head. Many types, however, will bloom the first year from seed.

Dwarf dahlias can be used as edging in a garden while the larger types are either massed according to individual color or mixed with a color definite scheme in mind. They are excellent cut flowers (singe the stem end over a flame after cutting). Most plants stay under 2 feet in height although a new cultivar, 'Showpiece', is said to reach 4 feet. Blossoms vary from 2 to 3 inches in width. Colors run the gamut except for blue. Plants need a fertile, deeply worked soil, well-drained, and in full sun.

Start seeds eight weeks before the last frost. Set seedlings outside when frost danger is past—the slightest frost will kill the leaves. Space the plants at least 10 inches apart depending on the type.

Datura (dah-toor'ra) from the Hindu name for this genus.

The thorn apple family of plants contains two species for the annual garden. The first is called angel's trumpet. *D. Metel* (T), an annual from Southwest China and the source of *scopolamine,* a drug used as a sedative and extremely dangerous. Trumpet-shaped yellowish white flowers, the outside washed with a chalky purple tint and often 8 inches long, hang down on a plant up to 5 feet high. Single- and double flowered cultivars are available, both with a heavy, sweet perfume and opening in late afternoon or evening. Start plants six weeks before the last frost using 3-inch peat pots with two seeds in each pot, removing the smaller seedling. Germination takes 10 to 12 days. Daturas will flower in 14 weeks from seed and do well in pots on a terrace. Plants will need soil that is good but not too rich or you'll get leaves instead of flowers. Plants like some shade during hot afternoons. Plants can be up to 5 feet in diameter so space them at least 2 feet apart.

The second thorn apple is the native American plant, *D. Stramonium* (T), the jimson weed, and source of *hyoscyamine,* a drug that acts as a heart stimulant and is known to kill cattle. Flowers are off-white, lasting but one day but soon followed by more until the plant is cut down by frost. Once again, these plants are poisonous.

Delphinium (dell-fin'ee-um) from the ancient Greek name of the larkspur.

Two perennial delphiniums, *D. cardinale* (T) and *D. grandiflorum* 'Blue Butterfly' (HH), are worth the trouble of sowing early for first year bloom. The first is an American native from California, has

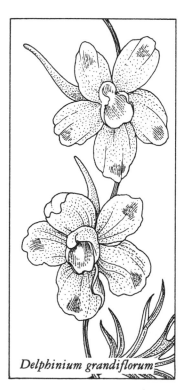

Delphinium grandiflorum

red blossoms on 3-foot stems and is beautiful in any garden setting only requiring well-drained but not overly acid soil. Start seeds indoors 12 weeks before the last frost. Space plants 8 inches apart and be careful of slugs: They love this plant!

'Blue Butterfly' is excellent both as a bedding plant and cut flowers bearing 1½ inch blossoms of an intense, deep blue on 14-inch plants. Start seeds indoors eight weeks before the last frost. Space plants 1 foot apart.

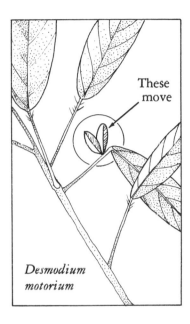

These move

Desmodium motorium

Desmodium (des-mo′di-um) from Greek for a chain, referring to the shape of the seed pods.

There is a strange member of this genus that deserves a spot in the annual garden if only as a curiosity piece: the telegraph plant, *D. motorium* (T). It hails from the tropics and can best be described as a plant that sends semaphore signals with its animated leaves. Unlike the sensitive plant (*Mimosa pudica*) or the caramba tree (*Averrhoa Carambola*) it's not necessary to touch the leaves: Just make sure the temperature is above 70°F. and the signals will begin. Start seeds eight weeks before the last frost. Plant out in the garden when all frost danger is past. Space plants 8 inches apart.

Dianthus (dy-an′thus) from the Greek for divine flower, named for the fragrance and beauty of the blossoms.

The Greeks had a word for it and that word perfectly describes the three common pinks grown for the annual garden. No garden is complete without these plants. Sweet William, *D. barbatus* (H), has been a favored biennial plant for the border since great grandmother's garden and before. But today there is no need to wait for the second year as new types will flower the first summer. Flat circles of tightly packed flowers sit on top of stems about 8 inches high in colors of red, pink, and white plus various combinations of these colors. Look for 'Indian Carpet', 'Summer Beauty', and 'Roundabout'; all of these will bloom if started early. Sow seeds indoors six to eight weeks before the last frost. Move seedlings outside to a cold frame when weather has settled as they like cool weather. Space plants about 8 inches apart, according to variety.

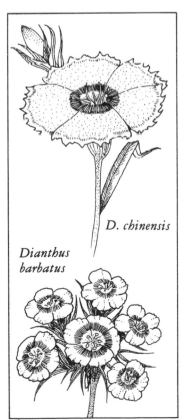

D. chinensis

Dianthus barbatus

The China pink, *D. chinensis* (HH), is another popular bedding plant often sold at garden centers for edging the garden. These are plants that will perform as annuals, biennials, or short-lived perennials. Grey-green grass-like leaves support charming flowers up to 1 inch

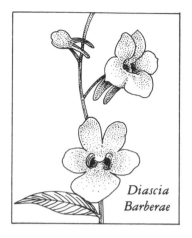

*Diascia
Barberae*

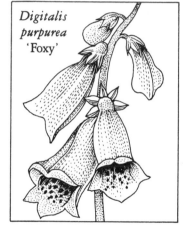

*Digitalis
purpurea
'Foxy'*

Dimorphotheca pluvialis

wide on stems up to 12 inches. Some cultivars have fringed petals. Flowers are not as fragrant as the true perennial pinks but are still sweet and spicy. Colors range from flaming red (look for 'Fire Carpet') to pinks, pure whites, and various combinations of these colors on the same petal. Plant as above.

Finally the Deptford pink, *D. Armeria* (H), though a biennial, will perform as an annual with seeds started early in the season. Rose-colored flowers about ³/₄ inch wide, the petals speckled with tiny dots of white, bloom on stems growing to 16 inches. Plant as above. Set plants 6 inches apart.

Diascia (dy-ass'si-a) Greek *di,* two, and *askos,* sac, referring to the two spurs of the flower.

The twinspur, *D. Barberae* (HH), is another annual plant that looks more like a perennial. Pink flowers are 1¹/₂ inches long with five petals in front, tapering in the back, and ending in two curved horns. Plants are about 1 foot tall and form a mound of green. Start seeds indoors six weeks before the last frost. Cut back severely after blooming for more flower. Set plants 8 inches apart.

Digitalis (di-ji-tay'lis) Latin for the finger of a glove, an allusion to the shape of the blossom.

Foxgloves are famous biennials but there is one cultivar that will behave like an annual, called *D. purpurea* 'Foxy' (H). Two-inch flowers of yellow, white, pink, or cerise will cover stems up to 3 feet tall. 'Foxy' looks beautiful at the edge of a woods and will take slight shade, but the soil must be well drained. Plants are also beautiful either massed in the border or just spotted about. Start seeds indoors in February and set the plants out when the weather is settled. Space plants 1 foot apart.

Dimorphotheca (dy-more-fo-thee'ka) from the Greek and referring to a technical character of the fruit.

Cape marigolds or star-of-the-veldt, *D. pluvialis* (T) and *D. sinuata* (T) are perennial daisy-like flowers from South Africa that will flower the first year from seed. Blossoms about 4 inches wide in colors of cream, orange, or salmon sport petal backs in shades of chalky blue, all on 12-inch stems. A mass of these flowers is spectacular in the garden. Cape marigolds—they have nothing to do with the other marigold of the garden—like a hot and dry climate as long as they have well-drained soil and, of course, plenty of sunshine. Start seeds indoors four weeks before the last frost or start outdoors when all danger of frost is past. Plants will bloom in six weeks from seed. Seeds germinate in ten days. Space plants 8 inches apart.

Dracopsis (dra-kop´-sis) from the Greek for dragon, and alluding to a minor character in the flower's ovary.

Dracopsis amplexicaulis

For years the clasping-leaved coneflower was included in the genus *Rudbeckia* but is now alone in a new one. The full name is *D. amplexicaulis* (HH) and it's a wildflower from Kansas to Texas and south to Georgia. The daisy-like flowers are about 2 inches wide with yellow petals surrounding a central cone. Leaves are a light, almost milky green and clasp the stems, a habit leading to the common name. They are wonderful cut flowers and most effective when planted in a drift for the wild garden and will take partial shade. Start seeds indoors four weeks before the last frost or plant directly outdoors by the end of April. Space plants 6 inches apart.

Dyssodia (di-so´-dia) from the Greek for evil-smelling, which applies to some species.

Dyssodia tenuiloba

The Dahlberg daisy or golden fleece is a daisy-like flower with bright yellow petals and a yellow center, each 1 inch across, on stems 1 foot high. *D. tenuiloba* (H) is the botanical name. These plants are perfect for summer beds, have a flowering period of several months, but prefer cooler weather and full sun. Start seeds eight weeks before the last frost or plant directly outdoors in early spring. They take four months to bloom from seed. Space plants 4 to 6 inches apart.

Echinacea (ek-in-a´see-a) is from the Greek word for hedgehog and refers to the sharp scales on the flower head.

Echinacea purpurea

The coneflowers are native perennial plants of North America and although many will bloom the first year if seed is started early, they've never really been considered for the annual garden. Now Thompson and Morgan have introduced 'White Swan', a cultivar of *E. purpurea* (HH), that will bloom in 16 weeks from seed. Blossoms are daisy-like with spiny centers, often over 4 inches wide, opening in

Echium vulgare

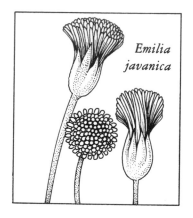

Emilia javanica

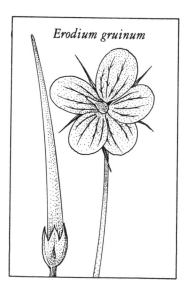

Erodium gruinum

lime-green to cream but turning the purest white as the petals age. Stems are 9 inches when plants start to bloom but can reach 20 inches by autumn. Then the plants can be discarded or moved to the perennial garden. 'White Swan' is perfect for cut flowers and easy to grow in most any soil and a sunny spot in the garden. Start seeds eight weeks before the last frost and you will have flowers by midsummer. Seeds germinate in 10 to 12 days.

Echium (ek'i-um) from the Greek word for viper, as the plant was once used to cure snakebite.

Last September I planted seeds of the biennial blueweed, *E. vulgare* (H), a member of the genus called viper's bugloss, in a 5-inch pot in the greenhouse. Plants began to blossom at the end of November with spikes of medium-blue flowers, the buds surrounded by thin green leaves covered with short silver hairs. In March, they were still flowering. This wildflower can reach 3 feet and grows in the worst of soils, including many rural roadsides. If given good soil, plants produce leaves but not flowers. Blueweeds are fine for the border. Start seeds outdoors when ground can be worked. They take two weeks for germination. Thin plants to 18 inches apart.

Emilia (e-mil'i-a) a commemorative name, but no one knows who the lady was.

Flora's paintbrush or tassel flower, *E. javanica* (HH), bears bright red-orange flowers, each 1/2 inch in length, on 1- to 2-foot stems. They look exactly like miniatures of the tassels you would find holding drapes in a Victorian living room, or like tiny paintbrushes used by the fairies living in the bottom of the garden, if dipped in scarlet paint. Foliage is neat and grey-green and flowers bloom over a long period. Store seeds away from light. Start seeds indoors four weeks before the last frost or outdoors in late spring. They will tolerate dry soil and need a sunny spot. Space plants 6 inches apart.

Erodium (ee-ro'di-um) from the Greek *erodios,* a heron, since the ripening seedpods resemble a heron's head.

The heron's-bill or storkbills are close relatives of the hardy geraniums and usually thought of as perennials. But one annual from Sicily and North Africa, *E. gruinum* (HH), is perfect for a dry and sunny location in the rock garden. Flowers of violet-blue, about ⅝ inch across, bloom on sprawling plants about 1 foot high. The fruit and namesake of the plant can reach a length of 4 inches. Start seeds indoors six weeks before the last frost and plant outside after frost danger is past. Space plants 6 inches apart.

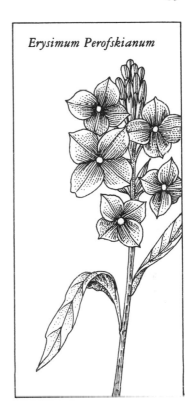

Erysimum Perofskianum

Erysimum (e-riss'i-mum) from the Greek word *erus,* to draw up, since some species are claimed to produce blisters.

Wallflowers are favorite flowers of England (and not at all like the botanical name would infer). Windowboxes all over London spill over in the spring with these charming flowers and their sweet fragrance. One species, *E. Perofskianum* (H), is an annual from the mountains of Afganistan and Pakistan. Stems 9 inches tall bear narrow leaves and dense spikes of showy yellow or orange four-petalled flowers, perfect for rock gardens or the edge of a wall. Plants like a well-drained, slightly alkaline soil. Start seeds six weeks before the last frost or plant outdoors in early spring. Germination takes two weeks. Space plants 6 inches apart.

Eschscholzia (esh-sholt'zee-a) commemorating Johann Friedrich von Eschscholtz, a nineteenth century naturalist.

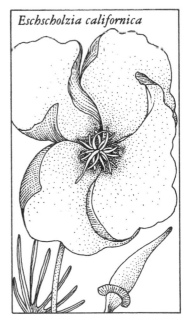

Eschscholzia californica

In the late sixteenth century, Spanish sailors journeying along the coast of California looked upon the hillsides awash with a golden hue and named the country "Tierra del Fuego"; others seeing the glowing shores would shout: "Gold! Gold!" and believe for a moment or so that they had found the true land of *El Dorado.* They had all seen the blooms of the California poppy, *E. californica* (H), a flower as close to the color of burnished gold as you're liable to find in the vegetable kingdom. Blossoms, which last three or four days, close at night. A perennial or biennial in California, these poppies are treated as annuals. They come in a bewildering array of colors including lemon yellow, purple-violet, golden yellow, and white, in single or double blooms (doubles are sterile). Look for 'Double Monarch Art Shades' and 'Cherry Ripe'. The disc at the base of the flower is called a "torus." Stems grow between 12 and 15 inches high. Even the foliage is attractive. Use them in drifts of color, along edges, or in a wild garden. Sow seeds directly outdoors as soon as the soil can be worked. Space plants 6 inches apart.

Eustoma grandiflorum

Exacum affine

Felicia amelloides

Eustoma (you-sto'ma) from the Greek for beautiful countenance.

Five years ago this plant was unknown to the general public. Now it is one of the most sought-after blossoms in the nursery trade with new varieties appearing every season. The prairie gentian or prairie rose, *E. grandiflorum* (HH), is a biennial that often acts as an annual. Many catalogs still list it as *Lisianthus*. The flowers look like a purple rose when opening, last up to two weeks when cut, and are truly beautiful—perfect additions to the border. Blossoms 2 inches wide and 2 inches long stand on erect stems to 3 feet. Colors are pink, blue, purple, or white, single or double. Leaves are oblong, about 3 inches long, and of a light milky green color.

Unfortunately they are not the easiest plants to grow. Start seeds indoors eight weeks before the last frost. Germination is in ten days. Move plants out to the garden when frost danger is past. They are slow growers for the first three months, remaining very small while only the roots grow. They need hot weather to flower. Nurseries keep the plants over winter in a protected frame for release the following spring. Space plants 6 inches apart.

Exacum (eks'a-kum) an ancient Greek name meaning out-going, and referring to the supposed expulsive power of the seeds.

From the Island of Socotra in the South Indian Ocean comes the German or Persian violet, *E. affine* (T), a biennial grown as an annual and generally used as a pot plant or along the edge of the border. The busy plants are covered with sweet-smelling blue flowers with yellow centers about 1/2 inch across. A healthy plant can reach a height of 2 feet. Start seeds in February or March for bloom in July. The seeds need light to germinate and sprout in fifteen days. Plants need partial shade from hot summer sun and a good, moist soil. Space plants 8 inches apart.

Felicia (fe-liss'i-a) Either a commemorative name for one Herr Felix, a German official, or from the Latin *felix* for cheerful, a reference to the bright flowers; I favor the second interpretation.

The blue daisy or blue Marguerite, *F. amelloides* (HH), is a charming perennial flower in South Africa that flowers the first year from seed with intense blue petals surrounding a yellow center. Blossoms are ³/₄ inch in diameter on 12-inch stems. Use them in the border, along edges, in the rock garden, and in pots. Start seeds six to eight weeks before the last frost. Germination takes two weeks. Plants want a sunny spot in well-drained soil. Space plants 6 inches apart.

Foeniculum (fe-nick'you-lum) from the Latin for hay, referring to the smell of the foliage.

Fennel has been grown for centuries as an herb, the leaves and stems used for seasoning and the seeds added to breads, stews, and liquors. It's not usually considered a plant for the formal garden but I use it for the overall effect of the lacy foliage coupled with the formidable size achieved over a short span of time. *F. vulgare* (H) is a chancy perennial usually dying out in cold winters, especially when denied snow cover. But as an annual it's perfect as a backdrop to a garden and can hide a multitude of backyard sins. The tiny, yellow flowers appear on large, flat discs in late summer and by then the plants are often 5 feet high. There is also a bronze-leafed form, smaller and used for its decorative foliage (see page 162). Fennel does not transplant well so start seeds in individual 3-inch peat pots, four weeks before the last frost. Cover seeds as they need darkness for germination, which occurs in 10 to 14 days. Plants need full sun and prefer a soil with some lime content but do well in our garden with very acid soil. Space plants 2 feet apart.

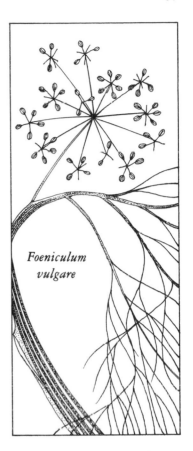

Foeniculum vulgare

Fragaria (fra-gair'i-a) from the Latin for fragrance, alluding to the sweet smell of the fruit.

Everyone knows the strawberry but few gardeners are aware that plants will bloom the first year from seed and make very effective edging plants and groundcovers. *F. vesca* 'Alpine' (H), the Alpine strawberry and *F. vesca* 'Mignonette' are the seeds to look for. Plants will form mounds of green, 8 inches high and bear tiny white flowers, ¹/₂ inch wide. When fruits form use them in the kitchen or allow them to remain on the plants as ornaments. Start seeds indoors in January but maintain a temperature of about 55°F.; seeds resent any heat. Germination is in 30 days. Plant out in mid-spring in a well-drained and fertile soil in full sun. Space plants 6 inches apart.

Fragaria vesca 'Alpine'

Gaillardia pulchella

Gaillardia (gay-lar′di-a) in honor of Gaillard de Marentonneau, a French patron of Botany.

The blanket flowers, *G. pulchella* (H), are beautiful, annual, daisy-like blossoms with large colorful petals named after their resemblance to an Indian blanket. Like their namesakes, they are Native Americans now popular around the world. Flowers are 2 inches across on stems up to 20 inches with colors of yellow, orange, red, or yellow with red bands. They are fine for bed or border, blooming most of the summer if flowers are cut for bouquets. Blanket flowers want full sun in most any soil and will tolerate a dry position. Start seeds indoors four weeks before the last frost or directly outdoors as soon as the ground can be worked. Germination is in 20 days and plants will bloom in 90 days from seed. Space plants 12 inches apart.

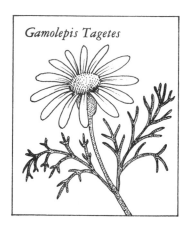

Gamolepis Tagetes

Gamolepis (gam-ol′e-pis) refers to the structure of the flower.

The sunshine daisy, *G. Tagetes* (HH), is an annual from South Africa bearing a host of 3/4-inch bright yellow daisy-like flowers on 1-foot wiry stems. It loves a spot in full sun, tolerates dry soil, and is perfect for the rock garden or the border's edge. Start seeds four weeks before the last frost or plant directly outdoors after frost danger is past. Space plants 8 inches apart.

Gazania (ga-zay′ni-a) named for Theodore of Gaza, a medieval translator of botanical works.

Gazania linearis

The African daisies, *G. linearis* (HH), are beautiful perennials in warmer parts of America, excellent houseplants, and will flower the first year from seed. Flowers can be 4 inches across standing on 10-inch stems. Leaves surround the plant's base and are dark green and felty white underneath. Colors are bright cream, yellow, gold, orange, pink, or red, with many petals sporting dark bands on their inner edge, surrounding yellow centers. They close at night. They are very effective when grouped in the border. Start seeds indoors four weeks before the last frost. They will germinate in eight days. Plant out after frost danger is past. Set plants 8 inches apart. Remember to dig up a few gazanias in the fall before frost for indoor plants where they will continue to bloom if given good light.

Gerbera (ger′ber-ra) named for Trang Gerber, a German naturalist.

Gerbera Jamesonii

The Transvaal daisy, *G. Jamesonii* (HH), is a true perennial, among the most beautiful of the African daisies bearing blossoms with thin, graceful petals of orange, pink, red, yellow, and carmine on 12- to 18-inch stems. Leaves are dark green, quite wooly underneath. They make long-lasting and exorbitant looking cut flowers. Gerberas are also fine pot plants. Start seeds eight weeks before the last frost, using fresh seed sown immediately upon receipt. Push the sharp end of the seed in the mix and do not cover, as they need light for germination. Seeds sprout in 15 to 25 days. Plants will bloom four months from seed. Plant outdoors after frost danger is past in full sun using a moist, well-drained, slightly acid soil. Space plants 12 inches apart. Remember to dig up a few gerberas in the fall before frost for indoor plants where they will continue to bloom if given good light.

Gilia (gil′li-a) in honor of Philipp Salvadore Gil, a Spanish botanist.

Gilia capitata

Queen Anne's thimble, *G. capitata* (H), are charming annuals with round 1-inch heads of small, pale blue flowers floating above finely cut dense foliage on 12- to 15-inch stems. Flowers are excellent for cutting and do well in pots. Plants want full sun and average to dry soil. They are perfect in a rock garden or for edging in the border. Start seeds directly outdoors in mid-spring. Plant in well-drained soil with full sun. Space plants 10 inches apart.

Glaucium (glaw′si-um) from the Greek word for glaucous, alluding to the gray-green bloom on the leaves.

Glaucium grandiflorum

The horned poppy, *G. grandiflorum* (H), is an annual member of the poppy family, 2 inches wide, with four orange or red petals often marked with a black or brown spot at the base. Stems are 18 inches high. The common name refers to the long seed pods. As most poppies do not transplant well, start seeds early in individual 3-inch peat pots or plant directly outdoors in any poor, sandy soil as soon as the ground can be worked. Horned poppies do well in seaside gardens. Space plants 6 to 8 inches apart. The roots of the horned poppy are said to be poisonous.

Gomphrena globosa

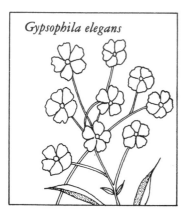

Gypsophila elegans

Helianthus annuus

Gomphrena (gom-free′na) taken from the Greek name given to an entirely different member of this family of plants.

The globe amaranth, *G. globosa* (HH), is a tropical annual with everlasting clover-like flowers in shimmering iridescent colors of orange, purple, pink, dark blue, and white. The flowers keep their color for a long time and are fine both for edging in a border and dried for winter bouquets. They also make an excellent pot plant. Plants grow about a foot high. Sow seeds indoors six weeks before the last frost or plant outdoors after all danger of frost is past. Seeds germinate in 15 days. Space plants 8 inches apart.

Gypsophila (jip-sof′fill-a) from the Greek word for gypsum-loving; some members of the family like limey soil.

Nothing in the garden is more beautiful than a cloud of baby's breath in full bloom. *G. elegans* (HH) is the annual plant and forms hundreds of small, 1/2-inch, five-petalled blossoms of white and now thanks to plant breeders, carmine, pale pink, and even purple. 'Covent Garden' and 'Giant White' are popular cultivars with larger than average white flowers excellent for cutting. Plants grow up to about 2 feet high and need a non-acid soil with good drainage. Baby's breath is so beautiful in the garden as a background to other flowers and a star in the cutting garden that it's worth the gardener's while to prepare a spot with the correct soil requirements. Start seeds directly outdoors in mid-spring. Plants bloom in six weeks from seed but only for a short time, so make successive sowings every three weeks. Space plants 10 inches apart.

Helianthus (he-li-an′thus) from the Greek words for sun and flower.

Everyone knows the sunflower but the days of seeing only 16-foot giants with ragged leaves and bending blossoms over 1 foot across, lined up in front of an old fence are, happily, gone. You can still buy seeds for the original, *H. annuus* (H), and use the 10-foot plants as a hedge to hide almost anything and keep the seeds for feeding birds in the winter. But now there are so many desirable cultivars including: 'Autumn Beauty' growing to 6 feet with 6-inch flowers of banded gold, lemon, bronze, and mahogany; 'Sungold' with double yellow flowers; 'Piccolo', 4 feet high with gold flowers and black centers; and my personal favorite, 'Italian White', 4 feet high with creamy white flowers with black centers surrounded by a narrow golden band. Sow directly outdoors in late spring when days are warm, in ordinary soil. Surprisingly enough, these flowers will tolerate partial shade. Sunflowers grow so fast it isn't usually necessary to start them indoors. Germination takes about two weeks. Space plants 2 to 4 feet apart depending on the type. They transplant easily.

H. annuus 'Italian White'

Helichrysum (hell-i-kry′zum) from the Greek words for sun and gold.

Strawflowers, everlastings, or immortelles are all common names of an Australian perennial that will easily flower the first year from seed. They are beautiful both as cut flowers and dried for winter bouquets. *H. bracteatum* (HH) is the species usually offered for sale. Daisy-like flowers have bright yellow-orange centers surrounded by stiff petals of red, orange, white, or yellow, up to 2 1/2 inches wide. Last summer some of our plants grew over 5 feet high, so make sure yours go to the back of the annual border or in the cutting garden. 'Monstrosum' is a cultivar with larger flowers but on smaller plants. Start seeds indoors six weeks before the last frost or plant directly outdoors when frost danger is past. Once established, plants will withstand temperatures to 26°F. Space plants 10 to 12 inches apart.

Helichrysum bracteatum

Heliophila (he-lee-o-fy′la) from the Greek for sun-loving.

Heliophilas are small annual flowers from South Africa. Three species are usually offered. *H. leptophylla* (HH), also called Capestock, grows about 9 inches high with blue-green leaves and 1/2-inch wide blue flowers with yellow centers. The petals close at night. It works best in the rock garden or as a border edging. Start seeds indoors six weeks before the last frost, and move plants outdoors in May. Space plants 6 inches apart.

H. linearifolia (HH) is a larger shrub-like annual up to 3 feet high and with the same type of flower as above. Grow as above. Space plants 1 foot apart.

H. longifolia (HH) grows to 15 inches with 2-inch linear leaves and 1/2-inch flowers of a rich blue with a distinct white throat. Grow as above. Space plants 6 inches apart.

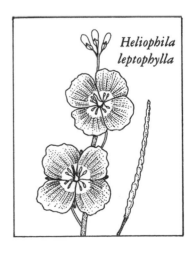

Heliophila leptophylla

*Heliotropium
arborescens*

Heliotropium (he-li-o-tro'pi-um) from the Greek words for sun and turning, referring to the old idea of plants bending to the sun.

These sweet-smelling plants are perennials from Peru and often cultivated in Europe for use in perfumes. Heliotrope or cherry pie, *H. arborescens* (T), bears many small violet or purple flowers ¹/₄ inch long on 15-inch plants with 3-inch oblong leaves on stout bushy stems. They are often used as bedding plants. But in order to have blooming plants for summer, seeds must be started in the beginning of February and that isn't always easy without adequate greenhouse space. The next best thing is to either buy plants from the nursery center. Or just buy one plant and root your own new plants by taking the young shoots and pegging them down into the soil, where they will quickly root. Then for winter plants indoors (temperatures of 50°F. are needed) take cuttings in September. Heliotropes want a good soil in full sun.

*Helipterum
Manglesii*

Helipterum (hel-lip'ter-rum) from the Greek for sun and wing, referring to a technical part of the flower structure.

The Swan River everlasting, *H. Manglesii* (T), is an annual everlasting flower that hails from Australia. Plants grow about 1 foot tall and bear solitary white, pink, or rose-colored flowers with yellow centers that bend over on wiry stems. The flowers are attractive in the border but not outstanding. They are best used in dried flower arrangements. Since seedlings do not transplant well, be sure if starting early to use individual peat pots or sow directly outside after all danger of frost is past. Flowering begins about 12 weeks after germination. Swan river daisies like a light, sandy soil in full sun. Space plants 6 inches apart.

*Heuchera
micrantha
'Palace
Purple'*

Heuchera (hew'ker-a) named in honor of Johann Heinrich von Heucher, a German botanist.

Including coralbells in a book of annual plants would seem surprising if it were not for one chance strain of plants developed by Brian Halliwell at Kew Gardens in England. The idea was to produce an original perennial bedding plant. Using *H. micrantha*, Mr. Halliwell bred 'Palace Purple', a plant that produces a mound of bronze-purple ivy-shaped leaves with a metallic cast, perfect in the border as an edger. It won't become a giant in the first year but will produce enough growth to be an effective color accent. Start seeds indoors ten weeks before the last frost. Keep temperature about 50°F. Light is beneficial to germination. Space plants 4 to 6 inches apart.

H. Sabdariffa 'Frisbee Hybrid'

Hibiscus (hy-bis'kus) from an ancient Greek name for a mallow.

This family of plants includes roselle or *H. Sabdariffa* (which see) and the swamp rose mallow, a perennial plant that has been cajoled into producing a number of cultivars behaving as annuals by plant breeders essentially from Japan. Using this mallow and two other species they have given us *H.* 'Frisbee Hybrid' (HH) a plant about 2 feet tall with disc-shaped flowers of red, white, pink, and rose, 8 to 9 inches across and blooming in three months from seed. They make quick-growing hedges and are spectacular in the border. Start indoors six weeks before the last frost, sowing seeds directly into 3-inch peat pots. Seeds usually need to be soaked in hot water (180 °F.) that is then allowed to cool for 24 hours, or nicked with a file, but most seed houses now treat the seed before packing so check the package instructions.

Hunnemannia (hun-nee-man'i-a) in honor of John Hunneman, an English botanist.

The Mexican tulip poppy or golden cup is a perennial that blooms the first year from seed. It's the only species in the genus. *H. fumarifolia* (HH) bears lovely poppy-like flowers with satiny petals up to 3 inches across on plants 1½ to 2 feet tall. The leaves are blue-green and finely cut, reminiscent of the California poppy but with more stamina. Tulip poppies are splendid spotted throughout the garden, planted in groups or in drifts. They resent transplanting and the roots are brittle so either start seeds in flats, pricking out into individual peat pots when tiny, or sow seeds directly outdoors in late spring. Space plants 10 inches apart.

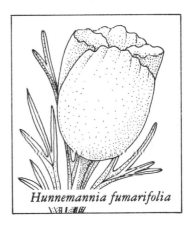

Hunnemannia fumarifolia

Hyoscyamus (hy-o-sy'a-mus) from the Greek word *hyos,* hog and *kyamos,* bean, an ancient name.

Henbane or stinking nightshade is a favorite plant of mine that friends always say should be grown in a torture garden or an out of the way plot devoted to the memory of Lucrezia Borgia. Opinions differ as to its beauty: Some people think it unusual and beautiful; others, loath it, calling it the Cutter Amberville of the plant world. *H. niger* (H) grows about a foot high with thick, downy leaves up to 8 inches long

Hyoscyamus niger

Iberis amara

Impatiens Balsamina

and 1¹/₂-inch wide flowers of a greenish yellow cast netted with purple veins. The dried leaves are sources of the alkaloidal drug *hyoscyamine* and all parts of the plant are poisonous. Start seeds indoors four weeks before the last frost or plant directly outdoors in late spring. Slugs seem to be immune to the sap of henbane and will devour it if found. Space plants 6 inches apart.

Iberis (eye-beer′is) named for Iberia, the ancient name for Spain and a home for many species.

Candytufts were aptly named as they often look good enough to eat. The annual species listed below are used either massed in garden beds, for edgings, and even for cut flowers. Rocket candytuft, *I. amara* (H), has been found in gardens since the sixteenth century. Plants grow about 12 inches high with thin leaves up to 3 inches long. Individual fragrant flowers are about ³/₄ inch wide and begin to open in the center of round terminal clusters that resemble Victorian jewelry. As more flowers open and mature the clusters gradually become elongated, with seeds forming on the bottoms. The colors have been traditionally shades of white but forms with pink, carmine, maroon, and rose are now available. The variety 'Giant Hyacinth' has white blossoms to 15 inches high. Sow seeds directly outdoors when the ground can be worked. Make successive sowings over the summer. Germination is in 20 days and bloom about 70 days later. Space plants 6 to 9 inches apart.

Globe candytuft, *I. umbellata* (H), is one of the most popular of edging plants. Flowers are small in neat, flat, 2-inch wide clusters on stems up to 16 inches high. Small scentless flowers are pink, violet, purple, rose, or white. Grow as above.

Impatiens (im-pay′ti-enz) from the Latin for impatience, referring to the bursting seed pods.

There are six common names for plants belonging to this group: impatience, touch-me-not, quick-in-hand, snapweed, busy Lizzie, and garden balsam. That shows just how popular they are for bedding plants either in full sun up north, and in a shady spot throughout the rest of the country. Impatiens are excellent edging plants or pot plants, perfect for window boxes, and fine as houseplants. *I. Balsamina* (T) is a true annual from India, China, and the Malay Peninsula, growing up to 2¹/₂ feet high and bearing everblooming, double 1- to 2-inch flowers, each bearing a short spur, that crowd the stems underneath leaves that are often 6 inches long. Blossom colors are dark red, yellow, salmon, lilac, pink, striped with white, and white. There are types with variegated leaves. Start seeds indoors six weeks before the last frost or start directly outdoors when frost danger is past. The exposure of seeds to light hastens germination, which usually takes 10 to 14 days. Since many of the newer types will bloom profusely on 10- to 12-inch plants, space according to the height listed on the seed packet.

I. Wallerana (T) is a perennial plant, originally from Tanzania and Mozambique, but usually treated as an annual in the garden. From a humble beginning there are now countless members to this species, ranging in height from 6 inches to 2 feet, forming mounded plants covered with single and double everblooming flowers in colors of tangerine, bright red, scarlet, orange, pink, rose, off-white, striped white, and pure white. There is no finer plant for bedding or border in light or filtered shade and moist soil that is liberally laced with organic matter and compost. Seeds may be started at any time of the year but you should begin ten weeks before the last frost for garden use. Do not cover seeds, for they need light to germinate, a process which takes 15 to 20 days. Plants can also be propagated by stem cuttings. Space them about a foot or more apart, depending on the variety.

The policeman's helmet or jumping Jack is a member of the group originally introduced to England in 1839 from the Himalayas and now naturalized in the northeast United States. *I. glandulifera* (H), sometimes *I. roylei,* is literally primed to explode and the slightest touch to a ripening seedpod scatters seed hither and yon; this plant can be invasive. Plants will reach over 6 feet with flowers about 1½ inches long in shades of deep purple, light blue, pink, or white.

A new type of impatiens, called the 'New Guinea' hybrids, are now found in garden centers. They feature leaves variegated with white and yellow and often 8 inches long along with very large flowers. And Thompson & Morgan in a continuing search for more new members of this family to use in breeding programs, now offer seeds for the golden impatiens, *I. oncidioides* (T), bearing 2-inch golden yellow blossoms perched above deep green foliage.

Ionopsidium (eye-on-op-sid'i-um) from the Latin like a violet, and alluding to the faint resemblance to some tufted kinds of violets.

Diamond flowers or violet cress, *I. acaule* (H), are not too well known annual plants. Originally from Portugal, they are perfect for a cool shaded spot in the rock garden or a small clay pot. White, lilac, or

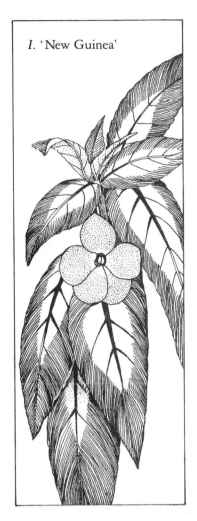

I. 'New Guinea'

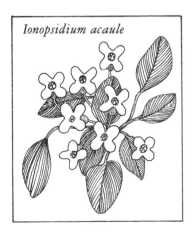

Ionopsidium acaule

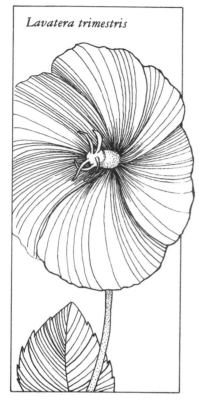

Lavatera trimestris

purple flowers with four petals, float above long-stemmed spatulate leaves on 3-inch high plants. Sow the seeds in early spring between flagstone paths and steps or next to rock walls. Plants will bloom about six weeks after germination. If grown in pots use a soil mix that includes small stones or sand to offer perfect drainage. They like cool weather and resent hot sun.

Lathyrus, the sweet peas are listed under vines.

Lavatera (la-va-tee'ra) named in honor of two Swiss brothers who were naturalists and physicians in Zurich.

The tree mallows are mostly perennial plants and shrubs but one species, *L. trimestris* (H), is an annual. Plants grow to 3 feet or more and are generously covered with hollyhock-like trumpets from mid-July until cut down by the frosts of fall. Give them good soil and full sun and you will be rewarded by a host of flowers. The cultivar 'Silver Cup' is usually offered and has petals of bright, shiny rose-pink, in flowers 3 or 4 inches across. Because of their growth habit, mallows look more like shrubs than garden annuals and are truly effective when massed toward the back of the border. 'Mont Blanc' bears all white flowers on bushes 2 feet high. Sow seeds directly outdoors in early spring where plants are to grow; tree mallows resent transplanting. Germination takes 15 to 20 days. Space plants 2 feet apart.

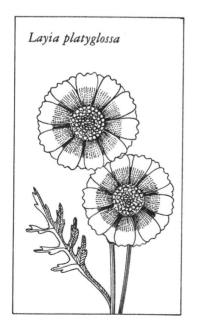

Layia platyglossa

Layia (lay'i-a) in honor of Thomas Lay, an English naturalist.

Tidytips, *L. platyglossa* (H), are annuals from California that I first ran across in English seed catalogs. They are as cheerful as their name would imply. Small, daisy-like flowers with sunny yellow petals, each with a dainty white deckled edge, are 2 inches across and excellent for cutting. Plants are between 12 and 16 inches high. Tidytips are perfect for dry, sunny banks, in the rock garden, and along the border. They will withstand temperatures of 26°F. Germination is in 12 to 14 days and they flower 14 weeks after sowing. Space plants 9 inches apart.

Legousia (le-goo'si-a) named in honor of Legouz de Gerland.

For centuries this charming annual was grown in European gardens where it was known as *Specularia Speculum Veneris* (H) or the mirror of Venus, a common name referring to the flattish, polished seeds, which suggested small mirrors. Another suggestion is that the shape of the flower resembles a hand mirror. Now its genus name has been changed to *Legousia*. Individual dark-violet flowers of 1-inch diameter, two or three to a cluster, are borne on 12-inch stems. Plants like a moist soil in a cool, shady spot. Only in the North can they take full sun at noon. Sow seeds directly outdoors in early spring. Thin plants to 4 inches apart.

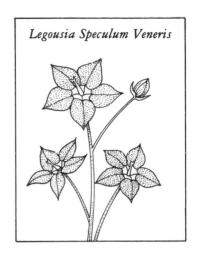

Legousia Speculum Veneris

Limnanthes (lim-nan'-thez) from the Greek for marsh flower, referring to the habitat.

Meadow foam, *L. Douglasii* (H), also known as fried eggs, is an annual from California. Inch-wide saucer-shaped flowers with five yellow petals edged with white appear above plants about 1 foot high. They have a sweet fragrance and are continually visited by bees. Leaves are shiny green and reminiscent of celery. Plants prefer cool weather and moist, but not wet, soil. Sow seeds directly outdoors when soil can be worked. Germination takes about three weeks. Meadow foam will often self-sow. Thin plants to 4 to 6 inches apart.

Limnanthes Douglasii

Limonium (ly-mo'ni-um) from the Greek for meadow, an allusion to the many species found in salt marshes.

Limoniums are a large family of plants, often called sea lavenders, from the Mediterranean region. Clusters of tiny flowers are each surrounded with bright, papery wraps ⅜ inch wide set on 2-foot stems. They are fine in bouquets either fresh or dried. Three species are usually sold—and often interchanged—by seed suppliers. *L. sinuatum* (HH) is a short-lived perennial or biennial that flowers the first year from seed. It is popularly known as statice, and flowers on 18-inch stems. Colors are red, apricot, deep blue, sky blue, yellow, and white. Plants need well-drained soil in full sun and because of their taproots should be sown directly outdoors in mid-spring. Space plants 9 inches apart.

L. Bonduellii (HH), an annual from Algeria resembles the other but has bright yellow flowers. Follow the same growing instructions.

L. Suworowii (HH) is the Russian statice or pink pokers, now called *Psylliostachys Surorowii*. Unlike the others, these plants have dense vertical spires covered with tiny pink flowers on 18-inch stems. Grow as above.

Limonium Bonduellii

Linanthus dianthiflorus

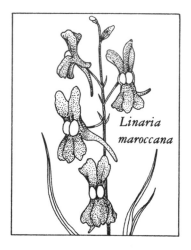

*Linaria
maroccana*

*Linum
grandiflorum*

Linanthus (ly-nan'thus) from the Greek word for flax, an unknown application.

The mountain phlox are mostly annual plants from North America and Chile. There are a number of species but usually two are offered: *L. grandiflorus* (H) bears white to lavender flowers about 1 inch long on plants about 18 inches high. *L. dianthiflorus* (H), the ground pink, forms 6-inch tufts of foliage with ³/₄-inch lilac or pink flowers. Both need full sun and well-drained soil and are fine in the rock garden. Many catalogs list them as *Gilia*. Sow seeds directly outdoors as soon as ground can be worked. Space plants 4 to 6 inches apart.

I have been looking over a number of years for *L. dichotomus* (H), called evening snow, where white flowers about 1¹/₄ inches long with a brownish throat open in the evening. If any readers know of a source, I would appreciate hearing from them.

Linaria (ly-nay'ri-a) from the Latin for flax, referring to the flax-like leaves.

Toadflax requires a stretch of the imagination to see the derivation of the common name: The tiny ¹/₂-inch flowers on 16-inch stems look more like snapdragons than mini-amphibians. *L. maroccana* (H) is an annual originally from Morocco and available in a number of colors, chiefly red, yellow, blue, lavender, violet, pink, and white. Look for the cultivar 'Fairy Bouquet'; it's aptly named. Flowers are excellent for cutting and look delightful in a rock garden. Toadflax likes well-drained soil in full sun or a bit of shade. It's also a cool weather plant so it dies out in hot weather. Sow seeds outdoors when soil can be worked. Thin plants to 6 inches apart.

Linum (ly'num) from the ancient Greek name for the plant.

Flowering flax, *L. grandiflorum* (H), is a 2-foot high annual happy in most any soil. It withstands dry conditions and revels in full sun. Flowers bloom up to 1¹/₂ inches across with petals that resemble the finest bolts of satin in an upholstery shop. Three cultivars to look for are 'Coccineum', with scarlet flowers; 'Roseum', with rose-pink petals; and 'Rubrum', with bright red flowers. Seedlings are difficult to transplant. Sow directly outdoors as soon as the ground can be worked. They will flower in about 100 days from seed. Flax does not have a long flowering season so make successive sowings three weeks apart over the summer. Space plants about 8 inches apart.

Common flax, *L. usitatissimum* (H)—the species name is Latin for most useful—is an ancient annual plant grown for the fiber to make linen and seeds that yield linseed oil. Clear blue flowers are ¹/₂ inch across on stems up to 3 feet tall and able to withstand any wind. Grow as above.

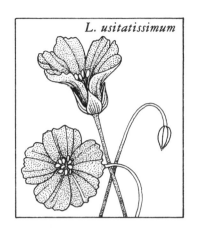

L. usitatissimum

Lobelia (lo-bee′li-a) named in honor of Matthias de L'Obel, English botanist to King James I.

Lobelia has to be one of the more popular plants for edging, groundcovers, planters, and windowboxes. The ³/₄-inch-long flowers are prolific bloomers that keep it up all summer long until cut back by frost. Most plants of *L. erinus* (HH) are annual, though a few live over two seasons in warm climates. They never grow more than 6 inches high. A number of cultivars have been developed, forming either compact clumps or trailing stems. The plants contain a poisonous alkaloid called lobelic acid and should not be eaten. Among the colors available are: 'Cambridge Blue', clear sky blue flowers; 'Pumila Snowball', pure white; 'Rosamund', cherry red with a white eye; 'Crystal Palace', deep blue against maroon foliage; and the most beautiful 'Queen Victoria', pure cardinal red. Start seeds indoors ten weeks before the last frost as the tiny seeds are slow to germinate. Plants should bloom about 100 days after sowing. Lobelia likes good, moist soil and will enjoy full sun in cooler parts of the country. Where summers are hot they like a bit of shade. Lightly cut back the plants in mid-summer and they will start to flower again. Space plants about 6 inches apart. They will quickly join together.

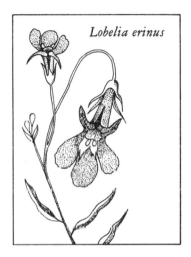

Lobelia erinus

Lobularia (lob-you-lair′i-a) from the Latin for little lobe, referring to the seed pods.

Sweet alyssum is a perennial in its native home of southern Europe, but it is grown as an annual in most gardens. *L. maritima* (H)—still called *Alyssum maritimum* in many seed catalogs—has a lovely honey-like odor and the charming little flowers bloom happily most of the summer and on into fall. Plants have tiny leaves and slender branches that usually trail over the ground bearing globe-like clusters of tiny ³/₄-inch-wide flowers. The original color was white, but alyssum is now available also in pink, lilac, purple, or rose. Look for 'Little Dorrit', only 4 inches high and covered with white flowers, and 'Rosie

Lobularia maritima

Lonas annua

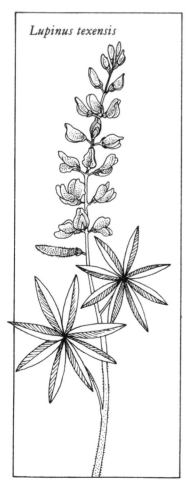

Lupinus texensis

O'Day', which is covered with sweet-scented rose colored flowers. Plant them as edging, in baskets, or let them ramble along a fieldstone path or tumble over rocks in the rock garden. Sow seeds directly outdoors as soon as the ground can be worked. Sweet alyssum wants full sun and well-drained soil. When plants get rather careworn in midsummer, cut them back and they will bloom anew. Space plants 6 inches apart.

Lonas (lo´-nas) the derivation of this name is unknown.

There is but one species in this genus, *L. annua* (HH), an annual called the golden ageratum, and native to Italy and northwest Africa. It's a daisy without petals. Flowers are a multitude of the discs found in a daisy's center, 1/4 inch wide, and grouped in 2-inch clusters on 10- to 12-inch plants with finely cut leaves. They need full sun and a well-drained soil and are excellent for seaside gardens. Start seeds indoors ten weeks before the last frost and cover them well as darkness is needed for germination. Seeds will sprout in five to seven days. Space plants 6 inches apart.

Lupinus (loo-pine´us) from the Latin for wolf, referring to the belief that these plants would destroy soil fertility.

The lupines include a number of annuals in their genus and all are attractive in the annual garden. They look like a less showy version of the perennial lupine with pea-like flowers whorling up a stem usually between 1 and 2 feet high. *L. densiflorus* (H) comes from California and bears 2/3-inch-long flowers with petals of white, yellow, or rose, to purple. Plants are fine for the annual border and good for cutting. They need well-drained soil and full sun. Lupines do not transplant well so either start seeds indoors in individual 3-inch peat pots, four weeks before the last frost, or sow directly outdoors as soon as ground can be worked. Make successive sowings to have flowers all summer. Space plants 8 inches apart.

L. Hartwegii (H) is originally from Mexico. Flowers are blue with the upper petals a light tint of rose on 3-foot stems. Grow as above.

L. luteus (H) bears fragrant yellow flowers on 2-foot stems. Grow as above.

L. subcarnosus and *L. texensis* (H) are both lovely wildflowers called the Texas bluebonnet, with blue blossoms on 1-foot stems. Grow as above.

Lychnis (lick'nis) from the Greek for lamp in allusion to the petals of some species that are flame-shaped and colored.

Lychnis Coeli-rosa

The rose-of-heaven, *L. Coeli-rosa* (H), looks more like a phlox than the typical lychnis. Flowers have rose-pink petals, each 1 inch across. Plants are true annuals, between 8 and 20 inches high and usually covered with flowers. They are fine for the rock garden or for cutting. Plants like full sun and any good garden soil. Start seeds outdoors in early spring when the ground can be worked. Space plants 6 inches apart.

Rose campions or mullein pinks, *L. Coronaria* (H), are biennial or perennial members of the genus, bearing 1-inch flowers of an intense magenta on stems up to 2 feet high. There is also a white-flowered form. Both the leaves and stems are covered with woolly white hairs hence are sometimes incorrectly called dusty millers. They are striking in the annual border. Rose campions will bloom the first year from seeds started outdoors in mid-spring. Space plants 6 inches apart.

Machaeranthera (ma-kee-ro-an'-ther-a) from the Greek for sickle-anther, referring to a botanical feature of the flower.

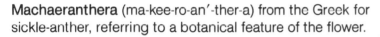

Machaeranthera tanacetifolia

The tansy or Tahoka daisy (named after a small town in Texas) is an annual aster and American native of great charm. *M. tanacetifolia* (H) bears 2-inch pale blue flowers with yellow centers on stems up to 2 feet tall. Leaves are up to 3 inches long. Wild plants are found in dry soil from South Dakota to Nebraska and Texas, and on into Mexico. Flowers are perfect in the border and for cutting. Sow seeds directly outdoors as soon as the ground can be worked. Space plants 6 inches apart.

Malcolmia (mal-co'mi-a) named in honor of William Malcolm, an English horticulturist.

Virginia stock, *M. maritima* (H), is an annual originally from the Mediterranean region and grown in country garden both here and in England for centuries. Pretty little blossoms 3/4 inch wide cover bushy plants usually about 9 inches high. Colors are red, lilac, or white. Use stocks in the rock garden and massed in the border. Plants will take full sun or light shade. Start seeds directly outdoors as soon as the ground can be worked in spring; they will bloom within six weeks and readily self-sow. Space plants 4 inches apart.

Malcolmia maritima

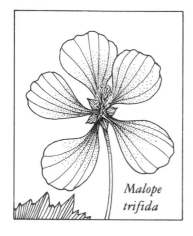

*Malope
trifida*

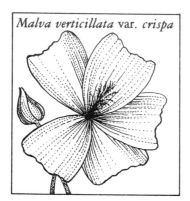

Malva verticillata var. *crispa*

Matthiola incana

Malope (ma-lo′pe) from an ancient Greek name for a kind of mallow.

Malope, *M. trifida* (H), are beautiful annuals from North Africa and Spain. Trumpet-shaped flowers of pink, purple, or white and 3 inches across, cover bushy plants 2 to 3 feet high. Malopes are excellent for the border and for cutting. Look for 'Vulcan', a free-flowering form with larger than type blossoms of brilliant red. Malopes like a good well-drained soil in full sun. Sow seed directly outdoors as soon as the ground can be worked. Space plants 9 inches apart.

Malva (mal′va) an ancient name from the Greek word to soften, referring to the sap's use as an emollient.

The crisped musk mallow, *M. verticillata* var. *crispa* (H), is an annual from Europe and Asia, now naturalized in the U.S. Although it's a bit weedy, it makes an excellent plant for the back of the border. Its 1/2-inch long white flowers cluster in the axils where the leaves meet the stems, the stems growing up to 6 feet high. The leaves are lobed, about 3 inches across, with the margins wrinkled and crisped. They are sometimes used in salads. Sow seeds directly outdoors as soon as the ground can be worked. Space plants 1 foot apart.

Matthiola (ma-thy′o-la) named in honor of Peter Matthioli, an Italian garden writer from the sixteenth century.

Stocks are biennial or perennial flowers first found growing on cliffs high above the sea in England. From the original wild plant, *M. incana* (HH), a number of garden flowers were developed, all with beautiful showy blossoms, single or double, and bearing a lovely fragrance. These stocks are unexcelled for garden beds, the border, pots, and cutting. All these new stocks are annuals and belong in a group called the ten week stock, belonging to the cultivar 'Annua', blooming within ten weeks of sowing. Included in this type are the following flowers: the Dwarf Large Flowering with a height of 1 foot and found in colors of yellow, crimson, pink, lavender, and white; the Column stocks, much taller with average heights of up to 2 1/2 feet and flowers of a similar color; the Giant Imperial stocks, usually 2 feet high and available in copper, gold, and yellow; the Mammoth stocks, usually about 1 1/2 feet high in colors of deep crimson, rose-mauve, white, pale yellow, and purple; and finally a new strain called the Trysomic stock, with short and tall varieties bearing double flowers 85 percent of the time and said to bloom in seven weeks. There is a very new cultivar called 'Dwarf Stockpot Mixed', 8 to 10 inches high, in colors of rose, bright red, purple, and white, that flowers in seven to nine weeks and the seedlings programmed to produce double flowers show a distinct notch in one of the young leaves.

Stocks need good garden soil in full sun and will tolerate light shade. Poor soil will need the addition of compost or well-rotted manure. Start seeds indoors six weeks before the last frost and do not cover as they need light for germination, which usually occurs in seven to ten days. Set them out in May as plants like a cooler climate. Space 8 to 16 inches apart depending on the type.

M. longipetala

M. longipetala (H) is the night-scented stock, a species with small, rather pedestrian flowers but a perfume of such beauty that every gardener should have a batch near a window for enjoyment under the moon on summer evenings. Plant anywhere as soon as the ground can be worked. Plants often reseed themselves.

Mentzelia (ment zee'li a) named in honor of Christian Mentzel, a German botanist.

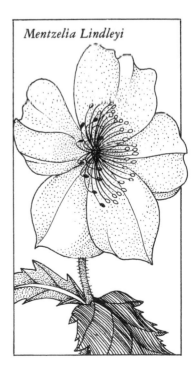

Mentzelia Lindleyi

Blazing star, *M. Lindleyi* (H), has been known for years as *Bartonia aurea* and no garden should be without it. English garden books listed it long before there was any interest in the colonies. And that's rather interesting since the flower was discovered by Thomas Henry Douglas, Forester of Leland Stanford University who found many new annual ornamentals in California and South America. One reference said he sacrificed his life to his botanical zeal but neglected to say just how. Many garden references claim the lovely and fragrant 2½-inch blossoms of bright yellow open only at night, authorities having confused the plant with *M. decapetala*, which does. Leaves are narrow, medium green, and somewhat cut. Plants grow to 1 foot tall but have a tendency to fall over and rest on the ground—perfect for the rock garden and at the edge of a wall. Since the plant is an American native from central California, it needs full sun and is happy in poor, even dry soil. Blazing star does not transplant well so plant seeds outdoors as soon as the ground can be worked. Thin plants to 6 inches apart.

Mesembryanthemum crystallinum

Mesembryanthemum (me-sem-bree-an'thee-mum) from the Greek for midday-flower as the flowers close in cloudy weather and at night.

Ice plants, icicle plants, fig marigolds, and pebble plants belong to one of those confused plant families where a number of species have been recently assigned to new genera. To save on confusion I'm only mentioning the two major species sold in most catalogs: *M. crystallinum* (HH), the iceplant, and the former *M. bellidiformis* which is now called *Dorotheanthus bellidiformis* or the Livingston daisy. The name of iceplant refers to the succulent leaves of *M. crystallinum* as the 6 inch high leaves have a surface that looks like myriad tiny slivers of ice. Flowers are daisy-like, up to 3 inches wide on the iceplant and 1¼ inches on the Livingston daisy. Colors are red, pink, lavender, yellow, and white and most open only on sunny days.

The plants are perfect for edging in the border, in windowboxes, and in the rock garden. They do best in dry soil and full sun and are very happy in seaside gardens. Start plants ten weeks before the last frost. Seeds are very fine and should not be covered. Keep flats away from light as darkness aids germination. Set plants out after the last frost and space plants 6 to 8 inches apart.

Mimosa pudica

Mimosa (my-mo'sa) from the Greek word for mimic, as the plants were thought to resemble animals in their sensitivity to touch.

When I was a child my mother always grew a few mimosa plants in the flower garden. Never for effect, because she always had towering delphiniums, peonies, hollyhocks, and a host of blatant annuals blooming in the border. No, the mimosa was an entertainment. When my friends visited the backyard I was able to walk over and gently touch the branches with my outstretched finger and the leaves would gently fold up against the stem, like a zipper in slow motion. *M. pudica* (T) is really too restrained for a bedding or border plant but well worth growing for amusement. Often termed a weed in the tropics, mimosas are about 2 feet tall with tiny green leaves, twelve or more on each side of the stem and pink blossoms like balls of fluff, ⅔ inch wide. Start seeds indoors ten weeks before the last frost using individual 3-inch peat pots. They make an interesting pot plant and will bloom indoors if given ample light.

Mimulus (mim′you-lus) from the Latin for a little mimic, referring to the grinning face in the flower.

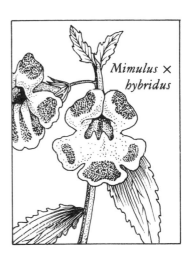

Mimulus × hybridus

Few flowers for the annual garden will do well in shade; choices always seem to be limited to begonias, impatiens, forget-me-nots, and just one or two others. But most gardeners overlook the monkey flowers, bright and pert blossoms dotted and stippled with color that are perfect for a spot in moderate shade. Originally a perennial from Chile, *M. × hybridus* (T), had been developed from a number of different species and are now available in colors of yellow, red, maroon, brown, and white, all with differing combinations of dots and spots of contrasting colors. Originally the 2-inch flowers were thought to resemble smiling monkeys but this seems to be even a bit more fanciful than the usual name derivations. Suffice it to say, they resemble bottom-heavy gloxinias riding above neat foliage usually about 1 foot high. Look for 'Calypso' in combinations of six to eight colors.

Plants prefer a good soil, well-drained but moist, and are perfect by a stream or garden pool. Start seeds indoors ten weeks before the last frost and plant out when frost danger is past. Space plants 6 inches apart.

Mirabilis (mi-ra′bil-is) from the Latin word for wonderful.

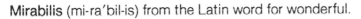

Four o'clocks or the miracle-of-Peru, *M. Jalapa* (HH), are one of my all-time favorite garden flowers. First, they bloom in late afternoon with fresh, bright flowers about 1 inch wide and 2 inches long on 1½-foot bushes of green; every evening the garden is aglow with fresh flowers. Second, they bloom faithfully until the first frost; and third, the long, thin black tubers can be dug up in the fall and used again the following spring. Perennials in their native home, I usually use four o'clocks as annuals in the border giving them a bright sunny spot— although they will do well in light shade—and well-drained soil. Colors are red, yellow, magenta, pink, crimson, and white, and some blossoms are striped. Start seeds six weeks before the last frost and set out when frost danger is past. Space plants 14 inches apart.

Moluccella (mol-lew-sell′a) named for the Island of Molucca where one species was reputed to be found.

The Molucca Islands are west of New Guinea and supposedly the original home of these unusual annual plants that bear enlarged green calyxes—the small leaves that usually wrap a plant's unopened blos-

Mirabilis Jalapa

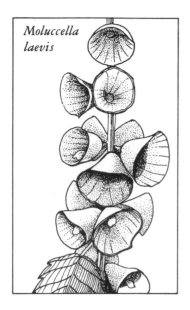

Moluccella laevis

soms—and contain tiny white flowers that sit within. Called bells-of-Ireland or Molucca balm, *M. laevis* (HH), these plants have stems up to 3 feet tall, the upper part ringed with the green bells. They are fine at the back of the border and perfect both as cut flowers and dried for winter bouquets. Start plants six to eight weeks before the last frost in individual 3-inch peat pots, as they are tap-rooted and will not transplant with ease. Don't cover, for the seeds need light to germinate, usually in eight days. Set out after frost danger is past. Space plants 1 foot apart.

Montia (mon′ti-a) named in honor of Guiseppe Monti, an Italian professor of botany.

Miner's lettuce is a little plant often found growing wild near old mining camps and prospectors' cabins in the American West. *M. perfoliata* (H) is an annual producing bright green, almost round, succulent leaves sitting on stems to 10 inches long, with tiny five-petalled white flowers emerging in little racemes from the leaf center. Settlers used them as salad greens and being slightly weedy, the plants continued long after the population moved on. They are charming plants for a moist, slightly shady area, either stream or poolside and can be raised in pots for winter greens for the table. Plant seeds directly outdoors in mid-spring. Space to 6 inches apart.

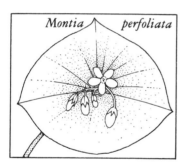

Montia perfoliata

Myosotis (my-o-so′tis) from the Greek for mouse ear, alluding to the shape of the leaves.

The garden or wood forget-me-not, *M. sylvatica* (H), is an erect annual, often biennial plant that is now known almost all over the temperate world. Flowers are blue, pink, or white and enjoy sun or partial shade, preferring a moist, well-drained soil either in the garden or at the edge of a woods. As an annual sow seeds directly outdoors in early spring. Remove dead blossoms for continued bloom. By mid-summer, a few will reseed and you'll have tiny plants by fall. Each will bloom the next spring, following the biennial habit. Nothing is more beautiful than a large decorative garden pot planted with forget-me-nots, either along with or surrounding spring bulbs, preferably yellow. Space plants 6 inches apart.

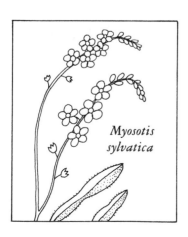

Myosotis sylvatica

Nemesia (ne-mee'she-a) from an old Greek name for a similar plant.

Nemesia strumosa

Nemesias, *N. strumosa* (HH), are annuals from the mountains of South Africa with brilliantly colored flowers. Plants are bushy and about 14 inches tall bearing 1-inch wide blossoms in pink, rose, yellow, scarlet, orange, blue, purple, and white. Nemesias are perfect in the border or in pots on a terrace, and are fine for cutting. Unfortunately the plants like cool weather and resent hot summers. Start seeds indoors eight weeks before the last frost. Move outside when the weather steadies using a cold frame if your area is threatened by heavy spring frost. Space plants 6 inches apart.

Nemophila (nem-off'i-la) from the Greek words for grove and love, referring to the plant's preference for a shady spot.

Nemophila menziesii

Baby-blue-eyes or California bluebells, *N. menziesii* (H), are native American wildflowers with attractive foliage and 1½-inch bright blue flowers with white centers on plants between 6 and 10 inches tall. We have naturalized them in part of our wildflower meadow and a sweeter flower you're not likely to find. Some cultivars are occasionally available, including white. But in this case the original flower is so pretty, stick with it. California bluebells prefer cool weather and are especially fond of moist soils with a high organic content. Sow seed directly outdoors in early spring. Thin plants to 6 inches apart.

Nicandra (ny-kan'dra) named in honor of Nikander of Colophon who wrote about botany in 150 A.D.

Nicandra Physalodes

Shoofly plants, *N. Physalodes* (HH), are said to be anathema to insects, especially whiteflies. If shoofly plant really lived up to its press, every garden would boast dozens of these plants. Unfortunately I've never seen them operate that way. Shooflies grow to a 3-foot height. Light green ovate leaves have a toothed edge. Flowers are small and bell-shaped, violet with a white throat, and open only for a few hours at midday. The developing fruits, each enclosed by sharply defined papery sheaths, are the most interesting aspect of the plant. They are shaped like either the headdress on Ming the Merciless' daughter in *Flash Gordon* or the shoulder pads on a medieval Japanese knight. They are excellent as dried flowers. Start seeds indoors six to eight weeks before the last frost. Set plants out when frost danger is past. Space plants 1 foot apart.

Nicotiana sylvestris

N. alata

Nicotiana (ni-ko-she-a′na) named in honor of John Nicot who introduced tobacco to France.

We've always had various members of the tobacco family in our annual garden, one, the true tobacco, for sheer size and the rest for a combination of lovely flowers and sweet perfume. The most common of the flowering tobaccos is *N. alata* (HH) or jasmine tobacco, a true perennial grown as an annual originally from Brazil and popular as a bedding plant, in the border, and as a cut flower. These plants are especially valuable as they not only withstand hot sun but will do well in light or open shade. Breeders have been at work and there are a number of cultivars: Plants from 1 to 3 feet tall bear 2-inch-long flowers open all day (they once held off opening until late afternoon). Flowers come in many colors: 'Crimson Rock' bears flowers of a bright carmine-crimson on 2-foot plants; 'Lime Green' blooms with the color of lime sherbert on 2½-foot plants; and 'Sensation Mixed' provides colors of maroon red, white, pink, and yellow on 3-foot plants. But it is at night when the sweet perfumes scent the air.

Seeds are very tiny. Sow them indoors six weeks before the last frost. Set plants out when frost danger is past. Space the plants from 9 inches apart depending on the size of the variety.

N. suaveolens (HH) is an annual from Australia and grows some 2½ feet tall. Leaves are somewhat sticky. The 2-inch long and 1-inch wide flowers are cream-colored tinged with green on the outside and white within. They prefer a shady spot, and are especially attractive to night-flying moths. Grow as above.

N. sylvestris (HH) is another beautiful perennial flowering tobacco treated as an annual and fine for a partially shaded position. Flowers are white and about 3½ inches in length and 1½ inches across at the mouth. Grow as above.

N. Tabacum is the true tobacco of commerce, usually an annual but occasionally living more than one year. This plant is a cultigen, a name referring to plants known only in cultivation and whose origins are unknown. First records of tobacco appear in pre-Columbian times. In our garden plants can easily reach 7 feet by the middle of August and are full of pinkish blossoms about 1½ inches long. Plants do well in pots for a patio.

Nierembergia (near-em-berg′i-a) named in honor of J. E. Nieremberg, a Jesuit professor of natural history in Madrid.

Cupflowers, *N. Hippomanica* (HH), are perennials in their native Argentina, but usually grown as annuals in American gardens. Plants are usually 6 inches high and bear cup-shaped violet flowers about 1 inch wide each with a yellow throat. They are excellent for edgings, in the front of a bed or border, and fine for hanging pots. Cupflowers like a good, moist soil, and in hot climates a bit of shade at midday. Start seeds six weeks before the last frost. Set plants out when frost danger is past. Space plants 6 inches apart.

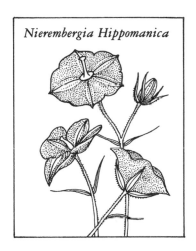

Nierembergia Hippomanica

Nigella (ny-jell′a) the Greek for black, from the color of the seeds.

Love-in-a-mist, *N. damascena* (H), or the fennel flower is a beloved plant cultivated for well over 400 years. The name refers to the pastel-colored 1½-inch blooms that hover just above a tangle of light green, fernlike foliage. The seeds are aromatic and used in eastern countries by oriental cooks and physicians. Seeds and leaves are used in India to prevent moths from chewing clothing. Plants are between 14 and 18 inches high and are especially attractive when massed in the front of the border. Two cultivars are worth seeking: 'Miss Jekyll' with bright blue semi-double flowers; 'Miss Jekyll Alba' of the purest white; and 'Persian Jewels' giving flowers of rose-pink, light blue, or white. Ripening seedpods inflate like balloons crowned with jester's caps only minus the bells. Plants do not transplant well and should be sown directly in the garden when the soil can be worked, or started in individual 3-inch peat pots four weeks before the last frost. Thin to 8 inches.

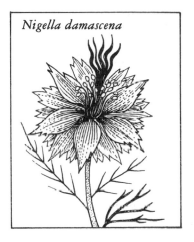

Nigella damascena

N. hispanica (H) is another species with black centers and scarlet stamens on 16-inch plants. Grow as above.

Nolana (no-lay′na) from the Latin for little bell, referring to the shape of the flower.

The Chilean bellflower, *N. paradoxa* (T), is a trailing perennial from South America commonly grown as an annual and only about 6 inches high. Flowers are dark blue, 2 inches wide, with a pale yellow or white throat looking somewhat like a morning glory with ruffled petals. Plants are perfect in the rock garden, trailing over walls, in edging, and in hanging pots. They prefer dry, well-drained soil and do well in seaside gardens. Bellflowers have a long taproot so either start indoors in individual 3-inch peat pots four weeks before the last frost or plant directly outdoors after all frost danger is past. Space 6 inches apart.

Nolana paradoxa

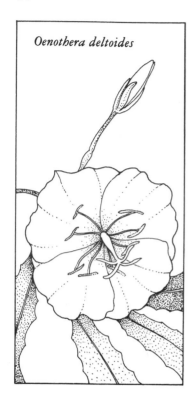

Oenothera deltoides

Oenothera (ee-no-thee′ra) from the Greek for *oinos,* wine and *thera,* pursuing or imbibing, referring to the roots of a similar plant thought to inspire a thirst for wine.

Evening primroses are vespertine flowers, a name describing their habit of blooming in late afternoon or twilight. They share a genus with the sundrops, bright yellow flowers that bloom by day. All are from North and South America. The flowers described below are only a few of the various species offered by the trade and the seed societies. Start seeds six weeks before the last frost and plant outside when frost danger is past. Space plants 6 to 12 inches apart, depending on the size of the species.

O. acaulis (HH) is an unreliable perennial that will flower the first year from seed and is best in the rock garden. Plants are usually 6 inches high, trailing, with long lance-shaped green leaves and 3-inch wide white blossoms opening in late afternoon. The flowers turn to rose with age.

O. Berlandieri (HH), or the Mexican rose, is another short-lived perennial blooming the first year with four-petalled rose-pink flowers on the top of slender 6-inch stems. It's very pretty grouped in the border.

O. deltoides (HH) is the desert evening primrose with white vespertine 2 1/2-inch-wide flowers that turn rose-pink with age. Plants grow 1 1/2 feet high.

O. Drummondii (H), the Texas evening primrose, is a short-lived vespertine perennial or annual with bright yellow flowers about 2 inches in diameter on 1 1/2-foot stems with lance-shaped leaves. These flowers are excellent for the wild garden or the rock garden. Start seeds in early spring when the ground can be worked and thin plants to 1 foot apart.

O. odorata (HH) is a perennial that flowers as an annual. Flowers, about 2 inches across with a sweet perfume, start to bloom with yellow petals that change with age to red. Plants are rangy and grow about 16 inches high.

Omphalodes (om-fal-lo′dez) from the Greek for navel-shaped in reference to the seeds.

The navelworts, navelseeds, or Greek forget-me-nots, *O. linifolia* (H), are annuals that produce long sprays of gray-green leaves surrounded by lovely white, faintly scented, 1/2-inch wide five-petalled flowers, followed by seeds that look exactly like their common name.

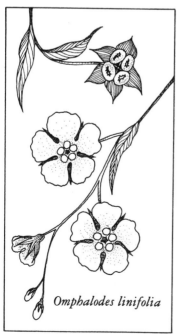

Omphalodes linifolia

The flowers are especially attractive when cut for bouquets. They are lovely in front of a stone wall or in the rock garden. Start seeds indoors four weeks before the last frost and plant out after frost danger is past. Or start seeds directly outdoors in mid-spring. Thin plants to 6 inches apart.

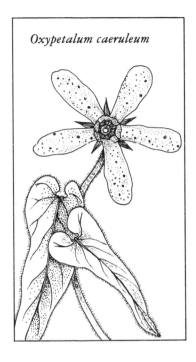

Oxypetalum caeruleum

Oxypetalum (ox-y-pet′a-lum) from the Greek for sharp-petalled.

Southern stars, or star-of-the-Argentine, *O. caeruleum* (T), bear five-lobed pale blue flowers about 1 inch across, that turn purple with age and turn to lilac as they wither. Plants are perennial shrubs with heart-shaped downy leaves that bloom the first year. They grow to only about 15 inches in height in the garden.

I first saw them blooming in the annual border created at Wave Hill, the lovely public garden in the Bronx, New York. Start seeds indoors eight weeks before the last frost and plant outside when frost danger is past. Plants like a good, well-drained soil in full sun. Space plants 8 inches apart.

Papaver (pap′a-ver) the ancient Latin name for poppies, said to refer to the sound made in chewing the seed.

My first memories of poppies were the glorious drifts of the perennial oriental flowers in my mother's garden of late May. Then I saw the *Wizard of Oz* and remember Dorothy and her companions falling asleep while running through a field of poppies cajoled into bloom by the wicked witch. And I can't forget Memorial or Veterans Day (the real holiday before the Congress saw fit to change it) and veterans selling Buddy poppies, a scarlet symbol of the tragedy of the First World War and Flanders' Field. The cultivation of these plants goes back to remote antiquity and the flowers are woven into the fabric of myth and romance both with pleasure and with dread.

The following plants are annuals or short-lived perennials that will bloom the first year from seed. All must be planted directly in the garden or started in individual peat pots as their taproots prevent the easy movement of the seedlings except when very, very little. With all except the alpine poppy, make successive sowings about twenty days apart until midway through the growing season to have bloom throughout the summer. The alpine poppy is usually called *P. alpinum* (H) but is more correctly known as *P. Burseri*. Plants are rosettes of

Papaver Burseri

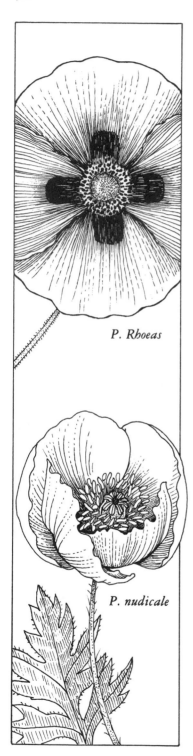

P. Rhoeas

P. nudicale

long wavy gray-green leaves that generally hug the ground but produce a number of satiny-petalled flowers on 8-to 10-inch stems. Flowers are white, orange, yellow, pink, and apricot, usually 2 inches across, and produce a faint, sweet aroma. These plants require perfect drainage or the taproot will surely rot, so are at their best in the rock garden. Sow seeds directly outdoors in early spring as soon as the ground can be worked. Thin plants about 6 inches apart.

The tulip poppy, *P. glaucum* (H), is native to Syria, Iraq, and Iran and was introduced to European gardens in the late nineteenth century. The gray-green leaves are lobed and surround $1\frac{1}{2}$-foot stems that bear tulip-shaped flowers up to 4 inches wide. The color is a vivid scarlet-red with a black center and the petals are the texture of satin. Plant in drifts; poppies look best when kept together to the exclusion of other plants. Thin plants to $1\frac{1}{2}$ feet.

"In Flanders' fields the poppies blow between the crosses, row on row." from the poem by John McCrae, refers to the field poppy of Flanders, *P. Rhoeas* (H). Flowers are often 3 inches wide and borne on 2-foot stems with colors of pink, scarlet, crimson, salmon, and white. The petals are unequal of size: two are large and two are smaller while the center of the flower is black. The petals have the texture of crushed silk. Leaves are a dark green. There are a number of different varieties on the floral market so check catalogs every year. Sow seeds directly outdoors as soon as the ground can be worked. They will bloom in 60 days. Thin plants to 1 to $1\frac{1}{2}$ feet and remove seedpods to keep blooms coming.

The Iceland poppy, *P. nudicale* (HH), is a perennial from the Arctic regions and has produced some of the loveliest flowers in the entire family. These plants are best as biennials and if the seeds are started early will bloom the first year from seed. Although they, too, resent transplanting, it's usually more successful here. My personal experience is with one of the newest Thompson & Morgan cultivars, 'Oregon Rainbow', semi-double blossoms of tissue-thin silk in colors of apricot, peach, pink, rose, and white. Blossoms are held on 6- to 8-inch stems above rosettes of light green leaves and are excellent for cutting—singe the stem tip in flame for this and other poppies. I started my seeds in early February. After a month the seedlings were moved to flats, six or eight plants per one 5- by 7-inch flat. Plants were hardened off in a cold frame and planted out in mid-May. They bloomed by the end of July and were quite beautiful.

Thompson & Morgan have also released another annual poppy for 1987. A plant of unknown origin found some 30 years ago in the Hadleigh garden of Sir Cedric Morris, an East Anglian artist, this plant is called 'Fairy Wings' (H). The blossoms are in colors of gray, soft blue, lilac, peach, dusty pink, and white with picotee edges of faint blue. Height is between 10 and 14 inches. Sow seeds directly outdoors in early spring. Germination is in 21 days. Plants should self-seed.

The final annual poppy in our list is the opium poppy, *P. somniferum* (H). The juice of the unripe pod is the source of opium and the production of this drug is illegal in the U.S. Strangely enough the seeds (along with the seeds of *P. Rhoeas*) are used for food since they contain not a trace of the toxic alkaloids that are present in the sap of the plants. In addition, opium poppies are the source of poppy seed oil. The flower is, however, of great beauty and available in a number of cultivars. Plants will often grow 4 feet tall and bear blossoms up to 5 inches wide. A large bed of these flowers is a breathtaking sight. 'Peony Flowered Pink Beauty' bears full double blossoms of salmon pink; 'Pink Chiffon' has doubles of bright pink; and there is a white form 'Alba' occasionally offered. 'White Cloud' is a double form often called *P. paeoniflorum,* but it is actually a cultivar name of the double-flowered blossoms in this species and not a recognized species of its own.

The dried seedpods, especially of the opium poppy, are valuable in dried bouquets. Look for *P.* 'Hen and Chickens', a type in which the central seedpod has arising from its base several little seedpods and according to Chiltern Seeds, gives the impression "of a mother hen surrounded by her brood of little chicks."

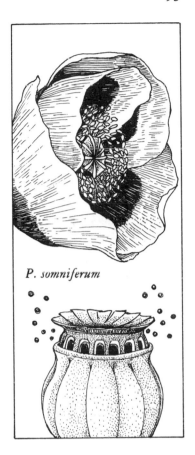

P. somniferum

Pelargonium (pee-lar-go′ni-um) from the Greek for stork, in reference to the shape of the fruit.

The garden geranium is unsurpassed as a bedding, basket, border, or cut flower and although often included in the genus *Geranium* (which see) they properly belong to the genus *Pelargonium* (T). These geraniums are perennials native to South Africa but usually grown as annuals. While most gardeners buy geraniums from nursery centers or take cuttings from either houseplants or others grown outside the previous summer, there are a fantastic number of cultivars that can easily be grown from seed and will flower the same year. In fact, the Geo. Park Seed Company catalog devotes two pages and Thompson & Morgan, three pages to seeds for these workhorse garden plants.

Garden geraniums fall into four groups: The show geraniums, *P.* × *domesticum*; the zonal geraniums, *P.* × *hortorum*; the ivy-leaved Geraniums, *P. peltatum*; and finally a number of species usually referred to as scented-leaved geraniums.

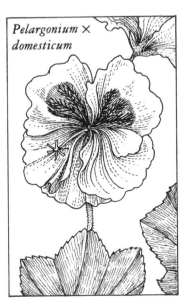

Pelargonium × domesticum

P. peltatum

Martha Washington, pansy-flowered, azalea, or regal geraniums are all common names for the show geraniums. These plants have the largest and fanciest flowers of all—individual blossoms between 2 and 4 inches wide—with the upper two petals having darker blotches of color. Leaves are between 3 and 4 inches wide and plants usually reach 1½ feet. Flower colors are red, rose, lilac, pink, or white. Show geraniums are best grown in pots but can be grown in the border if there is some protection from very hot sun at noon. In England, well-grown plants are often placed in antique oriental bowls for floral decoration in the home. Soil should be good garden or potting soil, well-drained, and at least ¼ of the mix should consist of composted manure. These geraniums prefer cooler nights and plenty of water when in active growth. Remove spent flowers.

Zonal geraniums are named for the various rings of color on the leaves. Plants usually grow about 2 feet tall with 3- to 5-inch leaves and flower colors of red, pink, salmon, rose, and white. These geraniums are best for beds, borders, and large containers. Grow as above but they can take much warmer weather and plenty of sun. Remove spent flowers.

Ivy-leaved geraniums are best as groundcovers or grown in hanging baskets where their glossy five-lobed, ivy shaped leaves can trail over the container edge, sometimes to 3 or 4 feet. Flowers are white, vermilion, red, pink, and various shades between. Grow as above.

Finally there are the scented-leaved geraniums, plants that are grown not for the flowers, which are small, but for the leaves that can smell like pineapple, coconut, rose, lemon, apple, peppermint, pepper, fern, orange, and other aromas. They are not planted in the bed or border but instead are used as pot plants. The leaves are often used to flavor cakes and jellies, to scent water for fingerbowls in fancy luncheons, and as an ingredient in potpourri. Grow as above.

Start seeds for all types of geraniums about ten weeks before the last frost. After the first true leaves appear move the seedlings to individual 2-inch pots and then on to 4-inch pots as they grow larger.

To propagate geraniums take cuttings 4 inches long, removing the bottom leaves and leaving three perfect leaves per cutting. Allow the cut end to dry for a day before placing in individual 3-inch pots filled with moist, clean sharp sand, vermiculite, or peat moss. Keep out of the direct sun and place the pots in a propagating unit or cover the pots with some plastic to retain moisture.

Remember, too, that geraniums will root in a glass of water, the way our great grandmothers took care of the problem.

Penstemmon (pen-ste′mon) from the Greek for five stamens, a botanical feature of this genus.

The penstemmons or beard tongues are a large genus of over 250 species, one from Asia and all the rest from North America. Quite a few are perfect for the wild garden and a number are useful in the perennial border. Yet one species, often called *P. gloxinioides* but more properly, *P. Hartwegii* (HH), is never reliably hardy in most of the U.S. and is generally grown as an annual. Plants are usually between 2 and 3 feet tall and bear stems liberally covered with bright, white-throated blossoms about 2 inches across. Colors are red, pink, lavender, and white. Look for the cultivar 'Sensation'. Start seeds indoors twelve weeks before the last frost and plant out when frost danger is past. Seeds germinate in ten to fifteen days and need light for germination. Make sure you remove spent flowers for continued bloom. Penstemmons need a reasonably good well-drained soil in full sun. Space plants 1 foot apart.

Penstemmon Hartwegii

Petunia (pe-too′ni-a) from *petun*, the Brazilian name for tobacco, to which these plants are closely related.

Everyone has their likes and dislikes and I'm afraid that along with African violets I'm not too fond of petunias. To prove to myself that I'm definitely swimming against the current I recently checked the petunia listings in the wholesale catalog for Dutch AGRI Products, one of the largest seedhouses in the world: Over 200 named cultivars of the common garden petunia, *P. × hybrida* (HH), are listed. Many come true from seed while others are propagated by stem cuttings. They include dwarf petunias from 6 to 8 inches; tall petunias growing to 1½ feet; hanging petunias that will cascade over a basket's edge; pollution resistant strains for planting in cities; the 'Recover' series for planting in unfavorable climates; and scads of petunias for bedding. Colors available are: red, salmon pink, dark scarlet, deep carmine, deep purple, a host of blues from the lightest of blue haze to cobalt blue, yellow, orange, lavender with darker veins, cream, and white, not to mention petunias with picotee ruffles and flowers that are striped and veined with contrasting colors. There are single and double flowers up to 3 inches across.

Petunias need sunshine at least for half the day and require a good, well-fertilized soil and you must be especially attentive with water.

Petunia × hybrida

*Phacelia
campanularia*

Start seeds indoors ten weeks before the last frost is due. Use flats and do not cover the tiny seeds as they need light to germinate. When they have three or four leaves transplant them to individual 3-inch peat pots and as soon as the weather warms take them out to a cold frame. Plant out when all danger of frost is past. Be sure you pinch back plants for bushiness. Space plants 8 to 12 inches apart.

One problem with most petunias is the excessive length of the stems. Since the blossoms are usually terminal the plants become rather messy by midseason. To remedy the problem, take a long stem about halfway up and roll it gently between your fingers, just to squeeze and soften the tissue. Then bend it gently backwards so the upper part is now pointing to the pot or container. This action prevents a hormone produced in the growing tip from reaching the side buds and inhibiting bloom. Now the side shoots will develop and flower and the top will continue to bloom and hide the growing process. Finally you can pinch off the top stem for a more compact plant.

Phacelia (fa-see′li-a) from the Greek for cluster, alluding to the flower arrangement.

The scorpion weeds are native chiefly to the U.S. and Mexico. While not as spectacular as many wildflowers they are noted for the intense blue of their 1-inch-wide flowers.

California bluebells, *P. campanularia* (H), are annuals that grow about 1 foot high with small grey-green leaves with a reddish tint. While flowering the leaves are hidden by the bell-like flowers, deep blue within and light blue without. Plants are fine as a groundcover and when grown in the rock garden. Start seeds directly outdoors in early spring as they do not transplant well. Bluebells want a sandy, well-drained soil in full sun. They flower over a longer period when days are cool. Thin plants to 9 inches apart.

Phlox (flocks) from the Greek for flame referring to the color of the flowers and the flame shape of the buds before opening.

Few annuals excel *P. Drummondii* (HH) in providing a constant show of summer color yet most people never realize that it's a native American plant discovered in Texas in 1835. Although some plants may reach 20 inches in height, the usual choice for the garden border are the newer dwarf varieties that stay between 6 and 8 inches high,

Phlox Drummondii

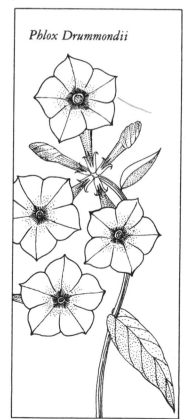

their busy plants covered with blossoms 1 to 1½ inches across. Colors range from pure white to purple, crimson, yellow, lavender, and some blossoms with mixed colors. Look for 'Petticoat', a low growing plant with many ½-inch blossoms of violet, lavender, white, and salmon or 'Twinkle' with very fancy star-shaped blossoms usually in two colors.

Phlox is often planted out in ribbon fashion or in separate beds with different colors and is quite adaptable for commemorative designs. They are fine for rock gardens and make excellent cut flowers. Phlox want a good well-drained soil in full sun but will tolerate a bit of shade. Sow seeds indoors six to eight weeks before the last frost and plant out after frost danger is past. Or plant directly outdoors in late spring. Space plants about 10 inches apart in good soil, closer together in poorer soil.

P. Drummondii 'Twinkle'

Phuopsis (fu-op′sis) named for the resemblance to *Valeriana Phu,* a European wildflower.

The Caucasian crosswort, *P. stylosa* (H), is called *Crucianella stylosa* in *Hortus Third* but *Phuopsis* everywhere else. It's an annual plant from Iran and central Asia that will sometimes winter over since its roots can be perennial when the spirit moves them. The stems are prostrate, about 8 inches long, and are covered with whorls of small sharp, leaves about ¾ inch long, attractive in themselves. Pink flowers are tubular with five petals and appear in bunches at the ends of the stems. Crossworts are fine in the rock garden and especially attractive planted along the edge of a wall. Start seeds indoors six weeks before the last frost and plant outside after frost danger is past. Space plants 6 inches apart.

Phuopsis stylosa

Physalis (fiss′a-lis) from the Greek word for bladder, referring to the balloon-like husks.

Ground cherries or husk tomatoes are the popular names for a genus of plants that include a number of species grown for the edible fruits. *P. Alkekengi* (H), is a perennial member that blooms the first year from seed and is also known as Alkekengi, winter cherry, Chinese lantern, Japanese lantern, and the strawberry tomato. They have been grown for years, not for flowers or foliage, but for the orange-red husks (really an enlarged calyx) that protect the fruit, which ripens in the fall. Hardly a flower arrangement in the 1930s (or painting on a tea tray) was produced without these colored balloons. They will last for weeks

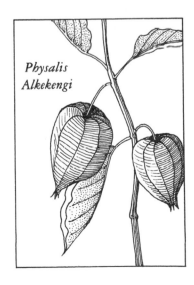

Physalis Alkekengi

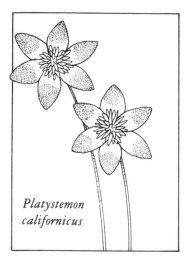

*Platystemon
californicus*

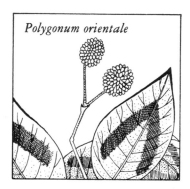

Polygonum orientale

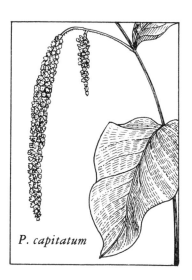

P. capitatum

when cut or can be dried for winter arrangements. Take care, the plants are weedy, spreading by a network of underground stems. Sow seeds outdoors in early spring in ordinary soil, preferably in a cutting garden. The plants want full sun. Thin to 1 foot apart.

Platystemon (plat-i-stee′-mon) from the Greek for broad stamen, referring to the form of the flowers.

There is but one species in this genus, *P. californicus* (H), or creamcups, another lovely flower from California. Solitary flowers 1 inch wide on foot high stems are light yellow or cream-colored with white centers and dance above gray-green narrow leaves about 3 inches long. They somewhat resemble poppies and are indeed members of that family. Use them in the rock garden, as an edging in the border, or plant them in a meadow garden. Sow seeds directly outdoors as soon as ground can be worked in spring. Thin to 4 inches apart.

Polygonum (pol-lig′o-num) from the Greek for *polys,* many, and *gonu,* a small joint, referring to the many joints in the stem.

The knotweeds are a large family of plants containing many pernicious weeds. But one, *P. orientale* (H), is an attractive annual plant with a number of common names including: prince′s-feather, princess-feather, and kiss-me-over-the-garden-gate. The plant can reach a height of 5 feet and then bear 4-inch sprays of tiny flowers like large BB′s in colors of bright pink or rose. The leaves are heart-shaped and large, often 8 to 10 inches long. Plants are excellent for a quick backdrop for the rest of the flower bed. Sow seeds outdoors in early spring in a good garden soil. They like full sun but will accept a little shade. Space plants about 1 foot apart.

P. capitatum (T) is a perennial from the Himalayas that may be grown as an annual groundcover. It is a spreading plant, rooting at every knot along the stem, and trailing over the edge of a wall or hanging basket. Be warned! In Zones 9 and 10 this can be a weed but everywhere else its rambling activities are cut down by a good old-fashioned killing frost. The heart-shaped leaves are green with a bronze-colored stripe, and little balls of tiny pink flowers float above on 4-inch stems. Start seeds indoors six weeks before the last frost. Space plants 1 foot apart; they will quickly fill in.

Portulaca (port-tew-lak′a) from the old Latin name for the purslane.

The rose moss or portulaca, *P. grandiflora* (HH), is an annual or short-lived perennial from Argentina and Uruguay and is able to survive *and* bloom in some of the most inhospitable places imaginable. Parched, dry, and poor soil plus bright, hot sun do nothing to diminish the onward march of this creeping plant. Pretty single or double flowers, up to 2 inches across, with satiny petals in colors of red, yellow, orange, scarlet, magenta, and white, bloom on succulent reddish stems and usually hide the cylindrical leaves. This is *the* annual to plant in that spot where nothing else will grow. It is fine for edging, between fieldstones or rocks, and along the edge of a wall in full sun. Start seeds indoors six weeks before the last frost. Use 5- by 7-inch flats as the plants can easily be transplanted to 3-inch peat pots or directly outside if frost danger is past. Mix the fine seed with sand for easier sowing and do not cover, as it needs light for germination. Thinning is not necessary.

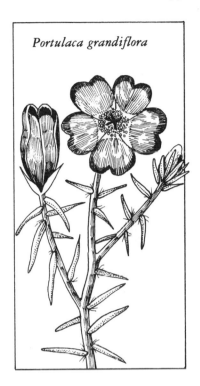

Portulaca grandiflora

I hesitate to mention another member of this genus, *P. oleracea* (H), because it's usually cursed as that pesky weed in the vegetable garden. Called purslane or pusley, the spatulate fleshy leaves on thick stems form living mats wherever there is any soil at all. Little yellow flowers quickly mature and form more seed and the beat goes on. The original plants probably came from India where it is used as a salad green or vegetable. I include it so that you know what it is and where it came from. There is a cultivar called 'Giganthes' with double flowers, 1 inch across, that is sometimes grown as an ornamental.

Proboscidea (pro-bos-sid′i-a) from the Greek for snout, in reference to the long-beaked fruit.

Before growing the unicorn plant, *P. louisianica* (HH), I was warned by many texts to beware of the flower's smell, an odor so obnoxious that advice is to plant it in an out-of-the-way place so the vapors never cross your path. If you do choose to stick your nose in the flower, you will detect an indelicate perfume reminiscent of rotten turpentine but not bad enough to make strong folk cry. The Navajos take black fibers from the seed pods and weave them into their baskets. Still called *Martynia* in many catalogs, the plant is a weak-stemmed annual that upon reaching a height of about a foot, falls over and starts to trail along the ground bearing three-lobed leaves about 6 inches wide. Stems and leaves are covered with short, sticky hairs. The

Proboscidea louisianica

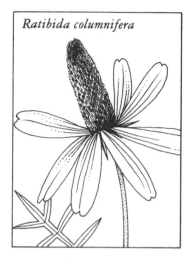

Ratibida columnifera

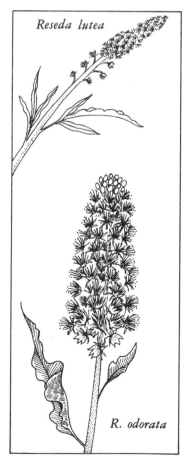

Reseda lutea

R. odorata

gloxinia-like flowers, 2 inches across, are quite beautiful, an off-white color dotted with violet about the mouth and orange-violet lines that lead to the bottom of the throat. However, the reason for growing this plant is not the flower but the seedpod, which is an arranger's delight. As the fruits mature, they look like a milkweed pod that soon splits at one end into two curling parts—hence the other common name, the devil's claw. Start seeds indoors four weeks before the last frost and plant outside after frost danger is past. Space plants about 2 feet apart.

Ratibida (rat'i-bi-da) has no known explanation.

The prairie coneflower or the Mexican hat, *R. columnifera* (H), is a native American perennial that will bloom the first year from seed. Most seed companies still list it as a member of the genus *Rudbeckia*. Of the two common names, Mexican hat is the best, for this flower looks like the kind of chapeau worn by the Ritz Brothers going Latin in a thirties movie. Flowers are yellow, on stems between 20 and 24 inches high. A Mexican hat with reddish-brown petals is called Forma *pulcherrima*. They are excellent massed in the border or the wild garden and make fine cut flowers. Start seeds indoors eight weeks before the last frost and plant outdoors after frost danger is over. Space plants 6 inches apart.

Reseda (re-zee'da) an ancient Latin name from *resedo*, to calm, as the plant was often applied to soothe external bruises.

Two species of mignonettes are usually found in our annual garden. *R. odorata* (H) is never grown for the flowers, which look very ragged and weedy but for the sweet perfume, an odor so delightful that it's grown commercially for an essential oil used in perfumery. Plants usually grow about 1½ feet in height with heavy stems and spatulate, limp leaves. Flowers are yellow-green to brownish yellow, small, in dense racemes, and nothing to write home about. But planted by the back door, underneath the kitchen window, next to a garden bench, or picked to add to a bouquet, they are wonderful. Seedlings resent transplanting so sow seeds directly outdoors as soon as the ground can be worked. Do not cover, as they need light for germination. Soil should be good and well-drained. Mignonettes prefer cooler climates and a bit of shade when the afternoon sun is hot. Space plants 10 to 12 inches apart.

R. lutea (H) is much more graceful in habit than others in the genus. Billed as an annual or a biennial, plants will flower the first year if started early. They bloom most of the summer on 2 1/2-foot stems covered with small, light yellow flowers. The leaves are three-lobed and deeply cut. We have built a raised bed of fieldstone set against a gentle hill in the backyard. I grow *R. lutea* along the top edge flanked by red coralbells, and by midsummer they lean over the wall, much like spires of yellow lace. Either plant can be seeded directly on the spot as soon as soil can be worked or you can start seeds indoors using 3-inch peat pots, thinning the seedlings to three per pot. Move out to cold frames when weather is settled and place in the garden in late May. Space plants 8 inches apart.

Rudbeckia (rood-beck'i-a) named in honor of the Professors Rudbeck, father and son.

Plant breeders have worked their wonders on black-eyed Susans, *R. hirta* (H), charming American wildflowers of the daisy family. By selective hybridizing of these annuals (and often short-lived perennials) the results have been the cultivars 'Gloriosa Daisy' and the 'Double Gloriosa Daisy', some of the most valuable flowers for the border, naturalizing in the wild garden, and for cutting. Flowers up to 6 inches wide on 2- to 3-foot stems will do well in almost any type of soil, withstand drought, and can even be transplanted in full bloom. Over the years they have self-seeded in our meadow. Petals are yellow, gold, orange, or reddish brown, and surround dark brown centers. The variety 'Irish Eyes' boasts a green center in place of the usual brown. Although impervious to the hottest sun, plants will also do beautifully in a bit of shade, especially in late afternoon. Start seeds directly outdoors as soon as the ground can be worked. Space plants about 1 foot apart.

Rudbeckia hirta 'Gloriosa Daisy'

Salpiglossis (sal-pi-gloss'is) from the Greek for tube and tongue, referring to a botanical feature of the flower.

One species of this genus is an annual in the garden bed or border or used as a cut flower or pot plant from the winter greenhouse. *S. sinuata* (T) comes from Chile. Its common name of painted tongue refers to the etched designs of color on the petals of the 2 1/2-inch flowers: Over basic tones of reddish-brown, carmine, violet, or black, the colors yellow, scarlet, pink, or blue are brushed over the tops of the

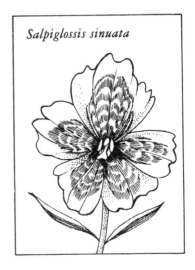

Salpiglossis sinuata

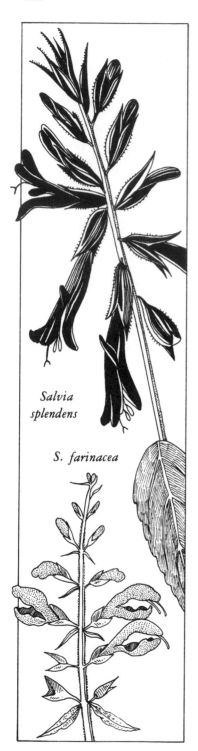

Salvia
splendens

S. farinacea

petals, then as though by an artist's hand, a network of veins in yellow, blue, maroon, or red is applied over all. Plants grow between 2 and 3 feet tall with narrow leaves.

Start seeds indoors eight weeks before the last frost. Do not cover the fine seeds with soil but blanket your flats or pots with black plastic as seeds must have darkness to germinate, a process completed in fifteen to twenty days. Plant out after all frost danger is past, in full sun and a rich, somewhat alkaline soil containing plenty of organic matter and with good drainage. If your soil is too acid work in some lime. Painted tongues will appreciate some organic fertilizer by midsummer, the best being dried blood dissolved in water. They might require some pea-stakes to hold the plants up. Space plants 1 foot apart.

Salvia (sal'vi-a) from the Latin *salveo,* to save or heal, referring to the healing properties of some species.

More than 750 species belong to this genus. Many of them are fine garden subjects, and a number of others are used for perfume oils, cooking, or in medicine. *S. farinacea* (HH) is a native perennial of Texas and New Mexico, not reliably hardy in most of the U.S. and thus usually treated as an annual. Violet-blue flowers 1 inch long grow in spikes to 3 feet high. The calyx, the cupped part of the flower that holds the petals, is dusted with a white powder, hence the common name of mealycup sage. Plants like any normal soil in sun or partial shade. Once happy, plants will self-sow over the years, becoming a large grouping. 'Silver White' bears free-blooming white flowers and 'Victoria' flowers of violet-blue. Both types look well together in the border, are excellent for cutting, and dry well for winter bouquets. Start seeds indoors six weeks before the last frost and set outdoors when frost danger is past. Seeds germinate in about fifteen days. Space plants about 1 foot apart.

The blue or gentian sage, *S. patens* (HH), is a perennial from Mexico with bright blue ultramarine flowers on 2-foot stems. A cultivar called 'Cambridge Blue' produces flowers of sky blue and forms tubers that can be dug up in fall, overwintered indoors, and used again the following year. Grow as above.

Scarlet sage, *S. splendens* (HH), is the plant usually thought of as the bedding sage. A perennial from Brazil that freely blooms the first year from seed, this semi-shrubby plant with deep green, glossy leaves has led to a host of cultivars. But the one usually remembered is the fire-red flower at home in every park planting in America. The height is between 3 and 30 inches, depending on the type, and flowers are available in red, white, violet, salmon, and pink. 'Rodeo' is a new variety with 10-inch plants bearing those fire red blossoms but in just seven weeks from seed. They do not make good cut flowers because the color will fade. 'Laser Purple' has flowers of a deep purple that are said to be resistant to fading. Scarlet sage is unexcelled as a bedding plant for it will bloom most of the summer and looks good in massed plantings. But handle the fire-red types with care as their intense color can outshine most of the other flowers in the garden. Start seeds indoors eight weeks before the last frost and plant out when frost danger is past. Space plants 1 foot apart.

S. viridis

S. viridis (HH), once called *S. Horminum,* is the only true annual (or sometimes biennial) member of this group. A native of Southern Europe, it's been grown in gardens since the late 1500s and was written up in the 1629 edition of John Parkinson's *Paradisi in Sole: Pareadisus Terrestris.* Plants have soft oval leaves with tiny hairs and bear erect spikes of purple, violet, or lilac-colored flowers about an inch long and surrounded by a bright purple bract. Grow as above.

Sanvitalia (san-vi-tal'ee-a) in honor of the Sanvitali family of Parma, Italy.

Sanvitalia procumbens

Creeping zinnias, *S. procumbens* (HH), are annuals from Mexico and perfect in the garden as an edging plant, in the rock garden, as spectacular flowers for a hanging basket, and a delightful pot plant for the greenhouse or sunporch. Flowers are 1 inch wide and do resemble zinnias. They stand above creeping stems never more than 6 inches high. The original flower is yellow but a new cultivar called 'Mandarin Orange' bears double flowers of a bright orange. A well-grown plant will cover an area of 2 feet and will start to flower in July. Sow seeds directly outdoors in late spring using light, well-drained soil in full sun. Do not cover, as seeds need light for germination, which takes five to ten days. Creeping zinnias resent transplanting but if you want an early start with flowering, sow seeds four weeks before the last frost using individual 3-inch peat pots. Space plants 14 inches apart.

Satureja (sat-you-ree'a) from the old Latin name for savory.

Summer savory, *S. hortensis* (H), is an annual herb growing about 1½ feet high and trailing with lilac-colored stems, green lance-shaped leaves, and pretty ½-inch flowers of white, lavender, or pink. Plants

Satureja hortensis

Saxifraga Cymbalaria

want full sun and well-drained soil and are perfect in the rock garden. Sow seeds directly outdoors in early spring. Space plants 8 inches apart. In the fall before the first frosts pull up the plants roots and all and hang them up to dry. The peppery thyme flavor is excellent in fresh sausages, stews, or soups. Summer savory was once thought to be an aphrodisiac.

Saxifraga (sacks-iff'ra-ga) from the Latin for rock, *saxum,* and *frango,* to break, referring to species that grow in crevices of rocks and assist in breaking them up.

There are some 300 species in the *Saxifraga* clan and many of them are stunning perennials usually grown in the rock garden and so diverse that plant authorities have divided them into groups. Group 5 are the Cymbalarias, small freely branched annuals with ivy-shaped leaves and golden or white star-shaped flowers. One charming member is *S. Cymbalaria* (HH). Its leaves are thick and fleshy, with five lobes, and very attractive in the rock garden or scree bed. Sow seeds directly outdoors in late spring or start indoors six weeks before the last frost. Space plants 6 inches apart. Plants often reseed themselves.

Scabiosa atropurpurea

S. stellata 'Drumstick'

Scabiosa (skay-bi-o'sa) from the Latin word for itch, alluding to the medicinal properties of some species.

Pincushion flowers, sweet scabious, or mourning brides are lovely annual plants perfect in the garden border either alone or with other plants and excellent as cut flowers. *S. atropurpurea* (HH) is the species generally offered in catalogs. Flowers are perfect 1-inch mounds of tiny blossoms with a sweet smell, on slender stems to 2 feet or more that rise from basal rosettes of deeply dived leaves. Colors come in maroon; red; pink; rose; purple; deep purple, almost black; lavender; cream; or white. Unopened buds look like colored raspberries or little Victorian brooches. 'Dwarf Double Mixed' are fully double flowers on stems to $1\frac{1}{2}$ feet. Butterflies love these blossoms. Plants like a sunny spot in any good garden soil. Start seeds indoors six weeks before the last frost and plant out to cold frames in May as they prefer cooler weather. Seeds germinate in fifteen days. Space plants 6 to 9 inches apart so flower stems help to support each other.

Paper moons, *S. stellata* 'Drumstick' (H), looks like typical, though somewhat anemic, pincushions in a washed-out shade of blue. But hold on, for as the flowers mature and go to seed, they ripen into bronze-colored, round seedheads that look more like coral fossils than flowers. Stems can reach 2 1/2 feet, making paper moons a decorator's delight for dried arrangements. Space plants 8 inches apart.

Schizanthus (sky-zan'thus) from the Greek for split flower, referring to a botanical feature of the flower.

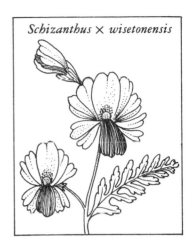

Schizanthus × wisetonensis

Butterfly flowers or poor man's orchid, *S. × wisetonensis* (HH), are unusually beautiful flowers and like many of our garden gems, from Chile. Plants reach 2 feet, have finely cut fernlike foliage and bear many 1 1/2-inch two-colored blossoms resembling little butterflies. Colors range from salmon, light pink, scarlet, and carmine to lilac, violet, and purple, all with exotic markings in the flower's throat. 'Morning Mist' is an improved Japanese variety in various shades of red and maroon, all with yellow centers. Start seeds indoors eight weeks before the last frost and plant outdoors after frost danger is past. Do not cover the fine seeds, but darkness is beneficial to germination so cover flats or pots with a sheet of black plastic. Germination usually takes 20 to 25 days. Move seedlings with care as the stems are brittle. Plants need a good soil with some moisture and prefer a spot in light shade where the climate is hot. Since butterfly flowers only last three or four weeks make successive sowings during late spring and summer for all-season bloom. Space plants 1 foot apart.

Schizopetalon (sky-zo-pet'a-lon) from the Greek for cut petals, alluding to the fringed petals.

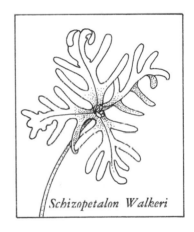

Schizopetalon Walkeri

A little known annual of great charm, *S. Walkeri* (HH), once again comes from Chile. Deeply cut four petalled flowers 3/4 inch wide have a sweet fragrance and are especially effective in pots or in the rock garden. Plants are usually 1 foot high and will bloom throughout the summer. Start seeds in individual 3-inch peat pots as plants resent transplanting, or start seeds outdoors in late spring. They take about eight weeks to bloom. Space plants 6 inches apart.

Sedum (see'dum) from the Latin to sit, a reference to the way plants grow on rocks and walls.

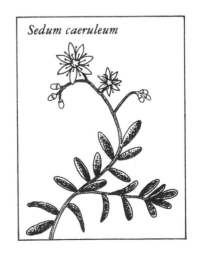

Sedum caeruleum

The sedums represent some 600 species of succulent plants but I only know of one annual worthy of growing in the rock garden, scree bed, or between the cracks in terrace paving and fieldstone walks. *S.*

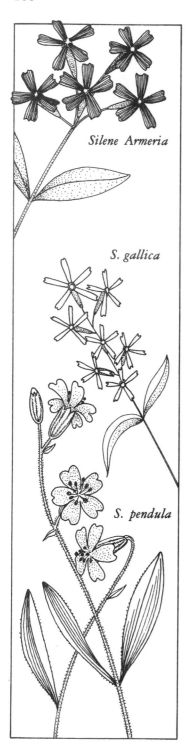

Silene Armeria

S. gallica

S. pendula

caeruleum (HH) comes from Southern Europe and Algeria. It only grows about 4 inches high, with glossy green and succulent leaves. The flowers are a pale blue and in a direct contrast to the plant stems, which turn a bronzy red as the summer heat progresses. Start seeds indoors eight weeks before the last frost and plant out in May. Space plants 4 inches apart.

Silene (sy-lee′ne) from the Greek *sailon* or saliva, referring to the sticky secretion on the stems of several species.

The catchflies—so called because the leaves of some species have a sticky surface that can trap tiny flies—are often common weeds, sometimes referred to as "seeds of troubled earth" because their seeds often lay in silent retreat for years until the earth is moved and they suddenly appear. The white campion, *S. alba* (H), is a perfect example, being found in fields and waste places across the U.S. But three annual species are excellent in the flower bed, border, or rock garden. Sweet William catchfly or none-so-pretty, *S. Armeria* (H), is a native of Southern Europe and has blue-gray leaves on stems to 2 feet high. It bears 3-inch clusters of pink flowers each ³/₄ inch in diameter. 'Royal Electric' bears masses of rosy pink flowerheads that virtually hide the leaves. An all-white cultivar called 'Alba' is also available. Sow seeds directly outdoors as soon as the ground can be worked. Plants like well-drained and slightly acid soil in full sun. Germination is in twelve to twenty days and plants will usually bloom for six weeks or more. Thin plants to 8 inches apart.

Nodding catchfly, *S. pendula* (H), is a native of the Mediterranean, and widely used as a dwarf bedding plant or planted along the edges of walls. 'Pendula Dwarf Mixed' produces plants 9 to 12 inches high and clusters of pink, rose, shell pink, and white flowers, ³/₄ inch wide. Grow as above.

S. gallica (H) is a pretty plant and not at all weedy. Flowers are small, ³/₈ inch long, white, and starlike. Blossoms form a one-sided row running down 1¹/₂-foot stem, opening slowly at dusk, just like twinkling stars on the garden's horizon. Space plants 6 inches apart using five or six to a grouping. Grow as above.

Stylomecon (sty-lo-me′con) from the Green *stylos*, style, and *mekon*, poppy, referring to a botanical feature.

Wind poppies, *S. heterophylla* (H) are one species of native American plants from California and the Baja peninsula. Flowers have four bright brick-orange petals with a large maroon blotch at the base of each petal and many yellow stamens in the center. Stems are 1¹/₂ to 2 feet high. They are beautiful in the rock garden or planted at the sea-side. Sow seeds directly outdoors in early spring as soon as the ground can be worked. Like most poppies they resent transplanting. Space plants 4 inches apart.

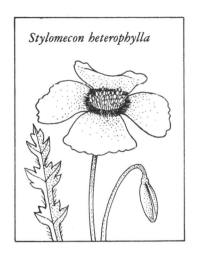

Stylomecon heterophylla

Tagetes (tay-gee′teez) from the Latin name of Tages, a grandson of Jupiter, who sprung from a clod of ploughed earth as a boy and taught the art of reading weather signs to the Etruscans.

What can one say about the marigold that hasn't been said already? First, the genus originally comes from Mexico and Central America. Its recorded history goes back to the Aztec Indians who used the plant for treatment of hiccups, being struck by lightning or "for one who wished to cross a river or a body of water in safety." In the 1500s native marigold seeds were taken to the Spanish court by explorers and were soon grown in monastery gardens. From there seeds went to France and Africa, and the American native eventually came to be called the African marigold. From Africa the seeds went on to India where the flowers are used to decorate village gods during harvest festivals. By the time of the American Revolution the marigold was re-introduced to colonial gardens. Then in 1915 David Burpee took over the William Atlee Burpee company and began investing money in marigold development. Today there are hundreds of cultivars and after years of searching, Burpees have developed a white marigold. Use the flowers in beds, borders, for edging, in containers, in baskets, and even in the vegetable garden where a chemical found in the marigold root does a good job of repelling nematodes.

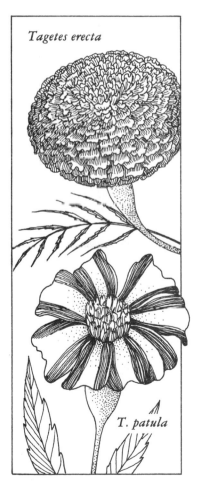

Tagetes erecta

T. patula

The African or American marigold, *T. erecta* (HH), has the largest leaves and flowers. Flowers are either semi-double or fully double from 3 to 4¹/₂ inches across in solid colors of orange, yellow, gold, cream, and the fabled white. According to the cultivar, plants vary from 9 inches for a dwarf to over 3 feet for the larger types and are usually placed at the rear of the bed or border. Start seeds indoors eight weeks before the last frost and plant out after frost danger is past. Transplant to larger containers as the seedlings grow. Space plants according to the variety.

The French marigolds, *T. patula* (HH), are smaller plants rang-ing in height from 6 to 14 inches. Colors are solid or bicolored with

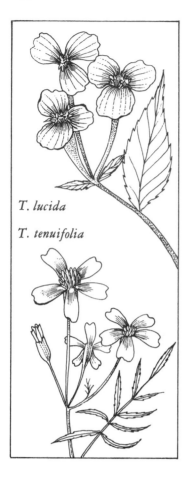

T. lucida

T. tenuifolia

orange, yellow, gold, or mahogany red combinations. They have been divided into five groups: single flowers; anemone flowering with rows of overlapping petals surrounding a central disc; carnation flowering with fully double flowers and numerous rows overlapping petals; and the crested flowers where the flower center is made of numerous short petals surrounded by either single or double rows of outside petals, French marigolds can be sown directly outdoors as soon as the soil temperature is 70°F. and will flower six to twelve weeks after sowing. Space plants according to the variety.

The signet marigolds, *T. tenuifolia* (HH), are also smaller plants reaching about 1 foot in height. Blossoms are single, about 1 inch wide, with a yellow center and surrounded by five yellow petals. 'Pumila' is a name applied to many dwarf and compact plants in this species. They are the most charming of the marigolds and useful as edging in the border.

Cloud plant or the anise-flavored marigold, *T. lucida* (T), is a perennial from Mexico but grown as an annual, usually in the herb garden. Plants are 1½ inches high with toothed, lance-shaped leaves and single orange-gold flowers blooming in high summer. The whole plant is sweetly scented and leaves are used to flavor soups or dried for making an herb tea. Plants can be dug up before frost and brought indoors for the winter. Sow seeds eight weeks before the last frost and plant out in a sheltered but sunny spot after frost danger is past. Space plants 8 inches apart.

Irish lace, *T. filifolia* (T), is grown for the foliage (see page 171).

Thelesperma Burridgeanum

Thelesperma (thell-e-sper′ma) from the Greek for wart and seed, referring to the surface of some fruits in the family.

A native of Texas, *T. Burridgeanum* (HH) look somewhat like coreopsis but have just a bit more snap to their posture and color. Flowers are 1½ inches across in maroon, with overlapping petals and golden yellow edges surrounding a purple center. Stems are 1½ to 2 feet high, with finely divided leaves and flowers suitable in the border or for cutting. Last year I planted them in front of the gray concrete stand for our sundial where they bobbed back and forth in the summer breeze until cut down by the autumn frost. Start seeds indoors six weeks before the last frost and plant out in late May. Space plants 6 inches apart.

Tithonia (ti-tho-ni-a) from Tithonus, beloved of Eos, a goddess who asked Zeus for immortality for her lover but forgot to ask for eternal youth.

Mexican sunflowers, *T. rotundifolia* (HH), are large dots of color for the back of the garden border or bed. The big, 3-inch-wide flowers are ablaze with fiery highlights. They are spectacular plants that can easily reach 6 feet in height so are excellent used as a temporary screen or hedge. Leaves are large and velvety to the touch. Plants will take a poor soil but need full sun to be at their best advantage, enduring drought conditions with ease. They are fine as cut flowers but remember to seal the hollow stem ends with a match or gas flame as you would with poppies. 'Goldfinger' is a new type in a bright orange-scarlet and 'Yellow Torch' is a bright, bright, yellow. Start seeds indoors six weeks before the last frost and plant outdoors after frost danger is past. Space plants 2 feet apart.

Tithonia rotundifolia

Tolpis (toll′pis) a name of unknown derivation.

Many of the hawkweeds are excessively weedy, but *T. barbata* (T) with its 1¼-inch daisy-like flowers of a sulfur yellow are a happy addition to the bed or border. There is no center disc like on the daisy, but the inner petals are reddish brown with yellow tips. Irregular filaments appear behind the flowers. Plants can reach 2 feet in height. Leaves are lance-shaped and stems have a milky sap like dandelions. Plants will do well in poor soil and withstand heat and lack of water. Start seeds indoors six weeks before the last frost and plant outdoors after frost danger is past. Space plants 6 inches apart.

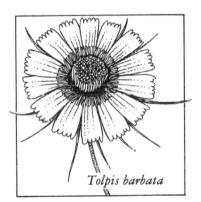

Tolpis barbata

Torenia (tor-ren′i-a) in honor of Olaf Toren, a Swedish clergyman and botanist.

Bluewings or wishbone flowers, *T. Fournieri* (HH), are annuals from Vietnam and fine for bedding, borders, edges, in planters and baskets, and make good houseplants after the summer is over, flowering until well into winter. Trumpet-shaped flowers like small gloxinias are sky blue with violet lips and a yellow throat. Two stamens (the filaments that bear a flower's pollen) bend about the top of the throat margin and look exactly like a wishbone from a Thanksgiving turkey. Lobe-shaped leaves are a bronzy green. Plants grow about 1 foot tall. They will take full sun only in the North and are often used in place

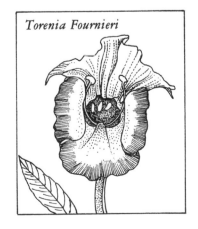

Torenia Fournieri

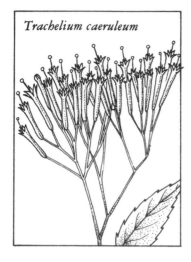

Trachelium caeruleum

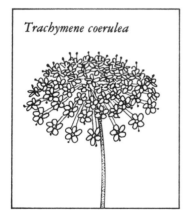

Trachymene coerulea

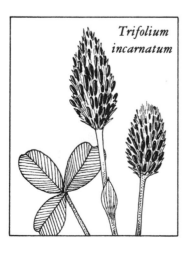

Trifolium incarnatum

of petunias in the Deep South. Start seeds indoors ten weeks before the last frost and plant outdoors when frost danger is past. Germination takes fifteen to twenty days. Space plants 6 to 8 inches apart.

Trachelium (tra-kee′li-um) from the Greek for neck, alluding to a supposed medical value in treating sore throats.

Throatworts, *T. caeruleum* (T), are perennials native to the Mediterranean region and grown as annuals in the North. Violet to blue flowers are small, less than ¹/₂ inch on a long tube, but hundreds make up the clustered blossoms, often 5 inches across. Stems are between 2 and 3 feet tall with oval leaves some 3 inches long. Flowers are fine grouped in the border and make excellent cut flowers. 'White Umbrella' bears white flowers. Plants are fine in ordinary garden soil, in full sun or a bit of shade, and grow well in pots. Start seeds indoors ten weeks before the last frost and plant outdoors when frost danger is past. It takes five months for the plants to bloom from seed. Space plants 1 foot apart.

Trachymene (tra-kee-mee′ne) from the Greek for rough membrane, referring to the fruit of some species.

Blue lace flower, *T. coerulea* (HH), is a true annual from Australia and looks like a scabiosa that has opened up and spread out. Small flowers of sky blue form discs up to 3 inches in diameter (the old genus name was *Didiscus*). These are popular cut flowers often found in flower shops. Plants grow 2 to 3 feet high and bear delicate, finely divided leaves. Blue lace flowers do best in cooler climates and stop blooming when weather is too hot. They resent heavy clay soils and want full sun. Start seeds indoors eight weeks before the last frost making sure the seeds are covered because they need darkness for germination, a process taking fifteen to twenty days. Or plant directly outdoors in late spring. Use individual 3-inch peat pots as the seedlings resent transplanting. Thin plants to 10 inches apart.

Trifolium (try-fo′li-um) from the Latin for three leaves.

Italian red clover or crimson clover, *T. incarnatum* (H), has never been overly popular in American gardens, probably because most people would think of it as a forage plant. But while the plant looks like any clover growing up to 2 feet high, the flowers are 2¹/₂-inch spikes of usually crimson but sometimes pink, or white flowers. To find the seeds look in English catalogs. We grow it for a pleasing addition to summer bouquets and a colorful member of the wild side of the annual border. Sow seeds directly outdoors in early spring. Space plants 8 to 10 inches apart.

Triodanis (try-o'dan-iss) a name of unknown derivation.

T. perfoliata (H) are native American wildflowers often confused with the *Specularias* (which see) but now are given their own genus. The plants grow to 2 feet, have few branches and the square stems bear leaves without stalks and blue to deep purple, five-petalled flowers about ¹/₂ inch long. They are used in woodland gardens where they will naturalize, and as pretty but unspectacular flowers for the garden border. Plant seeds directly outdoors in early spring. Space plants 6 inches apart.

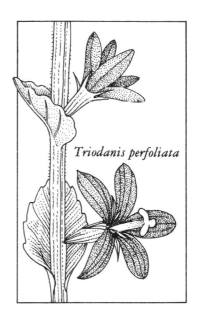

Triodanis perfoliata

Tropaeolum, the nasturtium genus is listed under vines and includes mention of the dwarf types that do not climb.

Ursinia (ur-sin'i-a) in honor of Johan Ursinus, a seventeenth century botanical author who wrote about plants mentioned in the Bible.

Jewel-of-the-Veldt is the common name for the *Ursinia* clan and it's a befitting name for these lovely flowers discovered in South Africa in 1836. They must have fertile, well-drained soil and do not flourish in areas of above-average rain. Instead they want warmth—not intense heat—and sunshine. These gems of the garden are beautiful planted in drifts or for edging in the border. Flowers close at night. *U. anethoides* (HH) is a perennial that flowers the first year from seed. Basically a sub-shrub, plants are between 1¹/₂ and 2 feet tall with finely cut leaves that are aromatic when bruised. Daisy-like flowers 2 inches in diameter with petals of a lovely shade of orange-yellow have a dark purple ring surrounding the central disc. 'New Hybrids' has flowers of both orange and yellow. Sow the fine seeds indoors six weeks before the last frost and plant outdoors after frost danger is past. Plants flower eleven weeks after sowing. Set plants 8 inches apart.

U. anthemoides (HH) is an annual species 12 to 16 inches high with flowers 1¹/₂ inches wide. They differ from the above species in that the petals are a violet-purple underneath. Grow as above.

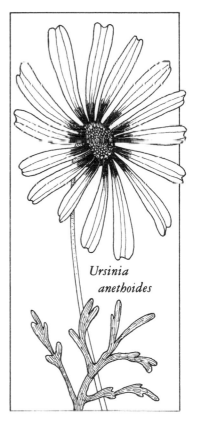

Ursinia
anethoides

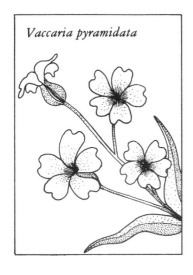

Vaccaria pyramidata

U. calendulifolia (HH) is a dwarf species under 1 foot with orange flowers with deep yellow centers deepening to purple and black spots near the base of the petals. Grow as above.

U. sericea (HH) is another perennial sub-shrub species known as the laceleaf ursinia. Plants grow about 2 feet high with lacy, silvery foliage and canary yellow flowers held high on thin stems. Grow as above.

Vaccaria (vak-kair′i-a) from the Latin *vacca,* cow, as the plant is said to be good fodder.

The cow herb, cockle, or dairy pink is now known as *V. pyramidata* (H), but most catalogs still list it as *Saponaria vaccaria* or *Lychnis vaccaria*. It's a lovely annual from Southern Europe with five-petalled, $1/2$-inch, deep pink flowers on 2 foot plants with smooth, ovate leaves. 'Pink Beauty' has more flowers than the type. Although it is often a weed in the grain fields of North America, it's still a beautiful flower for the garden. Sow seeds outdoors in early spring and thin plants to 9 inches apart.

Venidium fastuosum

Venidium (ve-nid′i-um) possibly from the Latin *vena,* a vein, referring to the ribbed seed pods.

The monarch-of-the-Veldt, Namaqualand daisy, or the Cape daisy are annual plants, again from South Africa, and fine in the bed, border, or a greenhouse, and, although they close at night, excellent cut flowers. The species usually offered is *V. fastuosum* (HH), bearing flowers between 4 and 5 inches wide, somewhat like sunflowers with bright orange petals marked with black feathering at the base and surrounding a disc of brownish purple to black. Plants are 2 feet tall with deeply cut leaves up to 6 inches long and covered with fine silvery hairs that sparkle in the sun. Plants need well-drained, sandy soil in full sun and dislike a damp climate. Sow seeds eight weeks before the last frost and plant out after frost danger is past. Do not cover seeds as they need light to germinate. Space plants 1 foot apart.

Verbena (ver-bee′na) possibly from the Latin *verbenae,* the sacred branches of laurel, olive, or myrtle carried by heralds and some priests.

The vervain or garden verbena, *V. × hybrida* (HH), is a perennial hybrid that freely blooms the first year from seed. This is a valuable garden plant: upright varieties are excellent for massing in beds and as edging plants, while others will commonly creep and are perfect for a spot along a stone wall in the rock garden or for pots and containers. They are great groundcovers and if you peg the plants down, the stems will root at the joints and nodes to fill in bare spots in the garden. Verbenas are also charming cut flowers. Heights now range between 6 and 12 inches according to the cultivar. Dark green lightly cut leaves form basal rosettes and individual flowers up to 1 inch wide make flat clusters of bloom, 2 to 3 inches across. Colors are blue, purple, red, pink, lavender, yellow, and white. 'Amethyst' bears vivid cobalt blue flowers with a distinct white eye; 'Tropic' has cerise-crimson flowers without eyes, and 'Blaze' is a vivid scarlet. Verbenas like good garden soil in full sun but adapt easily to sandy soils, too. Sow seeds indoors twelve weeks before the last frost and set out after frost danger is past. Plants will bloom in about 90 days from seed. On an average, space plants 10 to 12 inches apart or according to the variety.

Verbena × hybrida

V. rigida (HH), often called *V. venosa,* is a perennial species from Brazil that flowers freely the first year from seed. Stems up to 2 feet in length will tumble out of a planter or a large tub, and be completely covered with lavender-blue flowers. Grow as above.

Verbesina (ver-be-sy′na) from a supposed resemblance to some species of Verbena.

Crown-beards are American natives from the western U.S. and Mexico. Many of the genus are trees and shrubs but one annual, *V. encelioides* (HH), bears daisy-like flowers 2 inches wide on stems up to 3 feet. Leaves are about 4 inches long with a toothed edge. They are fine back-of-the-border plants and excellent as cut flowers. In our annual garden we plant them in front of the Mexican sunflowers. Start seeds indoors six weeks before the last frost using individual 3-inch peat pots, as the seedlings are difficult to transplant. Or sow seeds directly outdoors in late May. Seeds germinate in eight to ten days. Space plants 18 inches apart.

Vinca (vin′ka) from the Latin *vincio,* to bind, referring to the long runners.

The vincas are all evergreen perennial plants but one species, *V. major* 'Variegata' (T), is grown as an annual for its trailing stems and

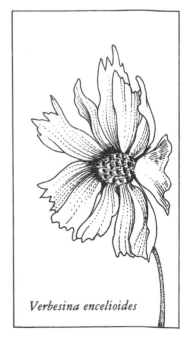

Verbesina encelioides

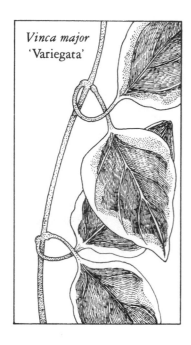

Vinca major
'Variegata'

green and cream-white foliage. Madagascar periwinkle once called *V. rosea,* was included in this genus but is now known as *Catharanthus roseus* (which see). This plant is often seen growing in containers and hanging baskets and is especially attractive growing from a second floor windowbox. Most nursery centers have plants in the spring and new plants are started from cuttings, not from seeds.

Viola (vy-o'la) from the old Latin name for violet.

Garden pansies are a relatively new plant. They were developed by plant breeders who started with a European annual or short-lived perennial, *V. tricolor* (H)—commonly called the miniature pansy, field pansy, or Johnny-jump-up—and two other perennials, *V. lutea* and *V. altaica.* The end result is the much-loved bedding plant, edging for the border, groundcover, and cut flower, *V.* × *Wittrockiana* (HH) the pansy. Flowers often reach a diameter of 4 inches. Colors are gold, yellow, blue, purple, rose, violet, orange, lavender, white, and bicolored, with most flowers having the markings that create the look of a fanciful face but some with only a center eye of yellow.

Although still perennial, pansies are best grown as annuals since they loose vitality by the second year. Because these plants like cool, cool weather, it's not always easy to grow them from seed. Most gardeners without a greenhouse generally buy pansies from a garden center. If you do try, sow seeds in a cool place (about 50°F.) twelve weeks before the last frost. Seeds will germinate in ten days. When the weather is settled, seedlings should be moved out to a cold frame as they really resent heat. Plant out in the garden in a good, well-drained soil with full sun or partial shade; summer heat, especially in the South, will do them in. Space plants 6 inches apart and remember to pinch off dead blossoms.

Pansy cultivars are legion. Look for 'Black Pansy' with a satiny black face and a bright yellow eye; 'Joker' with petals of light violet, white, and dark purple fading into the yellow throat; or the charming 'Baby Lucia', a true miniature pansy with 1½-inch blossoms of lavender-blue and perfect for the rock garden.

The field pansy, *V. Rafinesquii* (H), is now naturalized over much of the eastern U.S. It's an annual growing to 1 foot high with spatula-shaped leaves and small flowers to ½ inch wide in colors of bluish white to cream. Purple veins adorn the petals, leading to a yellow throat. Sow seeds in the wild garden early in the spring and thin to 6 inches apart.

Viola × *Wittrockiana*

V. Rafinesquii

Bishop's weed is the common name of *Ammi majus,* a field annual from Europe that makes both an effective blooming hedge in the garden and an excellent cut flower. Sweet alyssum carpets the foreground.

A wildflower from the American west, *Coreopsis tinctoria* is at home either in the wild garden or the formal border.

Coreopsis 'Tiger Flower' is an improved cultivar of the old standard coreopsis and is produced by Thompson & Morgan.

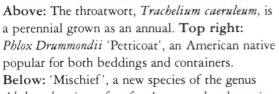

Above: The throatwort, *Trachelium caeruleum,* is a perennial grown as an annual. **Top right:** *Phlox Drummondii* 'Petticoat', an American native popular for both beddings and containers. **Below:** 'Mischief', a new species of the genus *Abelmoschus,* is perfect for the sunny border or in a pot on a windowsill. **Bottom right:** Garden verbenas, *Verbena* x *hybrida,* are perennial hybrids that bloom the first year from seed.

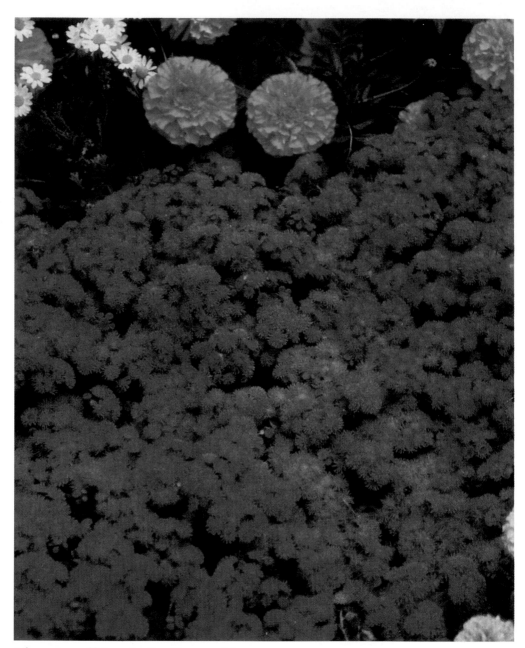

Like a river of blue, the flossflower cultivar
Ageratum Houstonianum 'Blue Danube' flows
between a field of marigolds. The compact
mounds of fluffy blossoms thrive in full sun
and average soil.

A new discovery by Thompson & Morgan is an annual poppy called 'Fairy Wings' originally found some 30 years ago in the Hadleigh garden of Sir Cedric Morris, an East Anglian artist.

A white variety of the annual poppy, *Papaver Rhoeas*, blooms in company with crisped musk mallow *Malva verticillata* var. *crispa*.

Opposite page, top: Bells-of-Ireland or Molucca balm, *Moluccella laevis,* are perfect plants for the annual border, cut flowers, or dried for winter bouquets. **Bottom left:** Spider flowers, *Cleome Hasslerana,* look more like blooming shrubbery than annual flowers and are especially effective when massed in the border. **Above:** One of the most beautiful of the flowering tobaccos is *Nicotiana sylvestris,* especially when given a bit of shade from the noonday sun. The companion flowers are black-eyed Susans, *Rudbeckia hirta.*

Opposite page, top: An annual garden featuring sweet alyssum, impatiens, and marigolds. **Bottom left:** *Linanthus grandiflorus,* a California wildflower, is most beautiful when planted in drifts. **Right:** The magnificent cardoon, *Cynara cardunculus,* is a close relative of the artichoke and welcomed for its fans of green-gray foliage and thistle-like blossoms.

Four o'clocks or the miracle-of-Peru, *Mirabilis Jalapa,* are perennials grown as annuals, noted for opening their flowers in late afternoon. The tubers can be wintered over for next year's garden.

Greek forget-me-nots, *Omphalodes linifolia,* are often called navelworts because their seeds look exactly like their common namesake. They are beautiful against stone walls and make excellent cut flowers.

The tree mallows, *Lavatera trimestris,* resemble hollyhocks but bloom throughout the summer. 'Silver Cup' is the form usually offered but an all-white flower called 'Mont Blanc' is sometimes available.

This unnamed variety of the bush morning glory, *Convolvulus tricolor,* bears variegated leaves and flowers of rosy red, pink, and sky blue, all with white margins.

Nothing is more
delightful than a rustic
fence covered with a
confusion of morning
glories. *Ipomoea tricolor*
are perennial vines that
bloom the first year
from seed. The garden
is Wave Hill.

A field of California
poppies in bloom in the
1985 hardy trials for
annuals held by the
Royal Horticultural
Society at Wisley. They
are *Eschscholzia* 'Double
Monarch Art Shades'
and have frilled flowers
on compact plants.

Clasping-leaved coneflowers, *Dracopsis amplexicaulis,* are native American wildflowers growing from Kansas to Texas and south to Georgia. They adapt to partial shade and are excellent as cut flowers.

Gloriosa daisies, a cultivar of *Rudbeckia,* are impervious to the hottest sun and the poorest of soils, yet reward the gardener with nonstop flowers from late July until the frosts of fall.

Opposite page, top: A patch of yellow cosmos, *Cosmos sulphureus,* bloom in a cutting garden. If dead flowers are removed they will flower steadily until well into fall. **Bottom left:** Feverfew, *Chrysanthemum Parthenium* 'White Stars,' a perennial that blooms the first year from seed. **Below:** Annual chrysanthemums, *Chrysanthemum carinatum* 'Court Jesters', are a mixture of single flowers with various colored zones and centers blooming in the field trials for annuals conducted by the Royal Horticultural Society at Wisley.

Even with
limited space, an
annual garden
will burst with
bloom. In the
tub a dwarf form
of the sunflower
*Helianthus
annuus* called
'Teddy Bear'
shares space with
blue salvia and
marigolds.

Flowers of the iceplant, *Mesembryanthemum crystallinum,* are perfect for edgings in the border or in windowboxes. Here they happily trail along in a rock garden setting.

Monkey flowers, *Mimulus* x *hybridus,* are perennials from Chile grown as annuals. They prefer a cool and moist soil with plenty of organic matter and flower well in partial shade. The other flowers are garden verbenas.

The brilliant colors of the garden nasturtium, *Tropaeolum majus,* coupled with their becoming blossoms make them attractive additions to any annual garden. The blue flowers are the florist's cineraria, *Senecio* x *hybridus,* greenhouse plants usually offered around Mother's Day.

Snapdragons, *Antirrhinum majus,* have been a perennial favorite in the annual garden for decades. The variety shown is the new 'Princess White with Purple Eye'.

One of the more beautiful native American annuals is the basket flower, *Centaurea americana.* The common name refers to the unopened flower head because the soft strawcolored fingers that overlap the bud resemble tiny woven baskets.

Left: The prairie rose, *Eustoma grandiflorum,* is one of the most sought-after annuals in the nursery trade. **Below:** *Reseda lutea,* is a biennial that often acts as an annual or a perennial depending on its whims. Here it shares space with perennial coralbells, *Heuchera* spp. **Opposite page:** A glorious field of wildflowers: Texas bluebonnets, *Lupinus texensis,* and California poppies, *Eschscholzia californica.*

Opposite page, top: Meadow foam, *Limnanthes Douglasii,* is a beautiful wildflower from California that likes moist soil and cool weather. **Bottom left:** A charming garden of annuals including California poppies, sweet alyssum, dahlias, and larkspur. **Above:** An annual border that uses castor beans as a backdrop, then in descending order, red and blue salvia, flossflowers, and dusty miller.

Above: Fennel, *Foeniculum vulgare,* is a chancy perennial best grown as an annual. Here in the author's garden it mixes freely with hollyhocks, summer phlox, and ornamental grasses.

Opposite page, top: A country garden features bands of scarlet salvia, signet marigolds, and sweet alyssum, planted in bands of color to resemble the composition of a modern painting.

Right: Flossflowers, sweet alyssum, marigolds, and salvia in another bed of annuals. All three gardens are in the Catskill Mountains of Sullivan County, New York.

138

139

Above: Coneflowers, *Echinacea purpurea,* are American native perennial wildflowers that will bloom the first year from seed if plants are started early in the spring. Here they are in company with sweet alyssum and signet marigolds. **Right:** The ripened seedheads of *Scabiosa stellata* 'Drumstick' are a decorator's delight for dried arrangements. **Opposite page:** A small composition of annuals features sweet alyssum, pansies, pinks, and an unusual white form of the flowering kale, *Brassica oleracea.*

Foxtail millet, *Setaria italica,* is one of the most valuable of the annual ornamental grasses both for the garden border and for cut flowers.

Witch grass, *Panicum capillare*—an annual grass that is called a menace by most vegetable gardeners—is quite beautiful when held at bay in a restricted part of the garden.

Not only are the flowers of love-in-a-mist, *Nigella damascena,* attractive, their ripening seedpods inflate like balloons adorned with jester's caps, minus the bells.

Holiday peppers, *Capsicum annuum,* are perennial natives of tropical America grown as annuals, not for the flowers but for the colorful fruits that come in shades of orange, yellow, green, red, and a purple so deep it almost looks black.

The silver-gray foliage of the dusty-millers, in this case *Centaurea Cineraria,* makes an effective foil for most annual flowers.

Summer cypress, *Kochia scoparia,* is an annual plant that closely resembles a dwarf conifer. Here a number of them are planted with geraniums, blue salvia, and look far more permanent than they really are.

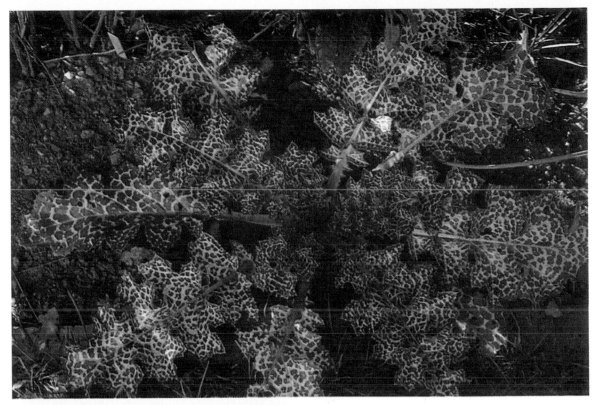

St. Mary's thistle, *Silybum Marianum,* is an annual or biennial grown for the attractive and spiny leaves that are dotted with a fine network of silvery veins and spots. The plants do well in very poor and dry soil.

The leaves of the flame nettles, *Coleus* x *hybridus,* come in an almost endless variety of colors including shades of red, orange, pink, yellow, chartreuse, bronze, and purple, and each year new color variations appear from the plant breeders. Pictured is 'Persian Carpet'.

A country garden features an unusual type of Prince's feather, in this case *Amaranthus hybridus* var. *erythrostachys*. The plant is grown for the showy clusters of minute flowers, the handsome foliage, and the edible seeds.

A bed of woolflowers, *Celosia cristata,* shimmer in the summer sun. These plants produce flowers that look like feathers, spires, or pieces of coral and are often called an acquired taste by many gardeners.

The Johnny-jump-up. *V. tricolor* (H), is an annual or short-lived perennial originally from Europe and now naturalized around the temperate world. Hardly an abandoned country garden does not have this flower still blooming every spring. Flowers are tricolored in purple, yellow, and white about 3/4 inch long. Look for 'Bowles Black', a variety with petals that are almost black and a tiny yellow eye at the center; often listed as *V. nigra,* a meaningless botanical name.

Viola tricolor 'Bowles Black'

Xanthisma (zan-this'ma) from the Greek word for yellow, the flower color.

The star-of-Texas, *X. texana* (H), or the sleepy daisy, is an American native and an erect annual about 2 to 3 feet tall and bearing 2 1/2-inch blossoms with citron-yellow petals surrounding a yellow disc. Leaves are toothed along the margin. Plant in drifts for the wild garden or in groupings for the border. The common name refers to the flower's habit of closing at night and in dull weather. Sow seeds directly outdoors in early spring. Germination takes 25 to 30 days. Thin plants to 6 inches apart.

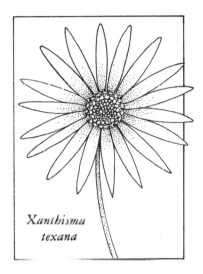

Xanthisma texana

Xeranthemum (zer-ran'the-mum) from the Greek *xeros,* dry, and *anthos,* a flower.

The immortelles or everlastings are annual plants from the Mediterranean region around Iran and *X. annuum* (HH) is one of the oldest such flowers in cultivation. They are attractive and easily grown flowers with white, woolly leaves and white or pink daisy-like blossoms 1 1/2 inches wide. Plants grow between 2 and 3 feet tall. Grow them in the garden border or in the cutting garden and use as cut flowers both in fresh or dried arrangements. Sow seeds directly outdoors in late spring in a sandy soil and full sun. Or start seeds indoors eight weeks before the last frost using individual peat pots, as seedlings resent transplanting. Seeds germinate in ten days and plants bloom about eleven weeks after sowing. Space plants 8 inches apart.

Xeranthemum annuum

Zinnia (zin'i-a) in honor of Johann Gottfried Zinn, an eighteenth-century German professor of botany.

Zinnias are true American natives originally from the southwest U.S., Mexico, and Central America. They are a perfect example of the genius of hybridizers who took the original plant, *Z. elegans* (HH), a rather dowdy purplish red wildflower of the Mexican deserts and turned it into one of the three most popular bedding plants in the country. As the flower develops and the petals around the disc start to fade, the tiny, true flowers in the central disc begin to open, hence the common name of youth-and-old-age.

Plants grow between 6 and 40 inches tall with blossoms either single or double and varying from a diameter of less than 1 inch to an astounding 7 inches. Colors are red, orange, rose, cherry, pink, salmon, purple, lavender, gold, yellow, cream, white, and even light green. There are multicolored petals, too. Leaves and stems are thick and of a good green color. Since the flowers are not fussy, they fill many empty shoes in the garden. They can be massed in beds, used for edging, planted in pots and containers, and the taller varieties make fine backgrounds to the border. They are also excellent as cut flowers. Zinnias want a reasonably fertile, well-drained soil in full sun. Make sure there is free circulation of air because plants are susceptible to mildew if subjected to too much damp.

Different flower shapes have been developed and named. A few of the groups are: California or giant-flowered with globular blossoms up to 6 inches across; cactus-flowered, featuring shaggy blossoms 4 to 5 inches across; giant doubles with double-flowered heads up to 5 inches in diameter; pumila or the cut-and-come-again zinnias being

Zinnia elegans

bushy plants to 2 feet tall, one of the easiest to grow, and blooming
almost continuously; scabiosa-flowered, with large, rounded crests with
a row of lower petals; and lilliput or pompom zinnias, dwarf plants
with small pom-pom flowers 1 to 2 inches in diameter. The only way
to keep up with the continuing development of the zinnia is to check
every seed catalog, every year.

Sow seeds indoors six weeks before the last frost and plant
outdoors after frost danger is past as young plants are susceptible to
chilling cold. In fact zinnias will not grow with any speed until
temperatures are above 50°F. Sow the giant varieties in individual
3-inch peat pots because these seedlings resent transplanting. Or sow
seeds directly outdoors in May for flowers by August and September.
Pinch young plants to make them bushy and always remove old
flowers. Space plants 6 to 12 inches apart according to the variety.

Z. Haageana (HH), the Mexican zinnia, is a smaller plant, 1 to
1½ feet tall, with narrow leaves and pretty single or double flowers
about 2 inches across in colors of red, mahogany, orange, and yellow.
Look for the cultivar 'Persian Carpet' a mix of bicolored blossoms in
maroon, gold, purple, chocolate, pink, and cream. Grow as above.

Z. angustifolia (HH)—once called *Z. linearis*—grows about 1
foot tall and bears single flowers of a golden yellow, about 2 inches
across. Grow as above.

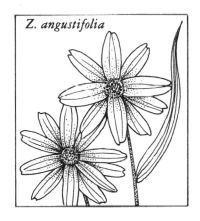

Z. angustifolia

Z. Haageana
'Persian Carpet'

CHAPTER 5

Foliage, Fruits, and Vegetables

George Cooper (who wrote the words to *Sweet Genevieve*) said: "After the shower, the tranquil sun; after the snow, the emerald leaves," and that image while not proving that leaves are more important than flowers, certainly goes a long way in reflecting such sentiment. And if that leaf, instead of being green, blares forth in strumpet colors, then our gardens can only benefit.

The following plants are grown not for their flowers, which are often too small or insignificant to be noticed, but for the leaves, the fruits, or the fact that some are welcome additions to both soup and salad.

Abelmoschus (a-bel-mos′kus) Arabic for musky-smelling seeds.

Okra, gumbo, and gombo are common names for *A. esculentus* (T), an annual herb quite popular in the South, grown for the large, green pods that are an essential part of chicken gumbo soup. The plants grow up to 5 feet high in the North and bear pretty yellow flowers, 2 to 3 inches across, each with a red eye. The pods are ribbed and beaked. It's a fine plant for the background of a garden but the ripening pods must continue to be picked if the plants are to stay in bloom. 'Okra Lee' is a shorter plant usually only reaching 3 feet. 'Okra Red' forms a 5-foot bush with reddish-brown leaves and bearing attractive red pods that later dry to a red-brown and make splendid dried flowers. Start seeds four to six weeks before the last frost. Soak the seeds for 24 hours in warm water before sowing. Germination is in 10 to 14 days. Do not move seedlings outdoors until the ground is warm. Plants need full sun and soil should be rich and well-drained. Space plants 1¹/₂ feet apart.

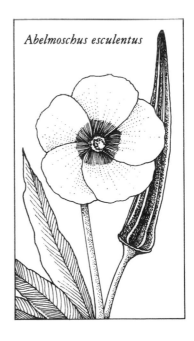

Abelmoschus esculentus

Amaranthus tricolor

Amaranthus (am-a-ran'thus) from the Greek *a,* not, and *maraino,* to fade, referring to the lasting quality of the flowers.

Tampala, *A. tricolor* (T), is a tender annual often called Joseph's-coat because of the yellow, green, and crimson leaves. The plants have been in cultivation since Elizabethan times, when it was written: "Every leaf resembles the most faire and beautiful feather of a parat." The plant is also a very nutritious potherb. The flowers are insignificant and plants are grown entirely for foliage which is extremely bright and tropical, more at home in Jamaca than a split-level in the suburbs. The taller varieties can be used as temporary shrubs, but these plants can often outshine everything else in sight. They are best used in pots to decorate a terrace or porch. 'Illumination' produces long, narrow leaves of scarlet widely brushed with gold on the top third of plants 4 feet high. 'Salicifolius Splendens' has foliage of a deep red on plants 2 feet high. Plants want an average soil in full sun. Start seeds indoors six weeks before the last frost and plant out after all danger of frost is past. Germination is in ten days. Space plants from 1 to 1¹/₂ feet depending on the cultivar.

Atriplex (at'ri-plex) from the Greek word for orach.

Mountain spinach or garden orach, *A. hortensis* (T), is a member of the goosefoot family that is grown both for the greens used in salads and the ornamental foliage in the garden. The flowers are insignificant. Since the plants can reach 5 feet they are excellent as quick hedges for the garden border. When young the leaves are often covered with a whitish bloom. References often suggest using the cut stems in flower arrangements. Plants want a good soil in full sun and well-drained. They are often used in seaside plantings. 'Cupreatorosea' has leaves and stems of red with a coppery luster; 'Rosea' bears leaves of light red with darker veins; and 'Rubra' is blood-red. Start seeds indoors six weeks before the last frost or plant directly outdoors when frost dangers are past. Space plants 1 foot apart.

Atriplex hortensis

Beta (bay'ta) from the Latin name for beet.

The beet, *B. vulgaris* (H), is one of those plants usually not thought of as being an attractive plant for the flower garden. But in addition to plants grown for the root vegetable (Crassa Group), there is a second division (Cicla Group)—Swiss chard—used both as a leafy vegetable and as a garden ornamental. The stems of this biennial are brilliantly colored, standing about 14 inches high, and quite effective when massed in the border or used as a different kind of edging. 'Ruby Chard' has red to purple stems with large, edible, wavy-edged leaves; 'Vulcan' is bright red; 'Lucullus' is light green; 'Rainbow' has stems of red, orange, purple, yellow, and white; 'Dracaenifolia' is dark crimson. Plants do best in cool weather and resent hot, dry climates. Sow seeds directly outdoors in early spring or start seeds indoors six weeks before the last frost in a cool place and using individual 3-inch peat pots, as Swiss chard resents transplanting. Thin plants to 6 inches apart.

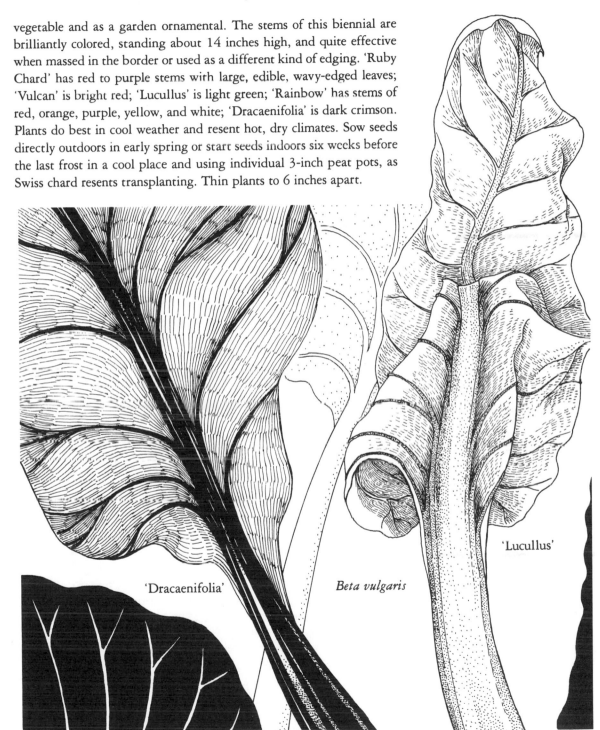

'Dracaenifolia'

Beta vulgaris

'Lucullus'

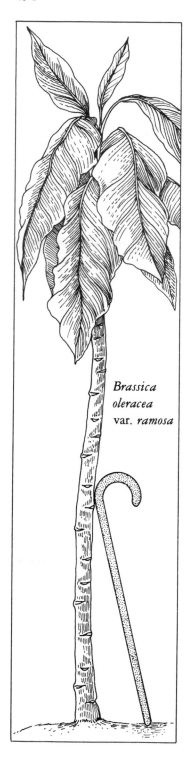

Brassica oleracea var. *ramosa*

Brassica (brass'i-ka) from the Latin name for cabbage.

Flowering cabbages and ornamental kales, *B. oleracea* (H), both belong to the Acephala Group of the cabbage clan. They are biennials grown as annuals, the kales having leaves with frilly edges and the cabbages with flatter leaves and a broader head. They are not flowers— these resemble tiny dandelions on a tall stalk and appear in the second year—but rosettes of leaves often a foot across and in colors of red, pink, white, light green, and mixed varieties. They're now "pop" plants with florists in the big cities and potted singles can go for $25 at a New York City florist. In fact, cut stems with heads can be put into water and you remove the lower leaves as they fade and shorten the bottom stem as the top continues to grow and expand. For bedding they are superb. Last year the Americana Hotel on Avenue of the Americas in New York City used these cabbages for an outdoor fall planting, right next to the spot where the BMW's and the Cadillacs pulled in. Since the plants are not that great until the fall coloration begins, keep them in a nursery bed or cutting garden and then transplant in the fall.

Start seeds indoors four weeks before the last frost, setting the plants into the garden when most frost danger is past. Seeds germinate in ten days. Although older plants thrive on cold, the seedlings raised indoors resent it. Seeds can also be started directly outdoors in early spring. Plants like average, slightly heavy soil in full sun. The colors start to gleam when nights become cold in the fall. 'Cherry Sundae' blends colors of carmine and cream while the 'Color Up' hybrids have luscious centers of red, pink, cream, and mixed green and white sur- rounded on the outside edges with green leaves and colored veins. Space plants 12 to 14 inches apart according to your designs.

The walking stick cabbage, *B. oleracea* var. *ramosa* (H), is more of a conversation piece than a garden ornamental. It's a perennial form of the common cabbage that grows up to 7 feet tall in the Channel Islands, the English-owned islands off the French coast. There the stems are dried, given hand grips, and sold as walking sticks. Plants look like ungraceful palm trees and often need propping up during or after a summer storm but they never fail to elicit a query as to where they came from. Grow as above.

Hon Tsai Tai, *B. Rapa,* Chinensis Group (H), is the purple- flowering Pak Choi, a Chinese vegetable grown not only for the kitchen but for the flower bed. The leaves are dark green, veined with purple, and plants produce purple flowers. Sow as above. Space plants 16 inches apart.

B. oleracea

Canna × generalis

Canna (kan'na) from the Latin word for cane or reed, referring to the tall flower stalk.

Cannas or Indian shot, *C. × generalis* (T), are tropical perennials usually started in gardens by rhizomes bought from nurseries in the spring. The plants are grown both for the foliage which comes in varying shades of green and bronze, and for the large and flashy, tropical flowers. Cannas are excellent for bedding, borders, pots, and planters with varieties growing from 1½ to about 4 feet.

Most gardeners do not realize that plants can be started from seed. Although they might not bloom the first year, especially in our Zone 5 climate, it's worth the effort for the attractive plants. Look for the new 'Seven Dwarfs' growing about 1½ feet high. The common name refers to the very hard seeds so nick the outer hull with a file, then soak them for 24 hours before sowing, starting sixteen weeks before the last frost. Germination should be in fourteen days. Seedlings should be transplanted into pots when they are about 2 inches high. Plant out after all frost dangers are past. Soil should be fertile with plenty of compost, well-drained, in full sun. Rhizomes can be dug up in the fall and stored for next year's use. Space plants 9 to 24 inches apart depending on the variety.

Capsicum (kap'si-kum) from the Greek word for bite, referring to the hot taste.

The holiday peppers, *C. annuum* (T), are perennial natives of tropical America grown not for flowers but for the pretty, colorful fruits and the attractive foliage. Ornamental peppers are perfect for beds, borders, edging, and pot plants both for the summer terrace or started in fall to produce fruiting plants for Christmas. Many kinds are available in heights from 6 to 12 inches. 'Holiday Flame' is a bushy dwarf, with scarlet-red finger-shaped fruits; 'Holiday Cheer' is 8 inches high and bears round, red fruit; and 'Midnight Special' has dark, dark green leaves in high contrast to intense scarlet fruit. These peppers are extremely hot and caution is advised in using them for food. Children should be warned. Plants need a fertile soil in full sun and will need adequate water. Start seeds indoors eight weeks before the last frost and plant out after frost danger is past. Do not cover seeds as they need light to germinate, a process taking about twenty days. Space plants 10 inches apart.

Capsicum annuum

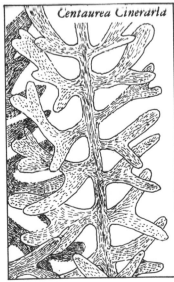

Centaurea Cineraria

Centaurea (sen-tor'ree-a) named in honor of the mythological Greek Centaurs.

Dusty-miller, *C. Cineraria* (T), is one of a number of perennials from the Mediterranean with the same common name. Others are members of the genus *Senecio* (which see). They are all grown as annuals for the lovely color and textures of the silvery gray foliage. The purple flowers of *C. Cineraria* are small and rather weedy looking, so should be removed if they appear. This plant is beautiful for edging and massed in the front of a bed or border. The variety usually offered is 'Silverdust' with finely divided foliage looking like it is brushed with powdered silver. Dusty-millers need a fertile, well-drained soil in full sun. They are excellent seaside plants. Sow seeds indoors ten weeks before the last frost and plant out after all frost danger is past. Germination is in ten days. Do not cover seeds as they need light for germination. Space plants 8 inches apart.

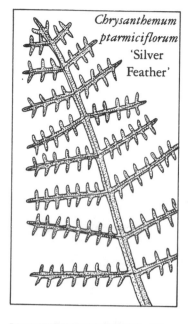

Chrysanthemum ptarmiciflorum 'Silver Feather'

Chrysanthemum (kris-san'thee-mum) from the Greek for golden flower.

Another plant called dusty-miller, this one from the Grand Canary Island, is known as *Pyrethrym ptarmiciflorum* but the correct name is *C. ptarmiciflorum* (T). 'Silver Feather' is the cultivar offered by most seed houses and closely resembles the plants described above. Sow seeds indoors sixteen weeks before the last frost; these seeds are slower to germinate, taking five to six weeks before sprouting. Space plants 8 inches apart.

Coleus (ko'lee-us) from the Greek word for sheath and referring to a character of the flower.

Flame nettle or coleus, *C. × hybridus* (T), are tender perennial plants originally from Indonesia and Java. They have been used as bedding plants in England for over 130 years. The leaf colors are legion: red, orange, pink, yellow, chartreuse, bronze, brown, purple, almost black, and white, some in various combinations, striped or spotted; every year plant breeders come up with new color variations. The original heart-shaped leaf is now long or short, wide or narrow, with wavy, scalloped, fringed, or filigreed edges. Older varieties would often grow to 4 feet but the present-day plants vary between 8 and 18 inches according to type. The dwarf varieties are good for windowboxes. Choice leaf patterns can be propagated by cuttings for use as houseplants in the winter. 'Scarlet Pancho' is quite lovely with leaves of deep maroon edged with lemon yellow and 'Fiji Mixed' bears leaves with fringed margins in all the bright colors.

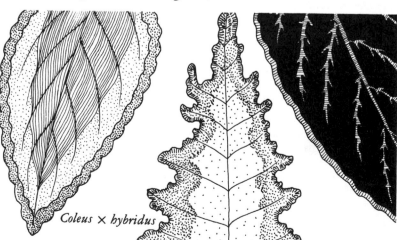

Coleus × hybridus

Average soil in full sun or light shade is fine. The flowers are not particularly attractive and should be pinched off as they appear. Start seeds indoors eight weeks before the last frost, planting out after all frost danger is past. Do not cover seeds as they need light to germinate, a process taking about ten days. Space plants 6 to 10 inches apart depending on the variety.

Cynara (sin′a-ra) from the Greek word for dog's tooth, referring to the bracts surrounding the flowers.

The cardoon, *C. cardunculus* (HH), a perennial in its native southern Europe, often grows to 6 feet in warmer climates but in our garden reaches about 4. It's one of the most ornamental plants I know and produces a mound of beautifully cut leaves in one season of easy growth, all topped with thistle-like flowers resembling small artichokes (a very close relative). The new leaves are a downy, whitish gray below and a green-gray above and fan out from a ribbed stem that resembles a stalk of celery. Blossoms continue to the end of October in our garden and withstand frost at least to −28°F. Cardoons can be used as a hedge, specimen plants, and even grown in a tub for a patio point-of-interest. Fertile garden soil in full sun is necessary and cardoons need plenty of water while in active growth. Start seeds indoors six weeks before the last frost and plant out in mid-May. Space plants 3 feet apart.

Cynara cardunculus

Wrapping a cardoon

In order to use the cardoon as a vegetable, you will need to blanch the stems. Just before the first frosts of autumn, on a bright sunny day when the plants are dry, draw the leaves together around the stem and tie them in place with garden twine. Then take strips of paper about 6 inches wide and starting at the bottom, wind them around the leaves right up to the top. Over this a 3-inch band of hay is tied. Bank up the plants with soil to help with the support. Leave about a month until the blanching is complete. Plants can be dug up and stored in a cool, dry spot with all the wrappings in place.

Euphorbia (you-for'bi-a) named in honor of Euphorbus, physician to a king of ancient Mauritania.

Two members of this genus are used in summer gardens: the annual poinsettia, *E. heterophylla* (T), and snow-on-the-mountain, *E. marginata* (T), both annuals native to the American Southwest and down into Mexico. They are excellent in the border and will grow in the poorest of soils, withstanding heat and drought, in full sun or partial shade. They can also be used in pots on a terrace. The milky sap or latex in the stems of both species of plant can be irritating to the skin and the eyes. The annual poinsettia closely resembles the Christmas plant growing about 2 to 2½ feet high with the top leaves turning bright red by midsummer. Snow-on-the-mountain is a shorter plant staying about 1½ feet tall with the upper leaves edged with white. Start seeds indoors six weeks before the last frost and plant out after all danger of frost is past. Or plant directly outdoors when frosts are over. Space plants 8 to 12 inches apart.

Euphorbia marginata

E. heterophylla

An enlarged flower

Foeniculum (fe-nick´you-lum) from the Latin word for hay, referring to the smell of the leaves.

The common fennel, *F. vulgare* (H), was mentioned in the section on flowers but there is a cultivar usually listed as 'Bronze Form'. It is quite similar to the species in all respects except the color of the foliage, which is a beautiful bronzy red tone, and the size of the plant, which is usually much smaller. Although usually not hardy in Zone 5, this spring new leaves are appearing from last year's roots. I first saw it at Kew Gardens in London where it was used as a bedding plant. Start seeds indoors four weeks before the last frost using individual 3-inch peat pots as fennel resents transplanting. Cover the seeds—they need darkness for germination, which takes ten to fourteen days. Space plants 6 to 8 inches apart.

Foeniculum vulgare 'Bronze Form'

Geranium (ger-ray'nee-um) from the Greek word for crane, referring to the shape of the ripened seed pod.

Herb Robert, *G. Robertianum* (H), is a biennial wildflower usually (but, of course, not always) producing light green, lacy foliage with reddish stems the first year and adding small pink or sometimes white flowers the second. The plants often reach a foot in height but soon bend over and become prostrate. Plants will grow in partial shade so I list it here not as a flower but as a most attractive groundcover, especially in a woodland garden. Plant seeds directly outdoors in early spring and thin to 6 inches apart.

Hibiscus (hy-bis'kus) from the Greek word for a mallow.

One member of the Hibiscus tribe, *H. acetosella* 'Red Shield' (HH), is a perennial plant treated as an annual in the North and grown for its unusual leaves that resemble those of a red maple. It usually takes eight to ten months for flowers, so they are generally overlooked. Since plants grow up to 5 feet tall, they make excellent temporary hedges and fine color accents in the back of the border. They will also grow in pots on a terrace. Plants want full sun in average garden soil. Start seeds indoors eight weeks before the last frost and set out after all frost danger is past. Space plants 12 to 14 inches apart.

Geranium Robertianum

Hibiscus acetosella 'Red Shield'

Hypoestes (hy-po-est'is) from the Latin *hypo*, under, and *estia*, house, referring to the structure of the flowers.

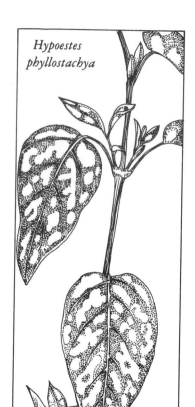

Hypoestes phyllostachya

The polka-dot plant, *H. phyllostachya* (T), comes from Madagascar and has long been popular as a houseplant, not because of its small purple flowers but because of the 2 1/2-inch oval leaves that are liberally spotted with tiny pink dots. Plants will take full sun or light shade in average but well-drained garden soil. The usual height is 1 1/2 feet and they are very attractive in a garden border. Polka-dots can be dug up in the fall and moved indoors for the winter. Start seeds indoors twelve weeks before the last frost, planting out when all frost dangers are past. Germination is in ten to twelve days. Space plants 12 inches apart.

Kochia (ko'ki-a) named in honor of W.D.J. Koch, a German botanist.

Summer cypress or burning bush, *K. scoparia* Forma *trichophylla* (HH), originally ranged from southern Europe all the way to Japan. It's an annual plant that perfectly resembles a dwarf conifer, especially a cypress. Plants are perfect for summer hedges, borders, single accents in the garden, and effective in pots on the terrace. With the arrival of fall, the foliage turns scarlet red, hence the plant's common name. During the summer the narrow and feathery leaves are a light green. The flowers are insignificant. Heights range between 2 and 3 feet, depending on the variety, with the width averaging 2 feet. Summer cypress likes full sun and a dry spot with excellent drainage. 'Acapulco Silver' is an especially fine cultivar with light green leaves dusted on the tips with silver. Plants can be sheared like a formal hedge. Sow seeds indoors six weeks before the last frost planting out when frost danger is past. Do not cover seeds as they need light for germination, a process taking about fifteen days. Space plants 1 1/2 to 2 feet apart.

Lactuca (lak-too'ka) from the Latin word for milk and referring to the milky juice of the plants.

Lettuce in the flower garden? It's really not as strange as it may sound. There are two new cultivars that make fine edging plants as long as the garden soil is moist and fertile. And they are always available for a quick salad. They are looseleaf lettuces and do not resent hot summers as much as other types. And when summer is over let a few plants bolt to seed, for the flower stalks on these red-leafed beauties are

Kochia scoparia

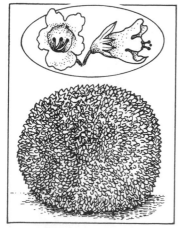

O. Basilicum 'Spicy Globe'

very pretty. Look for 'Red Sails', with deep red-bronze leaves, and 'Ruby', bearing finely crinkled leaves of red. Start seeds directly outdoors in early spring and do not cover for they need light for germination, a process taking seven to ten days. Space plants 4 to 6 inches apart.

Ocimum (os'si-mum) from the Greek word for an aromatic plant.

The basils, *O. Basilicum* (HH), have been found in herb gardens for centuries but in 1962, a new variety was introduced to the American scene, 'Dark Opal', bearing deep purple-black foliage and 2-inch spikes of small purple-tinged flowers—it was the first foliage plant to become an All-America Selection. Now in 1987 a new ornamental basil has been introduced and it too is an All-America winner: 'Purple Ruffles' with serrated leaves of the same deep purple color. Plants grow about 2 feet tall and about 2 feet wide, and are effective in both beds and borders. Try growing them next to some all-white annuals for a vivid contrast. 'Green Ruffles' has serrated leaves but no additional color. 'Spicy Globe' forms compact mound-shaped plants 6 to 8 inches high and 1 to 1½ feet across. According to the Park Seed Company, these new additions to the garden border will retain their shape throughout the summer without any trimming. Plus they can be used as the others to flavor your homemade tomato sauce. Start seeds indoors six weeks before the last frost and plant out after all frost danger is past. Germination takes seven to ten days. Space plants according to the type.

Ocimum Basilicum
'Purple Ruffles'

Perilla (per-rill′a) from the native Indian name for the plant.

Perillas, *P. frutescens* (T), are annual plants originally from India where they are cultivated for seed-bearing oils. Their attractive leaves are really too elegant to deserve the common name of beefsteak plant, an appellation given because the foliage is a reddish purple with metallic and bronzy overtones. Plants grow between 20 and 36 inches and resemble coleus in habit. 'Atropurpurea' has leaves of a very dark purple. The flowers are small, white, and best pinched off. Perillas make fine backgrounds for other brighter annuals. Start seeds indoors six weeks before the final frost planting out when all frost dangers are past. Use individual 3-inch peat pots as seedlings resent transplanting. Do not cover the seed; light is needed for germination, which takes about fifteen to twenty days. Space plants 12 to 16 inches apart.

Perilla frutescens

Petroselinum (pet-ro-se-ly′-num) from the Greek word for rock parsley.

Parsley is usually thought of as nothing more than a garnish on the dinner plate but it makes quite an attractive edging plant. 'Paramount' is a very dark green and makes an excellent plant for a hanging basket. 'Compact Curled' are 10-inch plants perfect for edging. A biennial grown as an annual, *P. crispum* (HH) has the reputation of being difficult to germinate. An old wives' tale says that "It goes to the Devil and back before it grows!" Soak the seeds in warm water for 24 hours before planting then sow directly outdoors, 1/4-inch deep, about three weeks before the last frost. Germination usually takes 14 to 21 days. Make sure the seed is covered because darkness aids germination. If starting indoors use individual 3-inch peat pots as parsley resents transplanting. Plants like full sun or light shade in a good, well-drained garden soil. Space plants 8 inches apart.

Petroselinum crispum

Ricinus (ris'i-nus) from the Latin name for tick, which closely resembles the seedpods of this plant.

Castor beans, *R. communis* (T), are grown for their immense tropical foliage, not the flowers, and were once a part of every garden. As a quick-growing screen or giant hedge they are unsurpassed. The seeds are the source of castor oil and are truly poisonous, capable of harming a child, which may explain why fewer seed companies carry them. This spectacular plant gives any garden the look of a Caribbean island with leaves often 3 feet wide on plants up to 6 feet tall. 'Gibsonii' has dark red leaves with a metallic sheen, while 'Red Spire' has bronzy green leaves on maroon stems. Plants need full sun, good drainage, and cannot tolerate wet feet. Flowers are small and nondescript but the developing fruits resemble bunches of small chestnut burrs. Start seeds indoors eight weeks before the last frost. Soak the seeds in warm water for 24 hours before planting. Germination should take fifteen to twenty days. Space plants 3 to 4 feet apart.

Ricinus communis

Senecio (sen-ee′si-o) from the Latin for old man, referring to white whiskers on some of the flowers.

Just when you thought you had seen all the dusty-millers, here are two more. *S. Cineraria* (HH) 'Cirrhus' is a perennial from the Mediterranean regions and often called *S. maritima* in English catalogs. The spoon-shaped leaves are woolly and silver-white, and plants can reach 2 feet. 'Silver Dust' is a dwarf plant about 8 inches high with deeply cut leaves covered with dense, woolly-white hairs and again, used as a foil for other bedding plants. The final dusty-miller is *S. Vira-vira* (HH) a native of Argentina easily mistaken for *S. Cineraria* but with foliage that is more finely cut. Start seeds indoors eight weeks before the last frost and plant out when all frost dangers are past. Germination takes about ten to fifteen days. Space plants 10 inches apart.

Silybum Marianum

Silybum (sil-ly′bum) from an old Greek name for thistle-like plants.

St. Mary's thistle or the blessed thistle, *S. Marianum* (H) is an annual or biennial depending on the weather. The basal leaves are about 12 to 14 inches long, lobed and very spiny, with a fine network of veins and spots of silvery-white on the surface. Towards late summer, light purple thistle-like flowers about 2 inches across appear on tall stems. They are not very spectacular so the plant is usually grown for the foliage. It can exist in poor and dry soil, reveling in hot weather, and makes a fine groundcover for a difficult spot. In Europe blessed thistle is used as a vegetable. Sow seeds directly outdoors in early spring. Space plants 2 feet apart.

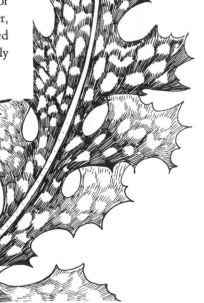

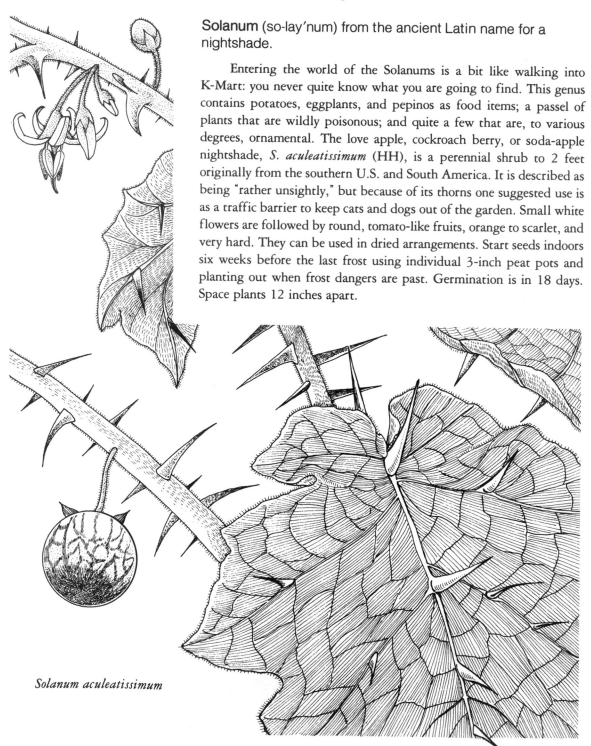

Solanum (so-lay′num) from the ancient Latin name for a nightshade.

Entering the world of the Solanums is a bit like walking into K-Mart: you never quite know what you are going to find. This genus contains potatoes, eggplants, and pepinos as food items; a passel of plants that are wildly poisonous; and quite a few that are, to various degrees, ornamental. The love apple, cockroach berry, or soda-apple nightshade, *S. aculeatissimum* (HH), is a perennial shrub to 2 feet originally from the southern U.S. and South America. It is described as being "rather unsightly," but because of its thorns one suggested use is as a traffic barrier to keep cats and dogs out of the garden. Small white flowers are followed by round, tomato-like fruits, orange to scarlet, and very hard. They can be used in dried arrangements. Start seeds indoors six weeks before the last frost using individual 3-inch peat pots and planting out when frost dangers are past. Germination is in 18 days. Space plants 12 inches apart.

Solanum aculeatissimum

And if the thorns of the love apple are not enough, there is *S. khasianum* (HH), a 2- to 4-foot perennial shrub from western Assam that is covered with spines and bears 1-inch ball-like fruits. Germination is in 24 days. Grow as above.

Next comes *S. laciniatum* (HH), a perennial shrub in Mexico that makes an excellent temporary shrub or background for the bed or border. The leaves are deeply cut, up to 20 inches long. It can reach a height of 6 1/2 feet in one season. In mild areas it will go on to become an 8-foot tree. Many lavender-blue flowers about 1 inch across are borne in summer, followed by oval fruits which ripen from green to light orange. Grow as above. Space plants 2 feet apart.

The last Solanum is the decorative eggplant, *S. Melongena* 'Golden Eggs' or 'Ornamental Mixed'. The first plant bears 3- to 5-inch fruits of a golden color, while the second cultivar bears a mixture of colored "eggs" chiefly white, pink, green, and purple. They are more a conversation piece than things of beauty. Try them in pots on the patio for a different approach to decoration. They are too small and mealy to be edible. Start seeds in individual 3-inch peat pots, six weeks before the last frost, planting out when frost danger is past. Do not cover seeds, they need light for germination, a process taking ten to twenty days. Space plants 2 feet apart.

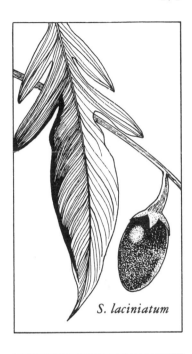

S. laciniatum

Tagetes (tay-gee′teez) from Tages, the grandson of Jupiter who sprang from plowed earth as a boy and taught the art of reading weather signs to the Etruscans.

Irish lace, *T. filifolia* (T), is a member of the marigold family that is grown for the leaves and not the flowers. Plants grow about 10 inches high, making neat green balls of fernlike leaves perfect for edging along walks and flowerbeds. The tiny white flowers appear in early fall. Start seeds indoors six weeks before the last frost planting out when frost danger is past. Space plants 6 inches apart.

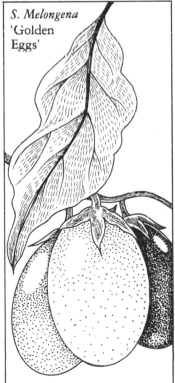

S. Melongena 'Golden Eggs'

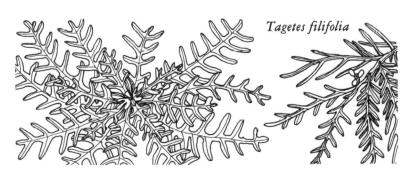

Tagetes filifolia

The Annual Grasses

". . . summer blessed earth's bosom bare with yellow dots of gold-star grass, and grey-black seeds of Job, entwined," is a quote from W. S. Lecher in his old *Garden Almanac,* written in the early 1700s and speaking to the beauty of the grasses, acknowledging their use long before the fashionable gardens of twentieth century England.

Most of the following grasses are best grown in the cutting garden and used for cut flowers both fresh and then dried for later use in winter bouquets.

To properly gather the blossoms, pick the stems on a dry and sunny day after the dews of morning have evaporated. Try to find flowers that have not completely opened and cut the stems as long as you can—they can always be trimmed later. To dry the grasses, strip off any excess leaves, tie small bunches of stems tightly together and hang them upside down on wire coat hangers leaving plenty of air space between each bunch. Hang the hangers well apart in a cool, dry, and airy room. Check the bundles every few days, for the stems will shrink as they dry, and some could tumble to the floor and shatter. It should take about three weeks for the drying process.

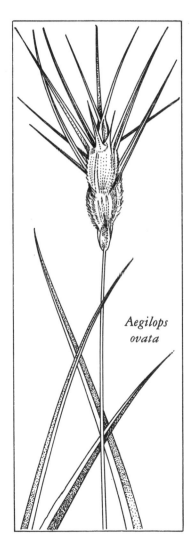

Aegilops ovata

Aegilops (ee´-gi-lops) from the old Greek name for a kind of grass.

Annual goat-grass, *A. ovata* (HH), is a native of the Mediterranean region that has been introduced in Virginia and California. It's a compact, tufted grass about 1 foot high that forms little mats. In central Europe it grows in dry, uncultivated ground and along paths and trails. In the garden, goat-grass is best with a rock garden type of existence. The chief feature is the inflorescence, somewhat resembling one of the one-celled animals found in a drop of pond water, with a number of spiked awns (bristlelike appendages that project from the grass flower) up to 1½ inches long, pointing in all directions. Start seed four weeks before the last frost or plant outdoors in early May. Space plants 8 inches apart.

Agrostis (a-gros'tis) from the Greek for a field and the Latin name for a kind of grass.

Cloud grass, *A. nebulosa* (H), is an annual grass as light as a feather moved by zephyrs, for when in bloom the effect is of a soft tan mist hovering over the edge of the garden. A native of Spain, blooming plants are about 15 inches high with each panicle some 6 inches long. Plants do not last long, dying soon after flowering, but consecutive sowings can help. They can be used in dried bouquets. Cloud grass is beautiful when planted in pots for an accent on the porch or patio. A dwarf variety termed 'Nana' is sometimes offered. Sow seeds outdoors in early spring. This grass will accept a spot in partial shade and still flower with ease. Space 6 inches apart.

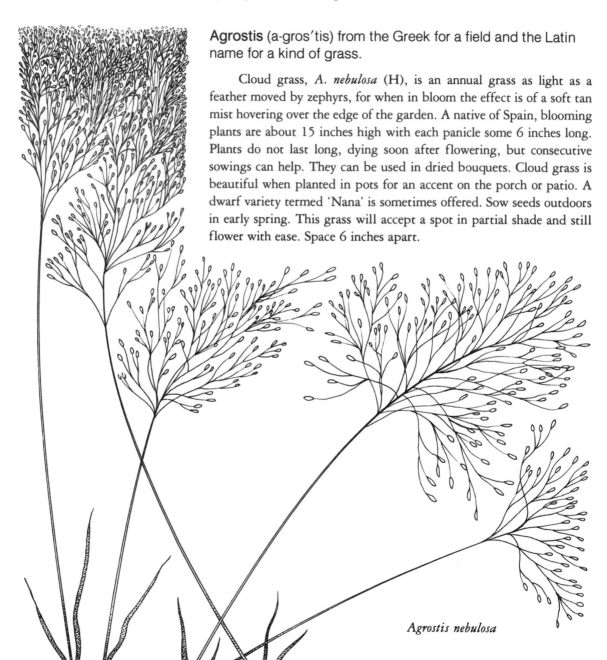

Agrostis nebulosa

Avena (a-vee'na) from the Latin for oat.

Three annual members of the oat family are grown not for the leaves but for the flowers, and are usually best in the back of the annual border or in the cutting garden where they can be gathered for fresh bouquets or dried for winter use. *A. fatua* (H) is known as wild oats, Tartarian or potato oats and forms clumps about 3 feet tall. It is found along the edge of fields or country roads and it's sometimes used for hay. The flowers are most attractive and a lovely shade of light brown. Sow seeds outdoors in early spring in any garden soil but with full sun. Space plants 2 feet apart.

A. sativa (H) is the plant usually cultivated by farmers and so close to the above that only botanists need be concerned about differentiating the two. Grow as above.

Animated oats, *A. sterilis* (H), has awns 2 3/4 inches long and the common name refers to their ability to move back and forth as the humidity changes. Because of this oddity the awns are often used in fishing flies. Grow as above.

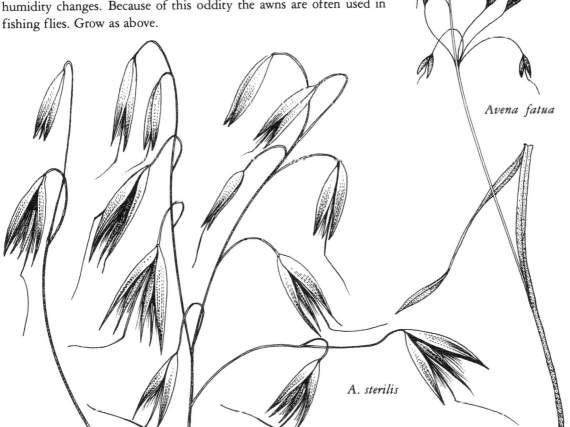

Avena fatua

A. sterilis

Briza minor

B. maxima

Briza (bry'za) from the Greek word for a type of grain.

The quaking grasses bear spikelets with the consistency of puffed wheat, each one on a very thin stalk so they continually bob and dance in the slightest breeze. They have been in cultivation as garden ornaments for well over 200 years. *B. maxima* (H), an annual, grows between 2 and 3 feet tall and is a bit rangy for a place in a formal bed or border. It's best in the cutting garden where the flowers can be used fresh or for dried bouquets. 'Rubra' has a crimson color to the top of the spikelets. Sow seeds directly outdoors in early spring or start seeds indoors about six weeks before the last frost, planting out when frost danger is past. Space plants 9 inches apart.

Little quaking grass, *B. minor* (H), is another annual of much smaller stature staying under 1½ feet in height. This species is fine as a grouping in a bed or border in addition to being used dried. Grow as above.

Bromus (bro′mus) from the Greek for food because this plant resembles wheat.

Rattlesnake chess, *B. briziformis* (H), is an annual ornamental grass suited both for the garden border and the cutting garden. The spikelets resemble those of quaking grass but are longer and the panicles are heavier. The plants are usually less than 2 feet high until in bloom. In order to save blooms for drying they must be picked very early or they will easily shatter. Plants want full sun and a good garden soil. Sow seeds directly outdoors in early spring or start indoors six weeks before the last frost planting out when frost danger is past. Make continuous sowings every two weeks into midsummer to have flowers all season. Space plants 1 foot apart.

Mediterranean brome, *B. lanceolatus* (H), has an airy bloom because of the spiky inflorescense. It's still offered as *B. macrostachys* (H) in many catalogs. Blooming plants are 2 feet high. Grow as above.

B. madritensis (H) is also from the Mediterranean and to my mind the prettiest of the brome or chess grasses. Blooming plants are 2 feet high with an airy inflorescence tinged with purple-red highlights. The flowers shatter too easily for dried bouquets but are lovely in the bed or border. Grow as above.

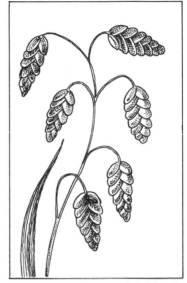

Bromus briziformis

B. madritensis

B. lanceolatus

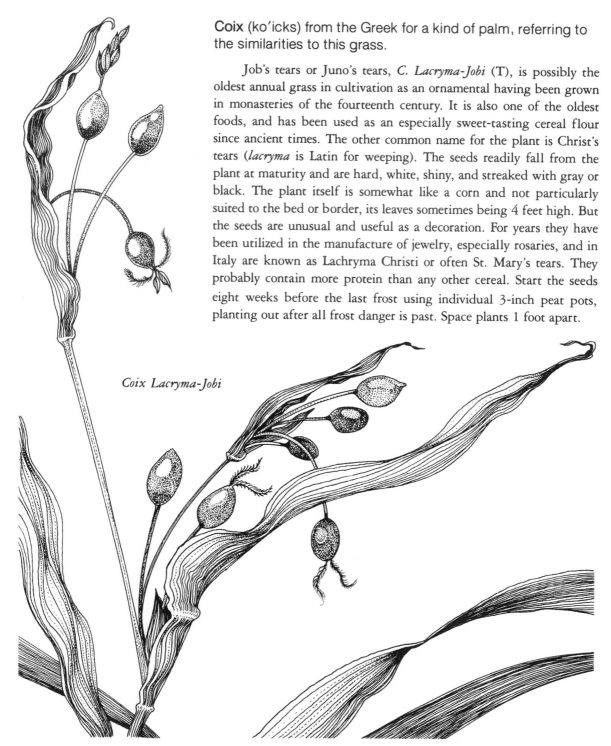

Coix (ko′icks) from the Greek for a kind of palm, referring to the similarities to this grass.

Job's tears or Juno's tears, *C. Lacryma-Jobi* (T), is possibly the oldest annual grass in cultivation as an ornamental having been grown in monasteries of the fourteenth century. It is also one of the oldest foods, and has been used as an especially sweet-tasting cereal flour since ancient times. The other common name for the plant is Christ's tears (*lacryma* is Latin for weeping). The seeds readily fall from the plant at maturity and are hard, white, shiny, and streaked with gray or black. The plant itself is somewhat like a corn and not particularly suited to the bed or border, its leaves sometimes being 4 feet high. But the seeds are unusual and useful as a decoration. For years they have been utilized in the manufacture of jewelry, especially rosaries, and in Italy are known as Lachryma Christi or often St. Mary's tears. They probably contain more protein than any other cereal. Start the seeds eight weeks before the last frost using individual 3-inch peat pots, planting out after all frost danger is past. Space plants 1 foot apart.

Coix Lacryma-Jobi

Cynosurus (sin-o-sur'-us) from the Greek *kuon*, dog, and *oura*, tail, alluding to the shape of the flowers.

My first seeds of rough dog's-tail grass, *C. echinatus* (H), were gathered in Greece of Elisabeth Belfer. The one-sided blossoms are a shiny green with purple highlights and physically resemble the tail of a collie or shepherd dog. It's an annual to 20 inches high that grows along dry banks and in sandy fields, so is perfectly suited for a place in the rock garden. Sow seeds directly outdoors in early spring or start seeds indoors about six weeks before the last frost. Space plants 10 inches apart.

Cynosurus echinatus

Cyperus (sy-peer'us) from the old Greek name for these plants.

Technically a member of the sedge family, *C. eragrostis* (HH) is an attractive semi-tropical perennial from Chile and is usually listed with ornamental grasses. Many references list it as *C. vegetus*. It will bloom the first year from seed, producing 20-inch triangular stems topped with a bright green inflorescence surrounded by many bracts, the plant closely resembling the popular umbrella sedge (*C. alternifolius*) of houseplant fame. Individual clusters of eight to twelve spikelets, each tinged with yellow-green and light brown, sit atop 2-inch stems. The flowers dry to a light tan. The leaves are about 1½ feet long and ½ inch wide, and are shaped like a V in cross-section. The plants are quite at home in wet, moist, or even dry soil. Start seeds indoors six weeks before the last frost planting out when frost danger is past. Space plants 1 foot apart.

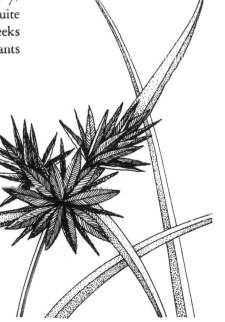

Cyperus eragrostis

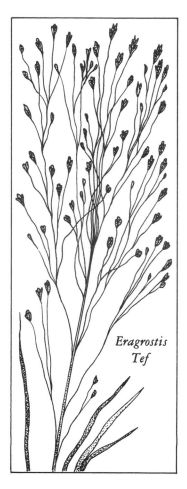

Eragrostis Tef

Eragrostis (e-ra-gros'tis) from the Greek for love grass, and no one knows why.

Teff, *E. Tef* (HH), is an annual grass from Africa where it's used as a cereal crop for making bread. Older catalogs list it as *E. abyssinica*. The narrow green leaves grow about 1 foot high with the airy and elegant, 6-inch-long inflorescences on stems about 1½ feet high. The plants are attractive in the border or relegated to the cutting garden for use in dried bouquets. Teff needs plenty of sun. Start seeds indoors four weeks before the last frost and plant out after frost danger is past, or sow seeds directly outdoors in late spring. Space plants 1 foot apart.

Hordeum (hor'dee-um) from the classical Latin name for barley.

Foxtail barley or squirrel-tail grass, *H. jubatum* (H), is a short-lived perennial or often annual grass that is frequently seen along highway medians, waving with a silvery effect as cars whizz by. The flower spike is about 4 inches long and often 4 inches across, looking like a pale green and silver feather. They turn brown and individual awns bend in all directions with age, finally shattering. Flowers must be picked early for bouquets. Green leaves are about 6 to 8 inches long and without the blooms would be easily mistaken for grassy weeds. Plants bloom in the heat of summer. These grasses are dangerous with livestock—the awns are able to cause puncture wounds so are not used as forage crops. Plant directly outdoors in early spring. Space plants 1 foot apart.

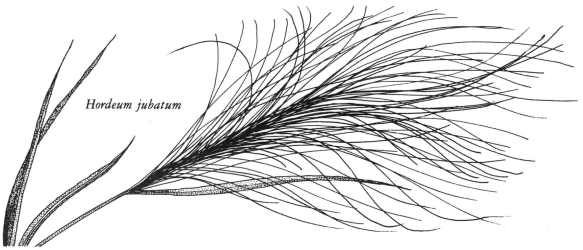

Hordeum jubatum

Juncus (jun'kus) from the classical Latin name for the rushes.

While not a show-stopper, the annual toad rush, *J. bufonias* (H), is a charming little plant for the rock garden or planted in a group in the front of a border. It's loosely tufted and bears tiny flowers of green in a forked cluster halfway up the stems. Toad rush can grow 18 inches high but usually stays under a foot. Sow seeds outdoors in early spring. Space plants 6 inches apart.

Lagurus (lag-you'rus) from the Latin for a hare's tail.

Hare's-tail grass, *L. ovatus* (H), is a beautiful annual grass from the Mediterranean and aptly named, for the flowers look exactly like the tail of Peter Rabbit. The light green leaves are often 1 foot long and all are covered with a soft down. Blossoms are spike-like panicles that can be 2 1/2 inches long and 3/4 inch wide. They are pale green as they open but turn off-white with age and are not only beautiful in the garden but excellent in dried bouquets. Unfortunately the seedheads will absorb dyes and are often found in gift shops garbed in colors of shocking pink or bilious green. A dwarf variety less than 6 inches high is called 'Nanus'. Hare's-tail is especially fine when massed in a bed or border or planted in drifts on a hillside. Plants need a light, well-drained soil in full sun. Space seedlings 4 inches apart.

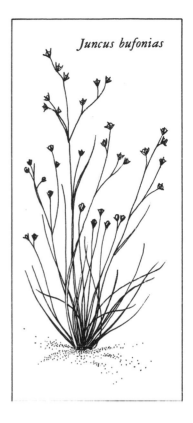

Juncus bufonias

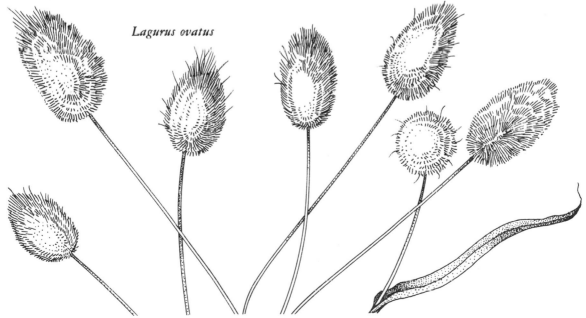

Lagurus ovatus

Lamarckia aurea

Lamarckia (la-mark'i-a) in honor of J. B. Lamarck, the French naturalist.

Goldentop, *L. aurea* (H), is the one species of grass in its genus. Named after the naturalist who lost out in the evolutionary sweepstakes to Darwin (Lamarck believed that the neck of the giraffe became very long after years of stretching) this annual grass from the Mediterranean is one of the most beautiful you can grow. The one-sided, 2 1/2-inch panicles, on stems to 16 inches high, have a shimmering golden effect when fresh that becomes silvery with age. By midsummer plants are turning brown, so a second crop should be prepared. The flowers shatter easily when dry so be sure and pick them before they are ripe. They are most attractive when used in an edging or massed in the front of the border. Sow seeds outdoors in early spring. Space plants 6 inches apart.

Mibora (me-bor'a) of unknown derivation.

Early sand grass, *M. minima* (HH), is an English native found growing on the dunes around the Channel Islands. At a mature height of about 1 1/2 inches, with tufts of narrow and short gray-green leaves and purplish one-sided panicles to 4 inches high, this is probably the smallest grass to be cultivated for an ornamental effect. There is no prettier little grass for use in the rock garden. If soil is reasonably moist, the plants stay green except in areas of very hot summers. New leaves often appear in the fall. Start seeds indoors six weeks before the last frost, planting out after frost dangers are past. Or sow directly in the garden in late spring. Do not thin plants.

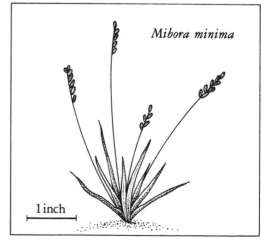

Mibora minima

1 inch

Milium (mil'i-um) from the old Latin name for millet.

E. A. Bowles was one of England's great gardeners. Among his contributions to the plant world were a number of rather odd plants that he termed "lunatics," and a few variegated or unusual forms of everyday members of the floral world. *M. effusum* 'Aureum' (H) is a beautiful grass, growing about 15 inches high. It's a variation of a common British native, where the whole plant—stems, leaves, and inflorescence—are suffused with a rich golden yellow. It's called Bowle's golden grass. A perennial south of New York City, it's generally used as an annual farther north. Try this grass as a color accent, as a edging plant, or massed in the border. Sow seeds outdoors in early spring or start indoors six weeks before the last frost, planting out after frost danger is past. Space plants 6 inches apart.

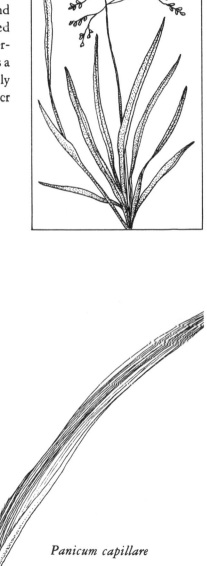

Milium effusum 'Aureum'

Panicum capillare

Panicum (pan'i-kum) from the old Latin name for Italian millet.

Broomcorn millet or proso millet, *P. miliaceum* (H), is an annual forage grass and one of the oldest in cultivation, known to the Romans as *Milium*. Used for hog feed and bird seed, the plants often escape from farms and turn up on waste ground across the country. Plants often grow 3 feet tall and though attractive when planted in groups in bed or border, are usually kept in the cutting garden where the drooping panicles make elegant additions to bouquets, fresh or dried. There is a purple-seeded variety called 'Violaceum' which is more suited to an elegant setting. Sow seeds directly outdoors in early spring. Space plants 1 foot apart.

Vegetable gardeners know the witch grasses, *P. capillare* (H), as small tufts of silky green much like fiber optic lamps that arise out of stout stems on 2-foot plants and enlarge to become over 14 inches wide, ripen, and blow about the garden like tumbleweeds, when they are often cursed. But these same annual grasses can be beautiful in the garden if relegated to one spot and kept there. In full bloom they become a very large cloud of silvery green mist hovering over the border. Blossoms are also effective in dried bouquets. Sow seeds in early spring. Space plants 1 foot apart.

Panicum miliaceum

Pennisetum (pen-i-see′tum) from the Greek for feather, referring to the plumes of some species.

Although this grass from Ethiopia is a perennial in Zone 9, it's treated as an annual in most gardens. Feather top, *P. villosum* (T), is rather floppy as the magnificent blossoms, often 9 inches long, can become quite heavy. If picked before they completely open, they can be dried for bouquets but will shatter with the slightest bump. Feather-tops are beautiful when used as fresh flowers and mixed with other garden annuals. Plants are about 2 feet high and like well-drained soil in full sun. Start seeds indoors six weeks before the last frost and plant out when all frost danger is past. Space plants 15 inches apart.

Fountain grass, *P. setaceum* (T), is another perennial grass from Ethiopia used as an annual. Plants are large often to 4 feet high, and bear 14-inch plumes of pink or purple. They are fine for the back of bed or border. The most attractive variety is 'Cupreum', with reddish leaves and copper-colored flower spikes. Grow as above.

Pennisetum villosum

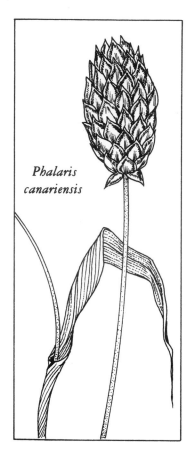

Phalaris canariensis

Phalaris (fal'ar-ris) from the old Greek name for some of these species.

Canary grass, *P. canariensis* (H), is another Mediterranean plant that has spread around the world, chiefly because the seeds are used for feeding canaries and often find their way to landfills along with the newspaper from the bottom of the cage. The tufted plants can reach over 3 feet high but usually stay 2 feet or under in most garden conditions. While the plant itself is not attractive enough for a spot in the formal garden, the 1-inch wide flowerheads of a variegated green and yellow-white sitting on top of long, slender stems are fine for winter bouquets. Sow seeds directly outdoors in early spring. Space plants 6 inches apart.

Polypogon (pol-li-po'gon) from the Greek, *polus,* much, and *pogon,* beard, in reference to the many awns.

Annual beard grass, *P. monspeliensis* (H), is also called rabbit-foot grass, the name referring to the 6-inch long spike-like panicles that are covered with very fine bristles of light green that turn to tan with age. Plants are about 2 1/2 feet tall when in full bloom. Like hare's-tail, these grasses look their best when planted in drifts or clumps and the silky flowerheads are massed together. The flowers can be dried for winter bouquets. Sow seeds directly outdoors in early spring. Space plants 4 inches apart.

Polypogon monspeliensis

Rhynchelytrum (rin-kel-i'-trum) from the Greek, *rhychos,* beak, and *elytron,* scale, alluding to a botanical feature of the seeds.

   Ruby, Natal, or champagne grass, *R. repens* (HH), is yet another short-lived perennial grass from Africa, which is usually grown as an annual that flowers the first year from seed. Most catalogs still list it as *R. roseum* or *Tricholaena rosea.* Plants bloom over a long summer season producing 6-inch reddish pink plumes that turn a soft silver with age. Since plants grow 3 to 4 feet tall they are best reserved for the back of the border. Blooms are fine as fresh cut flowers but easily shatter when dry. When gathering, pull the stems out of the leaf sheath, rather than breaking the stems. Ruby grass needs a well-drained soil in full sun. Start seeds indoors six weeks before the last frost using individual 3-inch peat pots, or sow directly outdoors in late spring. Space plants 12 to 14 inches apart.

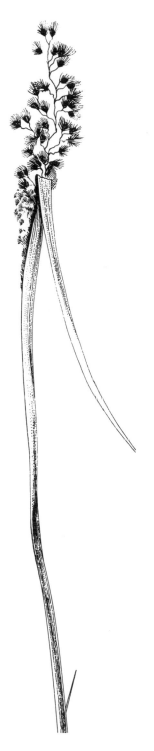

Rhynchelytrum repens

Setaria (see-tair'i-a) from the Latin word for bristle.

The foxtail millet, *S. italica* (H), is a striking member of the ornamental grasses that really looks like a foxtail ready to be tied on the rumble seat of an old Chevie during the 30s. The dense panicles are often a foot long and bow to the earth with the weight of the seed. Plants reach over 2 feet in height. First grown in ancient China around 2700 B.C., they reached Europe in the Middle Ages, and entered the United States in 1849 as an important fodder crop. Plants are much too ungainly for the front of the bed or border but are perfect as a back-drop hedge. The panicles make imposing additions to a dried bouquet. Sow seeds directly outdoors in early spring or start seeds indoors six weeks before the last frost using individual 3-inch peat pots, planting out when frost dangers are past. Space plants 14 inches apart.

Foxtail grass, *S. lutescens* (H), bears seedheads about 3 inches long and covered with fine bristles that are orange-red in color and gleam in the sunlight. The plants are just under 2½ feet in height and flop in all directions. They are a bit unruly for the bed or border but are splendid when planted in a drift on a hillside. They will also seed about and can become a bit of pest. But the flowering panicles are so beautiful they should be a part of any cutting garden. A massive bouquet made of 50 to 60 stems is a sight to be seen and not at all difficult to gather from a good planting. *S. persica* is similar to the above but with a beautiful purple-brown color to the bristles. Sow directly outdoors in early spring. Space plants 8 inches apart.

Green bristle-grass, *S. viridis* (H), is a weed of cornfields and often found growing along roadsides where its bright green panicles bend and sway as the cars whish by. Plants in bloom are about 3 feet tall and are best reserved for the cutting garden, and their flowers used in dried bouquets. Grow as above.

Sorghum bicolor

Sorghum (sor'-gum) from *sorgho,* the Italian name for this plant.

The sorghums are a confused family from a taxonomic viewpoint but when searching for seed to grow as an ornamental plant look for the name *S. bicolor* (T). These are important annual cereal crops originally from Africa and now grown all over the world. It is a source of syrup used to make molasses, grain for flour, and food for cattle. Somewhat corn-like in appearance, these are fine plants for the back of the border, often reaching 10 feet in height, and all with a tropical air. The dried panicles are usually orange, dark brown, or shiny black and really effective in arrangements. The corn-like leaves are a light green often spattered with brown specks. One variety called broomcorn is grown especially for the manufacture of brooms and brushes. Start seeds indoors using individual 3-inch peat pots, six weeks before the last frost and plant out after frost danger is past. Space plants 1 1/2 feet apart.

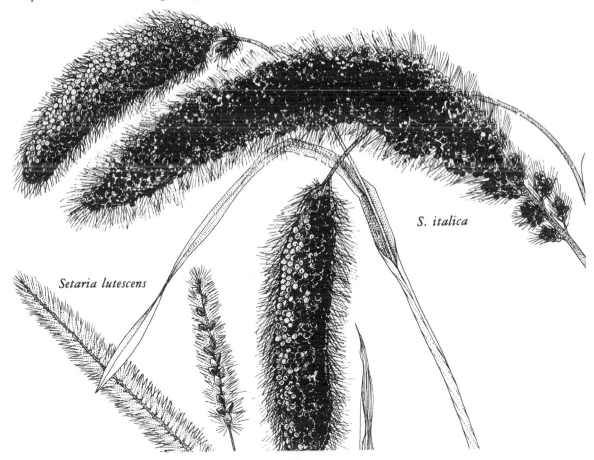

S. italica

Setaria lutescens

Triticum (trit'i-kum) from the classic Latin name for wheat.

Over the centuries, the original wheat, *T. aestivum* (H), has turned into a number of specialized cultivars and one of the most important cereals in the world. But as an ornamental, the tall flowering stalks are quite beautiful. You'll often see department stores use large bouquets of dried wheat artfully arranged in terra cotta pots to great effect in window displays. Flowering stems often reach a height of 4 feet but in the average garden stay about 3 feet high. Wheat is best kept to the cutting garden or planted in a drift on the hillside. Sow seeds outdoors in early spring. Space plants 1 foot apart.

Bearded wheat, *T. turgidum* (H), is the kind used for pasta flours. The long awns are unlike those of any other grass infloresence. Grow as above.

Triticum turgidum

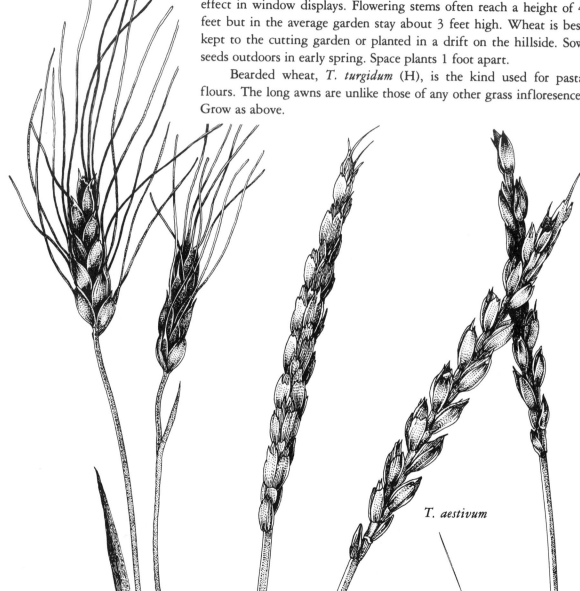

T. aestivum

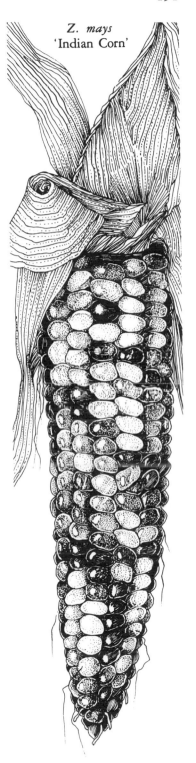

Z. *mays*
'Indian Corn'

Zea (zee′a) from the Greek word for a kind of grain.

Corn is one of the three most important cereal crops in the world and a number of different cultivars have been developed over the centuries. In the ornamental garden, Z. *mays* (T), is available in four varieties. Z. *mays* var. *gracillima variegata* is a dwarf type compared to the species, producing white-striped leaves on plants about 2 feet high. It does well in pots for terrace decoration or spotted about a small garden. Sow seeds outdoors after all danger of frost is past or start indoors six weeks before the last frost using individual 3-inch peat pots.

Z. *mays* var. *japonica* grows 4 to 5 feet tall and has leaves attractively striped with white, green, yellow, and pink. It's best at the back of the border for a striking hedge or in 6- to 8-inch clay pots for the terrace. Grow as above. This plant is often called *quadricolor*.

Z. *mays* var. *rugosa* bears 1½-inch strawberry-shaped ears crowded with deep red kernels. Not only is it a fine popping corn, it makes a beautiful decoration as well. Keep it in the cutting garden. Space plants 1 foot apart keeping them in a group for ease of pollination. Grow as above.

Z. *mays* 'Indian Corn' is grown for the ears that contain kernels of many colors and are dried to use for decoration. Space plants 1 foot apart, keeping them in a group for ease of pollination. Grow as above.

Zea mays var. *rugosa*

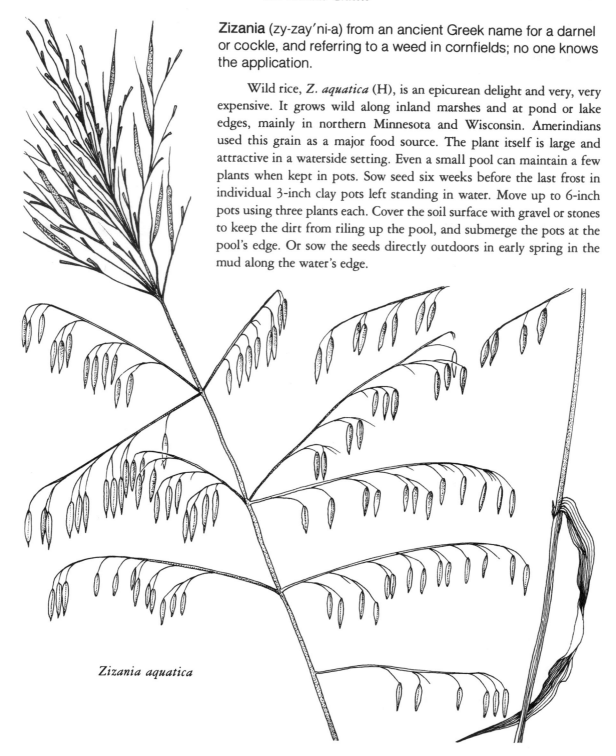

Zizania (zy-zay′ni-a) from an ancient Greek name for a darnel or cockle, and referring to a weed in cornfields; no one knows the application.

Wild rice, *Z. aquatica* (H), is an epicurean delight and very, very expensive. It grows wild along inland marshes and at pond or lake edges, mainly in northern Minnesota and Wisconsin. Amerindians used this grain as a major food source. The plant itself is large and attractive in a waterside setting. Even a small pool can maintain a few plants when kept in pots. Sow seed six weeks before the last frost in individual 3-inch clay pots left standing in water. Move up to 6-inch pots using three plants each. Cover the soil surface with gravel or stones to keep the dirt from riling up the pool, and submerge the pots at the pool's edge. Or sow the seeds directly outdoors in early spring in the mud along the water's edge.

Zizania aquatica

Zea mays var. *japonica*

_____ CHAPTER **7** _____

The Annual Vines

"As surely as the vine grew 'round the stump, she loved me—that old sweetheart of mine," said James Whitcomb Riley and the habits of that vine are not limited either to romance or to stumps. Many of the plants described in the next pages could not only be used to screen a romantic hideway but could easily hide a rubbish heap or an abandoned car. Japanese hops, for example, is a fantastic quick-growing cover-up for all sorts of eyesores about the home or farm.

At most garden stores you can buy ready-made, folding trellises of wood which expand to 12 feet in length, or supports made of plastic rods that screw together. A perfect movable support can be made from a frame of 1 by 3s using plastic fishing line strung on evenly spaced brass cup hooks. Or take aluminum clothesline and make a large spiral affixed to a pole stuck in a large pot.

If yours is not the handyman image, remember that vines are not particular and will grow on just about anything.

Anredera (anre'-der-a) from a personal name.

The madeira or mignonette vine, *A. cordifolia* (T), is a rapidly growing perennial vine twining to 20 feet and usually blooming the first year. Originally called *Boussingaultia baselloides* and still listed as such in most catalogs, the plant originates in Ecuador and Brazil. Throughout the southern states madeira vine is often found on porch trellises and covering summer houses. In late summer fragrant white flowers ⅛ inch long appear in spike-like clusters at the tips of the branches. The roots of the vines are tuberous and little tubers grow in the leaf axils and can be used to propagate new vines. Tubers are reported to be hardy as far north as New York City. Vines are hardy in Zone 9 and south, and will quickly become weedy in moist soil. Sow seeds indoors eight weeks before the last frost and plant out after all frost danger is past.

Anredera cordifolia

195

Asarina Barclaiana

Asarina (a-sa-ri′na) from an old generic word for gummy.

Barclay's maurandya, *A. Barclaiana* (T), is a perennial vine originally from Mexico that climbs with curling leaf stalks and reaches a length of 10 feet or more in one summer. Blooming the first year from seed, these vines are usually treated as annuals. Leaves are arrow-shaped and vines bear pretty longnecked flowers up to 3 inches long. Blossoms are pink when opening but turn purple with age. Sow seeds indoors eight weeks before the last frost and plant out when all frost danger is past.

Basella (ba-sell′a) a native Malabar name.

The Malabar nightshades are perennial twining vines classified as annual, biennial, or perennial according to which botanical reference you consult. Since they are not hardy at all, it's best to treat them as annuals. *B. alba* (T), is an attractive but rampant climber commonly called Malabar or summer spinach and as such is truly an ornamental vegetable (see page 16). The mild flavor of the leaves is reputed to be acceptable eaten raw in salads or cooked as a green but I frankly find them rather bland and prefer real spinach. In a good hot summer, these vines can grow up to 10 feet, especially when trained to grow up a stake and then allowed to cascade down to the ground. Oval leaves up to 5 inches long are on yellow stems and in midsummer, small pink or purple flowers about 1/8 inch long appear like purple BB's pasted on erect stems. A red-stemmed form called 'Rubra' is often offered. Start seeds indoors six weeks before the last frost and plant out when frost danger is past.

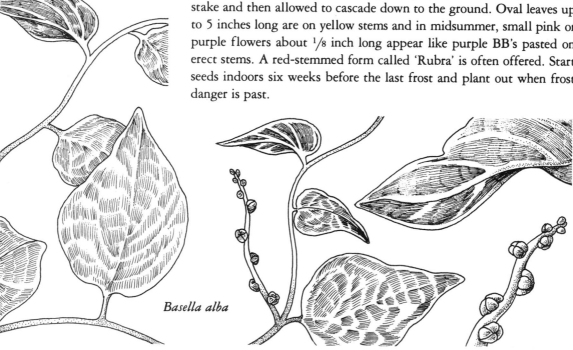

Basella alba

Benincasa (ben-in-kay′sa) in honor of Giuseppe Benincasa, founder of the botanical garden at Pisa.

There is only one species in this genus, *B. hispida* (T), an annual, pumpkin-like Asiatic vine that creeps along the ground, running 15 feet in a good summer season. When it does climb a trellis or strings, the vine is supported by tendrils or small coiling stems that wind about whatever they touch. Common names include: wax gourd, ash gourd, zitkwa, tunka, Chinese watermelon, and the Chinese preserve melon. Leaves are lobed and toothed, about 6 inches wide. Flowers are yellow, about 3 inches across and the fruit is a cylindrical melon, 8 to 10 inches long and about 2 inches wide, covered with a white waxy bloom. According to L. H. Bailey, the white flesh is used in the East in curries and also to make preserves and sweet pickles in southern Asia. While not terribly decorative it is an interesting vine in the garden. Start seeds indoors eight weeks before the last frost and plant outdoors when all frost danger is past. You will need at least 100 days of warm weather to produce fruit.

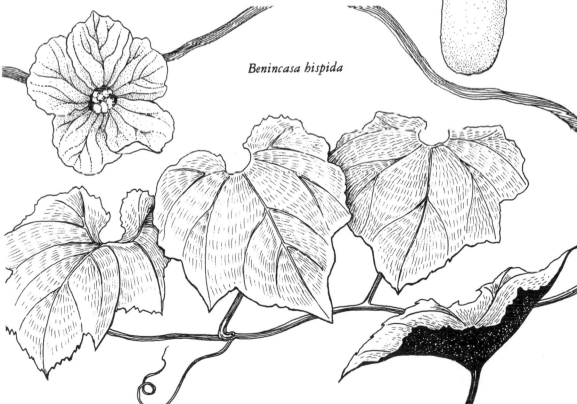

Benincasa hispida

Seeds of love-in-a-puff

Cardiospermum (kar-dee-o-sper'mum) from the Greek for heart and seed, referring to the heart-shaped mark on the seed.

Love-in-a-puff, balloon vine, and heart-pea are common names for *C. Halicacabum* (HH), a perennial vine from India and Africa that is treated as an annual in most of the United States. It has naturalized in parts of the country below New Jersey. The seed carries the mark of a heart at the spot where it was held in the ripening pod. Flowers are very small, 1/4 inch across, with four tiny white petals and four tiny sepals. Under a small lens they look like exquisite orchids. Leaves are deeply cut and attractive. And the balloons, each 1 1/2 inches across when mature, float like dozens of different sized light green bubbles and are so strong that you have to squeeze with your fingers to break them. In average soil and full sun, vines will grow up to 10 feet in one summer, needing the support of a trellis or strings. Space plants 12 to 14 inches apart to use as a screen.

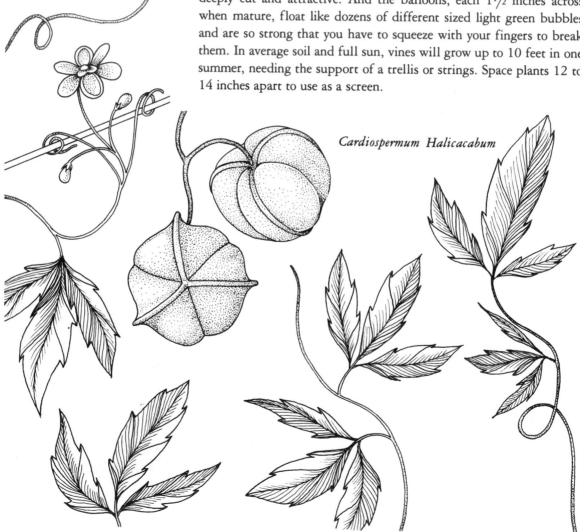

Cardiospermum Halicacabum

Cobaea (ko-bee′a) in honor of Father Cobo, a Jesuit
naturalist.

Cup-and-saucer, Mexican ivy, and monastery-bells are common
names for *C. scandens* (HH), a tropical perennial that will flower the
first year from seed. Rosy purple 2-inch-long flowers sit on a green,
saucer-shaped calyx and look for all the world like a cup on a saucer.
Flowers are greenish at first and have an unpleasant smell that makes
them attractive to flies. But upon opening the odor turns to honey for
attracting bees. Oblong leaves are 4 inches long and tendrils from the
tips of the branches cling to any available support, growing about 20
feet a year. Vines do well on arbors or a trellis and have been a favorite
greenhouse plant for over a century. Sow seeds six weeks before the last
frost using individual 3-inch peat pots. Plant two seeds per pot sticking
them in an upright position. After a fifteen to twenty day germination,
remove the weaker seedling. Or plant directly outdoors after danger of
frost is past. Vines want a good, moist, well-drained soil in full sun or
light shade.

Cobaea scandens

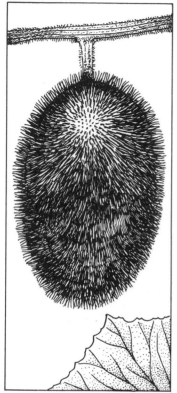

Cucumis dipsaceus

Cucumis (kew-kew′mis) from the Latin for a plant with a cucumber-like odor.

Queen Anne's pocket melon, *C. Melo* (T), belongs to the Dudaim Group of the *Cucumis* family. It's a small vine not growing more than 6 feet and bears yellow flowers 3 inches wide followed by oval fruits, green at first but turning to yellow stripes on brown when ripe. The rounded leaves are arrow-shaped and 3 inches wide. The best reason for growing this vine is the sweet perfume of the ripened fruit. It is said that good Queen Anne would carry this melon in her reticule as she walked the palace halls, inhaling its fragrance now and then to be revived from the odors that in those days permeated the castle. Start seeds directly outdoors as soon as all frost danger is past. Seeds can also be started indoors four weeks before the last frost using individual 3-inch peat pots and moving plants outdoors to a cold frame when the vines start to grow. Use three seeds per pot and discard the weaker two.

The snake cucumber, *C. Melo* (T), belongs to the Flexuosus Group of the *Cucumis* family and is another annual vine grown for the unusual fruit. Its origins have been lost in time. Linnaeus described the plant in 1763 and wondered if it came from India. The vine looks like other members of the clan, but the melon or fruit is between 1½ and 3 feet long, coiled and looped like a serpent in distress. L. H. Bailey mentions that the fruit is said to be usable as pickles. Grow as above.

Teasel gourds, *C. dipsaceus* (T), are annual vines native to Arabia and cultivated both for curiosity and for ornament. Leaves are small, rounded, almost heart-shaped, and grow from stems covered with tiny prickles. Flowers are yellow. The gourds are oblong, about 2½ inches long, and densely covered with bristles. Fruits stay green for a long time but eventually change to a straw color and last indefinitely. Grow as above.

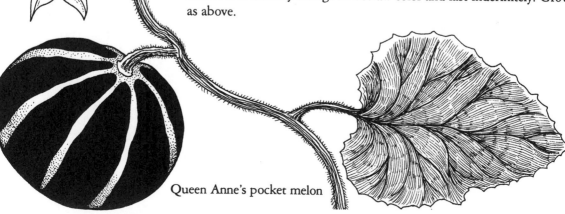

Queen Anne's pocket melon

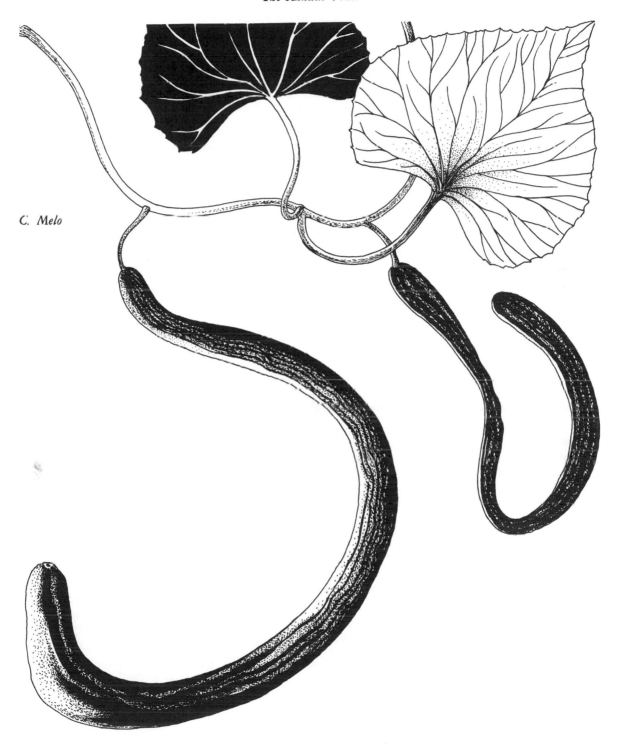

C. Melo

Cucurbita (kew-kur'bi-ta) from the Latin for gourd.

Most of the popular gourds grown for ornament are in this group of plants. The fig-leaf or Malabar gourd, *C. ficifolia* (T) is a giant among vines. Here is an ornamental to use if you wish to screen an entire barn. The large leaves—*ficifolia* means fig-leafed—look like their namesakes, being a healthy 9 inches wide. L. H. Bailey, in his book, *A Garden of Gourds,* called this vine the most vigorous species he ever grew. He measured the length of the main stem and branches of one plant that totaled 825 feet, and all of this in Ithaca, New York. The fruits are almost round, about 6 inches in diameter. They are beautifully marked with streaks of white on a dark green background. The fruit is eaten in tropical countries. Sow seeds outdoors after all danger of frost is past or start indoors as with the *Cucumis* gourds.

The Turk's turban, *C. maxima* 'Turbaniformis' (T), is an ornamental member with vines growing to 8 feet in length. Yellow flowers produce large gourds with bright orange, white, and green colorations, 6 to 7 inches in diameter. The gourds make excellent holiday decorations. Grow as above.

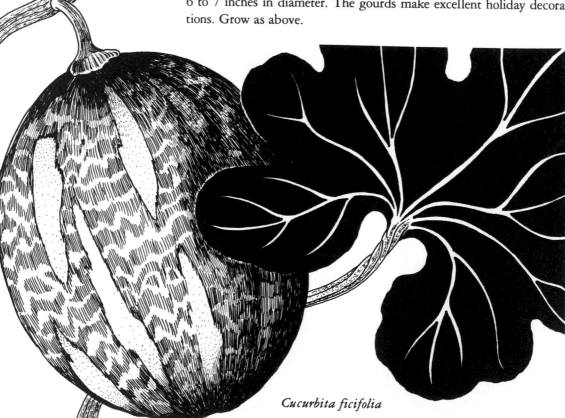

Cucurbita ficifolia

Among the newest novelty vegetables on the garden scene are the miniature pumpkins. Their tiny fruits are exact replicas of their giant brothers but fit to be carved by the fairies at the bottom of the garden. *C. maxima* 'Munchkin' (T), has fruits 3 to 5 inches across and 'Jack Be Little' is 2 inches high and 3 inches across. Sow seeds directly outdoors when danger of frost is past or start indoors four weeks before the last frost using individual 3-inch peat pots. Vines will usually bear fruit in 90 days.

The crown-of-thorns or finger gourd, the striped pear, and the spoon gourds, *C. Pepo* var. *ovifera* (T), are all members of the same genus yet look different enough to be families apart. And there are many more members: the white pear gourd, the goose-egg, the miniature gourd, the broad striped, the ladle or scoop gourd, the warty hardhead, the bell, and the big bell. The flowers are all yellow, and the vines grow about 12 feet long. Grow as above.

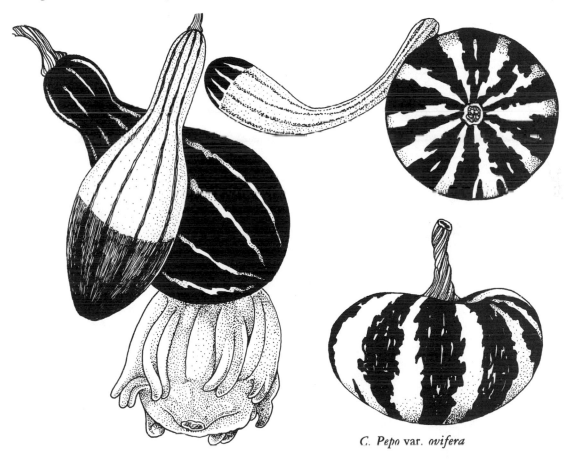

C. Pepo var. *ovifera*

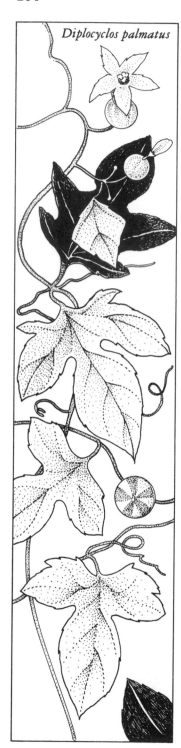

Diplocyclos palmatus

Diplocyclos (dip'lo-sic-los) from the Greek, *diploos,* double, and *kyklos,* circle, alluding to the double border on the seeds.

The marble vine, *D. palmatus* (T), is still called *Bryonopsis laciniosa* in many seed catalogs. It's a fast growing annual producing 10 feet of vine in a summer. In days gone by it was often used to shade the front porch, the overlapping, three-lobed leaves providing pockets of cool. The 3/4-inch flower blooms on top of the immature fruit and is nothing showy. But soon the fruits mature into marble-sized balls of apple green, striped with white, and changing with age to orange-red aggies striped with cream. Sow seeds outdoors when all frost danger is past. Germination will occur in eight to ten days. Use average, well-drained garden soil and provide a trellis or strings for the vines to grow upon.

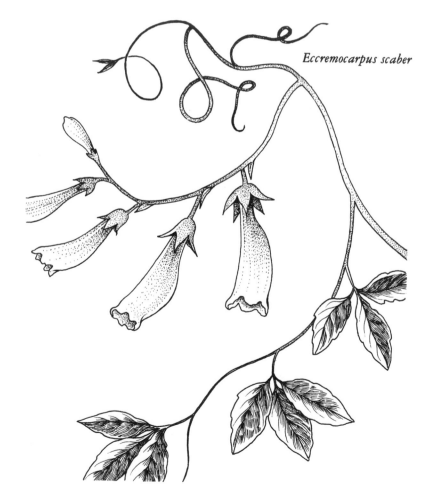

Eccremocarpus scaber

Dolichos (do'li-kos) from an old Greek word for a bean.

The hyacinth bean is known in various places about the world as lablab, the Bonavista bean, Lubia bean, Seim bean, Indian bean, and the Egyptian bean. *D. Lablab* (T) is a woody perennial twining vine from the Old World and is an important food in the tropics. Leaves resemble a lilac leaf in shape and occur in threes, each about 6 inches long. The vines are rapid growers, making a run of 15 or more feet in a summer. Flowers are fragrant, pealike, purple, producing decorative fruits about 2 1/2 inches long. 'Darkness' has flowers of deep purple with purple pods and 'Daylight' flowers are white. Sow seeds directly outdoors as soon as danger of frost is past. Or, since seedlings resent transplanting, start them in individual 3-inch peat pots six weeks before the last frost and plant outdoors when frost danger is past. Space plants 1 foot apart and provide a trellis or strings for the vines to climb.

Eccremocarpus (ek-krem'o-kar-pus) from the Greek for pendulous fruit.

The Chilean glory-flower, *E. scaber* (HH), is an evergreen perennial that will bloom the first year from seed. Leaves are featherlike, each leaflet 1 1/4 inch long and 1 inch wide, while tubular flowers are bright orange, blooming in clusters. They are excellent as cut flowers. These plants are really climbing shrubs using tendrils for holdfasts. In a good summer they will grow about 10 feet. Start seeds indoors six weeks before the last frost, using individual 3-inch peat pots and moving outdoors after all frost danger is past. Space plants about 1 foot apart in good, well-drained soil in full sun. Provide a trellis or strings for the vines to climb.

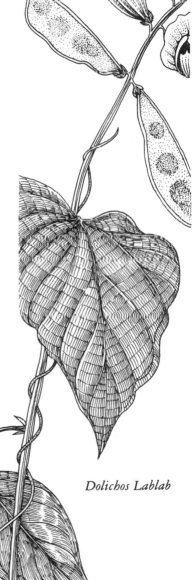

Dolichos Lablab

Echinocystis (ee-ky-no-sis'tis) from the Greek for hedgehog and bladder, referring to the spiny pods.

Wild or mock cucumbers, *E. lobata* (H), are high-climbing annual vines with lobed leaves somewhat like grape leaves, 3 to 5 inches long. They climb with tendrils, often reaching a height of 20 feet in a season. Use them to cover unsightly sheds, trash piles, and the like. Blossoms are small and white, blooming on flowering branches, appearing in late July and leading to oval fruits, 2 inches long, spiny and rather papery. Plants are wild natives and will grow in any soil with full sun. Seed should be nicked with a file and soaked in warm water overnight before planting out in early spring. Or start seeds indoors six weeks before the last frost and plant outdoors after frost dangers are past. Space plants 1 foot apart.

Echinocystis lobata

Humulus (hew'mew-lus) from the Latin word for ground, as the plants will tumble to it without support.

According to the *Flora of Japan* published by the Smithsonian Institution, there are two hops: Japanese hops, *H. japonicus* (HH/H), is an annual and common hops, *H. Lupulus* (HH), is a perennial twining vine. The first is a valuable ornamental plant often growing 30 feet in a good year. The second is the commercial source of hops and not as attractive a plant. But be warned: Japanese hops can be a rambling terror, wild enough to cover not only an unwanted trash pile or rubbish heap, but actually crawling up an entire garage. And it will

self-sow. The leaves are rough to the touch, deeply divided into five to seven lobes, and the stems are serrate (a nice word for covered with sawlike teeth), making them cling to shirt sleeves and garden gloves. Flowers are tiny, green, full of pollen, but not particularly attractive and luckily usually hidden by the leaves. Start seeds indoors six weeks before the last frost. Germination takes about ten days with a heating cable but 25 days outdoors in early spring. To cover an unwanted object, space plants 1½ feet apart. There is a variegated form, 'Variegatus', with a very attractive motley effect on the leaves.

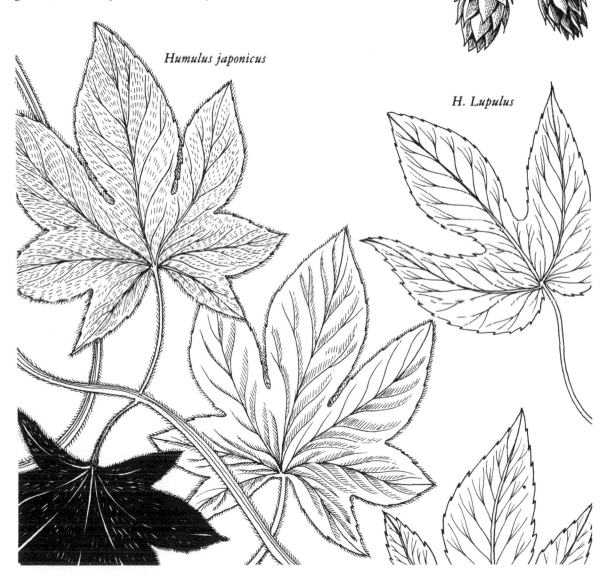

Humulus japonicus

H. Lupulus

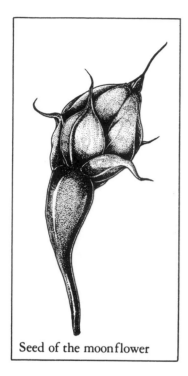

Seed of the moonflower

Ipomoea (ip-po-mee'a) from the Greek *ips*, a vine tendril, and *homoios,* similar, referring to their method of climbing with tendrils.

 The morning-glory family is quite large with over 500 species of plants. The group includes a few that made news during the 1960s because of their hallucinogenic properties and of course, the popular food plant, sweet potatoes (*I. Batatas*). The price of the seeds is often tagged to the amount of money needed to insure that collectors will not become involved with the pharmaceutical aspects of what they are reaping. The morning glories are often confused in seed catalogs with the *Convolvulus* (see page 57) or bindweeds but the first have blossoms shaped like a funnel while the bindweeds resemble bells. All the flowers mentioned need a support to twine upon, good, light, well-drained soil, and a position in full sun. For quick germination nick each seed with a file before planting or soak them in warm water for a day. Germination takes five to ten days. Sow seeds indoors six to eight weeks before the last frost in individual 3-inch peat pots, as the seedling resent transplanting. Seeds can also be sown outdoors after all frost danger is past. Space plants 8 to 12 inches apart.

 The moonflowers, *I. alba* (T), are perennials in the tropics but grown as annuals up north. The plant is a vine that will grow to 10 feet in a good summer season but up to 40 feet by the jungle's edge. The

Ipomoea alba

sweet-scented flowers are pure white, with a faint touch of light green along the floral folds, 6 inches long and 6 inches wide. They are highlights of a night garden for they bloom in early evening, opening as in a slow-motion nature film on flowers. But like Dracula, they quickly fold with the first touch of dawn. They will flower in eight weeks from seed. The developing seed pods are unique and interesting to watch.

I. coccinea

Star flowers, *I. coccinea* (T), are annual twiners once included in the genus *Quamoclit* and bearing 1½-inch scarlet flowers with a yellow throat. Leaves are heart-shaped, about 6 inches long. Vines can reach a height of 10 feet, blooming most of the summer.

Cardinal climbers, *I. × multifida* (T), are annual twiners with arrow-shaped leaves deeply cut almost to the mid-rib in ten to fifteen sections and about 4 ½ inches wide. The bright red flower resembles the trade mark of Chrysler Corporation and is ½ inch wide with a white throat. Vines can reach a height of 10 feet.

Morning glories, *I. Nil* (T), are annual or sometimes perennial twiners bearing leaves shallowly divided into three sections and up to 6 inches wide. Flowers are very showy, 4 inches wide, and come in colors of purple, red, blue, pink, and white. These flowers have been grown in gardens since the 1600s. One of the most famous varieties is 'Scarlet O'Hara' with scarlet flowers and splashes of white on the leaves. The Imperial Japanese morning glories belong in this genus. These plants are grown in pots, continually pruned above the third set of leaves, and eventually producing spectacular flowers. Vines can reach a height of 10 feet.

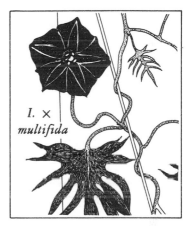

I. × multifida

The common morning glory, *I. purpurea* (H), is an annual vine from Mexico and now naturalized in many parts of the U. S. This is probably the most cultivated species and the most hybridized. Heart-shaped leaves are up to 5 inches long and flowers are often 4 inches across. This plant will often self-seed in the northern garden and can become quite a pest. There are single and double flowers in white, blue, dark blue, purple, crimson, scarlet, and pink. Look for 'Madame Anne' from 1865 and having flowers striped red on a white background. Vines can reach a height of 8 feet.

Cypress vine, *I. Quamoclit* (T), often called *Q. pennata,* is an annual climber with beautiful 3-inch leaves so finely cut they look like feathers. Flowers are scarlet, about 1½ inches long. Vines will grow to 15 to 20 feet.

Flag-of-Spain has been confused for years. Usually called an *Ipomoea* or known as a *Quamoclit* it is now called *Mina lobata* (T), and is all

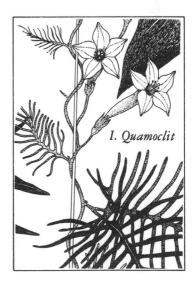

I. Quamoclit

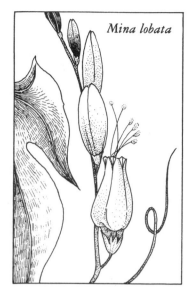

Mina lobata

alone in this genus. Leaves are divided into three pointed lobes. The common name refers to the tubular flowers, each about 3/4 inch long and blooming in a 4-inch spike. Unopened buds are red, and slowly—often over a period of weeks—turn lemon yellow as they mature. The only reason I know that the flower takes this long to change color is from growing the plant years ago. This native of Mexico will usually reach about 10 feet in length.

The morning glory, *I. tricolor* (HH), is a perennial climber blooming the first year from seed. This is the genus used by the Aztecs as a hallucinogen in religious ceremonials and as a medicine. A native of tropical America, the flowers are 3 to 4 inches in diameter with a white throat. Leaves are heart-shaped and usually 3 inches wide. This is the vine usually planted on fences and rural mailboxes. 'Heavenly Blue' is the one to look for. Flowers have an intense blue shading, lighter to the center, and the newly improved types have flowers that remain open for most of the day. Vines will grow about 10 feet long.

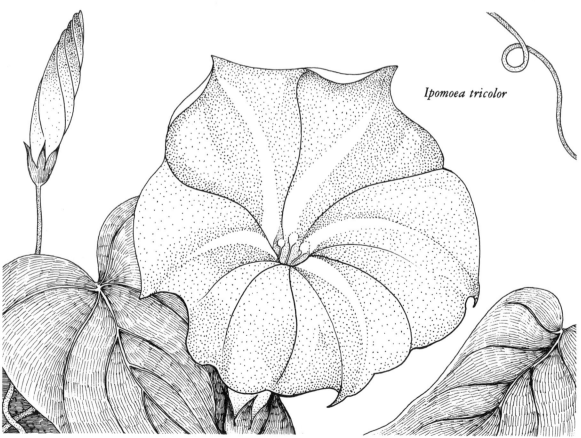

Ipomoea tricolor

Lagenaria (laj-en-a′ri-a) from the Latin for bottle, referring to the shape of the fruit.

The bottle gourds, bushel basket gourds, and powder horn or penguin gourds, *L. siceraria* (T), are all variations within one species. The flowers are large, sometimes up to 5 inches across, with white, paper-thin petals. They are sweet-smelling and bloom at night or on gloomy late afternoons. Vines can reach up to 25 feet in a good growing season. Leaves can measure a foot across. Last year in the garden we grew powder horn gourds of a light, pastel green that hung down 15 inches from the vine above their heads; bottle gourds 8 inches wide at the bottom and 10 inches high; and a bushel basket gourd that is meant to be the size of its namesake and weighed in at about 50 pounds.

Since these vines require a long growing season to set mature fruit, start seeds indoors eight weeks before the last frost using individual 3-inch peat pots. Soak the seeds in warm water overnight before sowing. Plant three seeds per pot and keep only the largest seedling. Germination takes eight to fourteen days. Soil should be rich and well-drained in full sun. These plants will need a lot of water during the growing season. Set plants 2 feet apart and provide a trellis or heavy strings for the vines to climb.

Lagenaria siceraria

Lathyrus (la'thi-russ) from the ancient Greek name for
the pea.

Remember the name of Popeye's little boy? It was Sweet Pea, a
name also given to one of the most popular garden flowers of all time
(Thompson & Morgan devote four catalog pages to sweet peas). The
original vining plant, *L. odorata* (H), came from Italy and in 1699
reached the shores of England, where it was grown in the garden of one
Doctor Uvedale. Soon strongly scented red and blue pea-like flowers
were for sale in all the flower markets in London. By 1730 sweet peas
were available commercially and the first variety appeared: It was
called 'Painted Lady' and was pink and white. In the 1850s the flowers
were also well-known in what is today Czechoslovakia for a monk,
Father Gregor Mendel, used them for his experiments in plant genetics
(unhappily, because of monastery politics, his discoveries were not recognized until 1900). Unfortunately for lovers of flower smells, the last
288 years have not been for the best, for the majority of the modern
sweet peas have sacrificed most of the perfume for size and color.

Lathyrus odorata

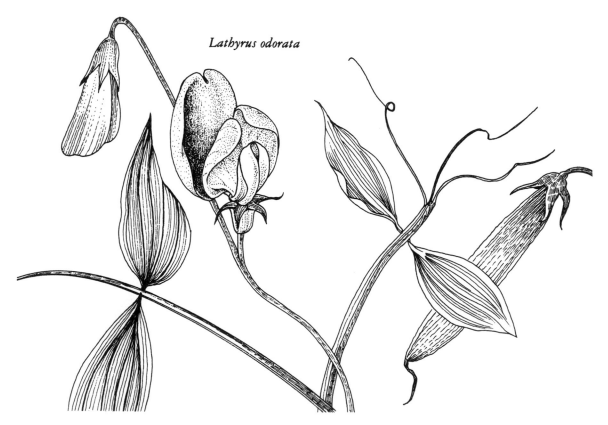

Thanks to plant genetics the present day sweet pea not only climbs up to 8 feet high but also crawls, so strings or staking for a vining support are not always necessary. Besides being excellent cut flowers, sweet peas can be used as flowering screens with the dwarf and trailing types at home in a bed or border. The plants prefer cool surroundings so gardeners in the warmer spots of America should look for 'Giant Mixed', heat-resistant varieties that come into bloom in early summer. 'Super Snoop' is an early-flowering dwarf strain with a long blooming period but spent flowers must be removed to guarantee continued bloom. The 2-foot plants do not need any support and come in colors of white, red, crimson, pink, and blue.

Sweet peas need a deep, moist, cool, and well-prepared soil and the gardener should start as soon as the ground can be worked. Then sow the seeds directly outdoors, or start them indoors in a cool place about six weeks before the last frost using individual 3-inch peat pots. Soak the seeds overnight in warm water. Space them according to the variety used.

Luffa (luf'fa) from the Latinized version of *louff,* the Arabic name for these gourds.

Dishrag gourds, *L. aegyptiaca* (T), are grown both as ornamental vines and for the fibrous interior of the fruit that is cured and used as a bath sponge or a dishcloth. Leaves have five to seven lobes about 6 to 8 inches long. Flowers are yellow, very showy, about 3 inches across. The fruit is cylindrical with shallow furrows, usually about a foot long. Special varieties that yield large fruits are grown in warm climates to produce the sponges available commercially. Start seeds indoors eight weeks before the last frost using individual 3-inch peat pots. Plant three seeds per pot and keep the largest seedling. Luffas want a good, well-drained soil in full sun. Space plants 2 feet apart and provide a trellis or heavy strings for the vines to climb.

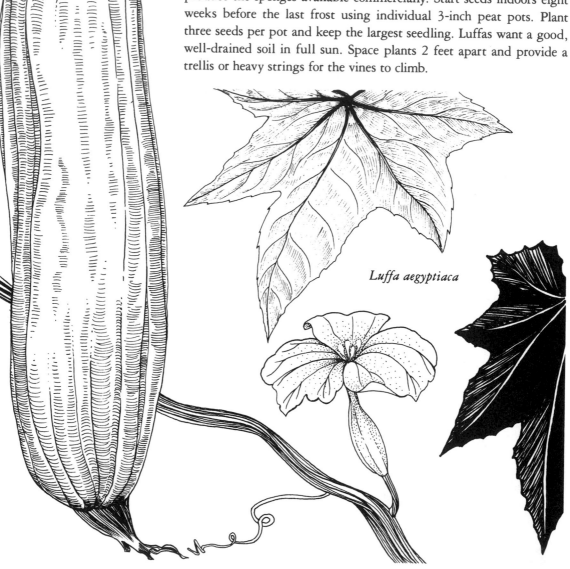

Luffa aegyptiaca

Momordica (mo-more′di-ka) from the Latin for bite, referring to the jagged seeds of some species.

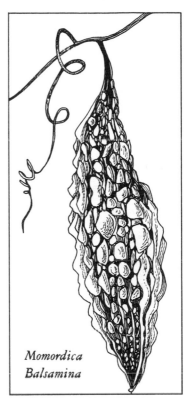

The balsam apple, *M. Balsamina* (T), is a fast growing annual vine from Africa and Australia, cultivated for the ornamental leaves, pretty flowers, and the unusual fruits. Ivy-like leaves of dark green are 4 inches across on vines that will grow 6 feet or more, climbing with tendrils. The flowers are yellow with black centers, about 1 inch across, and are followed by orange, 2- to 3-inch-long, warty, egg-shaped fruits. When the fruits are mature, they split along three sides, much like the pods in the movie *Alien,* revealing a red interior and large white seeds. These vines make excellent screens and are good for covering rock piles or old stumps in the garden. The vines need a long growing season to mature fruits, about sixteen weeks after sowing, so start seeds indoors eight weeks before the last frost using individual 3-inch peat pots. Plant out when frost danger is past. Balsam vines need a good soil, moist but well-drained, in full sun. For a screen space plants 1 foot apart.

M. Charantia (T) is the balsam pear. The annual vines can grow to 12 feet and the fruits are larger, spindle-shaped, tapering from the middle to either end, orange-yellow in color, about 8 inches long. The fruit bursts at maturity from the blossom end to reveal a scarlet lining. Grow as above.

Momordica Balsamina

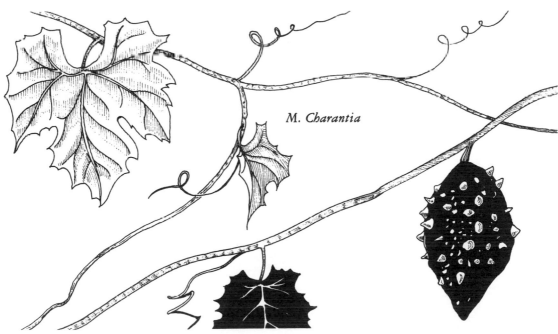

M. Charantia

Phaseolus coccineus

Phaseolus (fa-see′o-lus) from the Latin name of the bean.

Scarlet runner beans, *P. coccineus* (T), are perennial twining vines grown in American gardens for decades, blooming the first year from seed. Some authorities think this plant is the original bean grown by the Aztecs. Dark green leaves are compound with three leaflets, growing on vines that often reach 8 feet by midsummer. Pealike flowers are scarlet red and very showy, blooming in clusters, each flower about 1 inch long. Runner beans need a good well-drained soil and plenty of water during hot summers. Years ago my mother grew these vines in window boxes along the front porch by stretching strings about 10 inches apart from the porch rail to the edge of the roof above. About the middle of May in Zone 5, sow three seeds each within 3 inches of the base of each string. Seeds will germinate in about five days if the soil and the days are warm. Keep the strongest seedling. Pinch the tips of the vines when they reach the top of the strings. The beans are edible if picked when the pods are still green.

Pueraria (poo-er-ray′ri-a) in honor of M. N. Puerari, a Swiss botanist.

Kudzu vines are the black-belt karate champs of the vine world. They are a threat in many parts of the South and their uncontrolled growth has led to jungle thickets where once there were open woods and fields. Originally from Asia, *P. lobata* (HH), is a perennial vine usually not flowering the first year from seed but still valuable as a temporary screen or arbor plant growing up to 15 feet in one northern summer. Sometimes in a mild winter the roots will survive in Zone 4 or 5, but they never become a threat. Leaves resemble those of a bean plant and are abut 6 inches long. Purple flowers are fragrant and pea-like on spikes up to a foot long. The vines are not fussy as to soil but need full sun. Sow outdoors after frost danger is past placing seeds within 2 inches of the base of each support. Seeds germinate in fifteen days.

Pueraria lobata

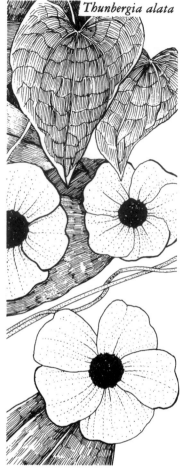

Thunbergia alata

Thunbergia (thune-ber'ji-a) in honor of Carl Peter Thunberg, a Swedish botanical author.

The black-eyed Susan vine, *T. alata* (T), is a perennial from tropical Africa that blooms the first year from seed. These vines are not rampant growers and usually stay 6 feet long or less. Leaves are arrow-shaped. Because the vines have a tendency to trail, they must be encouraged to climb by occasionally fixing them to a string or trellis, or allowed to trail from hanging baskets. Plants can be used at the edge of a wall so the stems will twine down between the rocks or creep as a groundcover. The flowers are 1½ inches across, available in white, orange, and yellow, each having a purple to black throat or eye. 'Susy Mixed' is a mix of the three colors, some flowers without an eye. As with most tropical perennials, black-eyed Susan vine makes an excellent houseplant. Start seeds indoors six weeks before the last frost using three seeds per individual 3-inch peat pot, keeping the strongest seedling. Germination is in 14 to 21 days. Plant out after all frost danger is past.

T. fragrans 'Angel Wings' (T) is another species with 2-inch wide flowers of white, blooming about four months from seed. These vines are common in California as groundcovers or trailing container plants. In spite of its name the blossoms are not very fragrant. Grow as above.

T. grandiflora (T) bears flowers up to 2½ inches across of a light sky blue. Grow as above.

T. Gregorii (T) has oval leaves about 3 inches long and plain orange flowers, 1¾ inches wide on stems covered with silky hairs. This is a stronger vine and will grow to 20 feet in warm climates. Grow as above.

Trichosanthes (try-ko-san'theez) from the Greek for hair and flower, and referring to the filaments on the petals.

The snake gourd, *T. Anguina* (T), is truly unusual. The white flowers are a little over 1 inch wide, with petals that are incredibly fringed. The fruit grows like a snake, long and coiled, and the warmer the climate, the longer the serpent. In *Handbook of Tropical Gardening*, H. F. Macmillan writes: "A quick-growing climbing gourd, bearing long cylindrical, green (sometimes greenish-white) fruits, which not unfrequently reach the length of five or six feet. In an unripe state these pot-like fruits are sliced and cooked in the manner of French beans. Seeds are sown in the monsoons [and] it is customary to suspend a small stone at the end of each fruit whilst growing, so as to weight it down and induce it to grow straighter." Grow as the *Cucurbita* species.

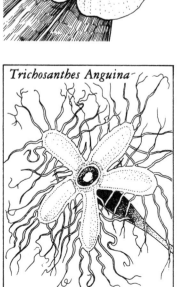

Trichosanthes Anguina

Tropaeolum majus

Tropaeolum (tro-pee'o-lum) from the Latin *tropaeum,*
a trophy, because the flowers and leaves are thought
to resemble the helmets and shields that were presented
at Roman triumphs.

Nasturtiums are mostly annual plants from the cool highlands of
Central and South America. The common name is from the Latin for
nose, *nasus,* and torture or twist, *tortum,* referring to the wry face that
one can make when biting into the leaves, which contain mustard oil.
Leaves are often used as a salad green and young seed pods can be
pickled like capers. Although one of the old favorite varieties listed
below is *T. minus* (T), which forms a dwarf bush about 1 foot high,
nasturtiums are usually thought of as vines and hence they are listed in
this section.

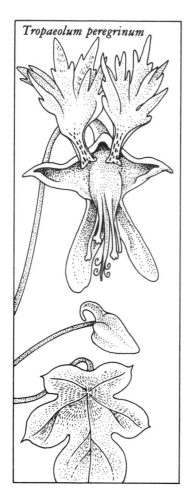

Tropaeolum peregrinum

T. majus (T) is the true old-fashioned flower having been in cultivation for over 300 years. Five-petaled and usually fragrant funnel-shaped flowers, 2 inches wide and bearing a prominent spur, come in colors of deep red, mahogany, scarlet, orange, yellow, and white. The leaves are almost round on smooth stems. The vines will grow 6 to 8 feet and will be at home on a trellis, strings, or chicken-wire forms. They are also excellent in pots or containers where they can trail over the edge of a wall or along the ground. Plants need well-drained but not especially rich soil or you will have more leaves than flowers. Plants also want full sun but resent hot summers. Nasturtium seeds are fairly hardy but the tender new leaves are quickly killed by frost. In addition the seedlings do not transplant well, so start seeds directly outdoors when the soil is warm, about two weeks before the last frost could happen. Cover the large seeds with three times their width in soil. They need darkness to germinate, a process that takes seven to twelve days. Plants grow quickly. Space the dwarf types 1 foot apart and the larger vines 2 to 3 feet apart. With nasturtiums watch out for aphids. Every garden book will warn of this and they are not kidding. Use a pyrethrum spray. A clump of nasturtiums grown next to a vegetable garden will actually draw these insects away from other plants.

Canary-creeper vines, *T. peregrinum* (T), are annuals from the Andes mountains and bear elegant leaves like those on a small fig, with five deep lobes. Flowers are 1 inch across with fringed, canary-yellow petals. Grow as above.

The flame flower, *T. speciosum* (T), is a perennial vine grown as an annual with red flowers with a spur about 1¼ inches long. Grow as above.

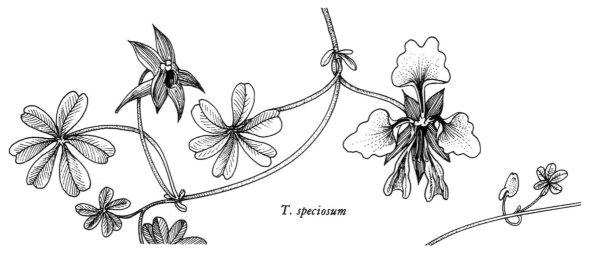

T. speciosum

The dwarf nasturtium, *T. minus* (T), is a fine edging specimen, groundcover, or pot plant. The flowers are typical of the species but the plant height is under 12 inches. 'Alaska Mixed' has leaves that are conspicuously marbled and striped with cream on a light green background; 'Peach Melba' has a beautiful blossom of light yellow with each petal blotched with scarlet at the throat; 'Whirlybird Blend' are semi-double flowers in colors of scarlet, rose, cherry, mahogany, orange, tangerine, gold, and cream, and perfect for growing in baskets.

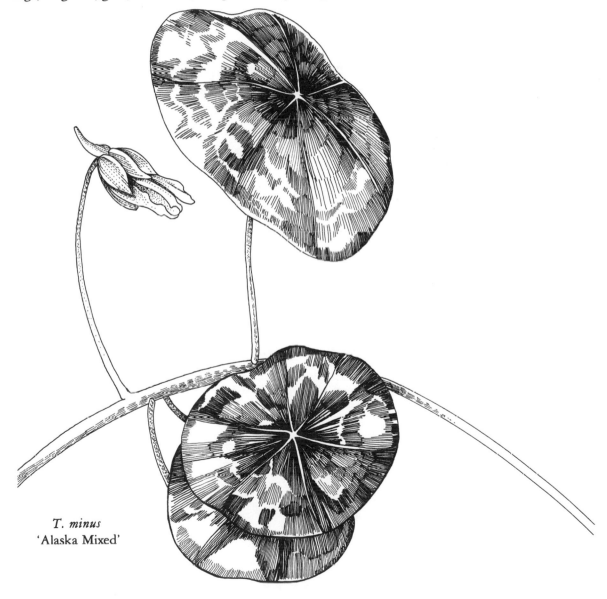

T. minus
'Alaska Mixed'

Appendixes

Appendix 1:

The Cutting Garden

I hate to cut flowers. My esthetic sense is somehow maligned when I find an empty spot in the garden, a spot that perhaps held a mass of cosmos, larkspur, or burgeoning phlox and now lacks those dots of vibrant pink or mellow orange and has become open space because blossoms were either clipped for the table or given to visitors who recently walked through the garden.

The solution is a cutting garden, a place set aside somewhere on the property where seeds can be planted without anything but the slightest of thoughts given to overall design—just a momentary pause about putting brilliant red next to a soft blue. For here the only concern should be flower production and the eventual masses of bright petals surrounding yellow centers, not grown to fill places in the border but to produce armloads of bloom for adorning tables, highboys, formal dinner parties, or the merest of picnics on the grass.

Our cutting garden is about 20 by 20 feet just beyond the vegetable patch. It's convenient to the kitchen and to the water faucet but not so noticeable that if I run out of time to spend on garden maintenance, I can overlook it and not be taken to task.

The plan will change from year to year but the general scheme calls for tall plants to the rear and shorter up front. Quite often I'll try out experiments in color using the cutting garden as a test area for the unusual.

Soils should be well worked and reasonably fertile but don't overdo as too much fertilizer leads to lush growth in contrast to fewer flowers.

If you are starting with very poor, and up to now, unworked soil, work in a good deal of compost including some peat moss and perhaps composted cow manure from the garden center.

223

Try to leave some open space to allow for successive plantings over the season. There should also be room for some truly weedy flowers like Queen Anne's lace (*Daucus carota* var. *carota*) and the sculptural teasel (*Dipsacus sylvestris*).

It's here that we grow our stock of dahlias and gladiolus so that we don't have to rush in digging them up in the fall after their tops naturally brown and become unsightly.

Maintenance of a Cutting Garden

Blooming plants use a great deal of water: All those petals unfurl and expand because of the pressures of water moving through their veins. You should water regularly and always keep an eye open to spot any wilting. When you do water, water well, soaking the soil not just lightly wetting the surface. A mulch might help if you live in an area of the country exposed to hot sun, daily winds, and limited rain fall.

Common sense should rule your maintenance program. Remove dead or dying leaves, dispose of the plants when they are finished with blooming, and continue to remove spent blossoms to encourage the production of flowers. Keep the weeds down.

A Year in the Cutting Garden

With careful planning, a cutting garden will provide bloom from April until well after the first frosts of fall. Daffodils and narcissus can begin the season; their leaves left to mature and die naturally, offend no eye.

By June, the annuals that bloom within eight weeks of sowing, should begin their floral show. Bachelor buttons and coreopsis, larkspur and cosmos should then brighten up July and August.

By now the dill is blooming, ready to be grouped with zinnias and marigolds for a table display of the best of summer. In the back of the cutting garden, a patch of early goldenrod is waiting to be picked and the Mexican sunflowers (*Tithonia* spp.) are shining orange blossoms on six-foot stems.

September brings glads, more dahlias, and ornamental grasses. Then the flowering kale begins its climb to glory: Cool nights with a nip of frost turn the filigreed edges to a frothy white with touches here and there of purple and pink.

When November does roll around and winter hovers in the wings, the cutting garden should be straightened up by removing dead plants and taking all the refuse to the compost bin to help the soil in another year.

After cutting the last of the dried grasses, I roll the snowfence across the front of the vegetable garden in a vain attempt to keep the deer away from the last of the Brussels sprouts.

Appendix 2: On Cutting Fresh Flowers

Always cut fresh flowers early in the morning, when they have had the benefit of night's cooler air. Stems are now tight with water, leaves dappled with dew, and most blossoms have recovered from the excesses of the day before.

Whenever possible, choose burgeoning buds and flowers just beginning to show pollen rather than older blossoms that have already been trod upon by an army of bees.

Bring a bucket of tepid, not cold, water into the garden and plunge the cut stems directly into it. Use a sharp knife or scissors to cut the stems, taking more length than you think you might need to ensure plenty of stem for flower arranging. When cutting, never pull at the stem. This can bruise and damage cell walls, restricting the free movement of water. Cut flowers continue to live and need all the water the stems can take in.

Either cut the stems straight across or at a slant. For years there have been proponents of either course of action, stem-cutters claim that the slant exposes more of the stem end to water and at the same time allows more water intake because the stem end is not resting on the vase bottom. I've found no irrefutable evidence to support either method so opt for the easiest. And keep the bucket in the shade if possible.

Back in the kitchen, check again to see that each stem has a clean cut. Experts advise making a second cut, this time under water, although I've never bothered with that extra step unless I missed the first time around. Now remove the bottom leaves. Those left above the water line continue to lose moisture to the air and those below begin to rot and restrict the water flow into stems.

The next step is most important: Use a sparkling clean container that has been scrubbed of any bacterial growth left over from the previous floral tenants, and change the water every day if possible, always using tepid water to prevent shock to the flowers.

Adding raw sugar to the water, or pennies, or diet soda does nothing except help the growth of bacteria. The University of California conducted an experiment in which a lemon-lime soft drink was added to water (1 part soft drink to 2 parts water) and tests did show that flowers lasted far longer than in plain water. The sugar in the soda apparently feeds the flowers and the acidity inhibits bacterial growth.

The same results can be had by mixing 1 tablespoon of corn syrup and 10 drops of bleach in a quart of warm water. Commercial preparations are available, but I've never tried them.

A few flowers, like poppies, tithonias, and snow-on-the-mountain, contain a milky fluid or sap that will clog stems of other flowers unless it's hardened by a quick pass of the stem end over a candle flame or lighted match. Dahlias also survive for a longer time if their stems are singed.

Appendix 3: Magazines and Newsletters

The following publications are all available by subscription in the United States and Canada, and in addition to many features on gardening in general, include a number of articles on annual plants every year.

The Avant Gardener is a monthly newsletter costing $15 per year and dealing with all aspects of horticulture. It's for the serious amateur and professional, covering news items and developments in horticulture and related subjects.
—Box 489, New York, New York 10028.

Flower and Garden is a bimonthly magazine that's been a friend to gardeners for years. It covers all types of gardening and features a number of articles on annual flowers. Price: $6 per year.
—4251 Pennsylvania Avenue, Kansas City, Missouri 64111.

Green Scene is published by the Pennsylvania Horticultural Society and appears on a bi-monthly schedule with fine articles on gardening. They recently published an entire issue devoted to annuals (July, August 1987). Price: $8.50 per year.
—325 Walnut Street, Philadelphia, Pennsylvania 19106.

Growing from Seed is a new quarterly published by the Thompson & Morgan Seed Company. It deals with all aspects of growing plants from seed and includes much information on annuals in every issue. Price: $9.95 per year.
—P.O. Box 1308, Jackson, New Jersey 08527.

Horticulture is a monthly magazine covering all aspects of gardening and has been one of the more accomplished publications for many years. Price: $18 per year.
—755 Boylston Street, Boston, Massachusetts 02116.

National Gardening was originally *Gardens for All*. It's a monthly magazine dealing with both flowers and vegetables, and a number of annual flowers. Cost: $15 per year.
—180 Flynn Avenue, Burlington, Vermont 05401.

Practical Gardening is Britain's number 1 garden monthly and absolutely fun to get. Much of the information is as useful here as in England and they cover many annuals every year. Cost: $18 per year but exchange rates fluctuate.
—Competition House, Farndon Road, Market Harborough, Leics LE1 9NR, England.

Rodale's Organic Gardening is no longer just for the backyard vegetable garden but today deals with many more sophisticated ideas in gardening and features many articles on annuals. Cost: $12.97 per year.
—33 East Minor Street, Emmaus, Pennsylvania 18098.

Appendix 4: Seed Exchanges

One of the best ways to find unusual seeds for the annual garden (or the perennial garden as well) is by joining one or more of the following organizations. Once a year they send out seed lists to the members and everyone is given an opportunity to choose a set number of species as part of their membership. At the same time interested gardeners are asked to donate seeds from their own gardens in an effort to continually expand the collections.

The Alpine Garden Society is mainly concerned with alpine and rock garden plants. Its quarterly bulletin is stocked with valuable information and photos of rare and unusual plants. The seed exchange is annual and lists well over 4,000 species and include a number of annuals. Both are available to members for $20 per year but varies with the exchange rates.
—Lye End Link, St. Johns, Woking, Surrey GU21 1SW, England.

The American Gourd Society is more American than apple pie. Located in Mount Gilead, Ohio, they publish a newsletter called *The Gourd* that is full of things done with gourds that boggle the imagination and a seed exchange among members. The cost is $2.50 per year.
—Box 274, Mount Gilead, Ohio 43338.

The American Horticultural Society sponsors a seed exchange for members that includes many annuals. It is included with membership

in the society and features a subscription to the *American Horticulturist* at a cost of $20 a year.
—American Horticultural Society, Mount Vernon, Virginia 22121.

The American Rock Garden Society publishes a fine quarterly bulletin and sponsors the biggest seed exchange in the United States and Canada. Over 3,500 different species are offered as part of membership and include many annuals. Cost is $15 per year.
—15 Fairmead Road, Darien, Connecticut 06820.

The Hardy Plant Society is a fine old English organization that publishes various news bulletins and sponsors a fine and select seed exchange that features many annual species. Cost is $8 and varies with the exchange rates.
—10 St. Barnabas Road, Emmer Green, Cabersham, Reading RG4 8RA, England.

Major Howell's International Seed Collection stocks hundreds of varieties of seed from all types of botanical collections throughout the world and includes many unusual annuals. Membership and lists are $10 per year, including the first six seed choices.
—Fire Thorn, 6 Oxshott Way, Cobham, Surrey, KT11 2RT, England.

The Royal Horticultural Society is one of the all-time greats. In addition to *The Garden,* the monthly magazine, a membership includes a free pass to the Chelsea Flower Show, and the seed exchange that covers the world with 1,200 entries, and includes many annual species. The cost is $20 a year but exchange rates vary.
—Vincent Square, London SW1P 2PE, England.

The Scottish Rock Garden Society publishes two fine bulletins a year that deal with alpine plants and sponsors a seed exchange of surprising diversity with 3,200 entries and includes many annual species. Membership is $12 per year.
—21 Merchiston Park, Edinburgh EH10 4PW, Scotland.

Appendix 5: Commercial Seed Companies

The following list consists of catalogs issued by seed companies mostly involved with flowers including a large number of annual varieties. Because of changing costs, I've not included any charges incurred with receiving their publications, so write first.

Remember, too, that each seed company is—at least up to now—unique in one way. Each carries a few species or cultivars that are theirs and theirs alone. Many items will be repeated from house to house, but every catalog will have a few surprises. Over the years, I've dealt with most of the businesses listed below. They will all, I think, deliver satisfaction.

And don't be afraid to send to England for seeds. Your letters should be sent air mail and will usually arrive safely. It just takes longer for shipments.

This list is in no way a complete count of seed companies in business today. Every year there are more.

Abundant Life Seed Foundation, P.O. Box 772, Port Townsend, Washington 98368. Dedicated to keeping species from disappearing from the garden scene.

Applewood Seed Company, 5380 Vivian Street, Arvada, Colorado 80002. A full line of wildflower seeds.

The Banana Tree, 715 Northampton Street, Easton, Pennsylvania 18042. Exotic seeds like bananas and unusual flowers.

Burpee Seeds, Warminster, Pennsylvania 18974. One of the oldest seed companies in the country and developer of the white marigold.

John Chambers, 15 Westleigh Road, Barton Seagrave, Kettering, Northants NN15 5AJ England. A large collection of annual wildflower and grass seeds.

Chiltern Seeds, Bortree Stile, Ulverston, Cumbria LA12 7PB, England. A wonderful seed house with a full line of unusual annuals and something new every year. The home of *Solanum aculeatissimum.*

Companion Plants, Route 6, Box 88, Athens, Ohio 45701. Many annual plants including 14 types of basil (*Ocimum* spp.).

The Cook's Garden, Box 65, Londonderry, Vermont 05148. Unusual gourmet vegetable seeds including lettuce.

The Country Garden, Route 2, Box 455A, Crivitz, Wisconsin 54114. Probably the largest collection of annuals to be found in the U.S. Another excellent place to look for the rare and unique.

DiGiorgi Company, Inc., Council Bluffs, Iowa 51502. Another old American seed house in business for over 80 years. A good selection of annual grasses.

Far North Garden, 16785 Harrison, Livonia, Michigan 48154. Another unusual catalog including a number of rare and different annuals.

The Fragrant Path, Box 328, Fort Calhoun, Nebraska 68023. A wonderful collection of fragrant plants and nightbloomers.

Gleckler's Seedsman, Metamora, Ohio 43540. Giant marigolds are a specialty.

Good Seed, P.O. Box 702, Tonasket, Washington 98855. Vegetables and flowers including the California scorpion weeds, *Phacelia* spp.

Grianan Gardens, P.O. Box 14492, San Francisco, California 94114. A small but charming catalog that lists, for example, six colors of cornflower, *Cyanus* spp.

Gurney's Seed & Nursery Co., Yankton, South Dakota 57079. An old-fashioned catalog with old-fashioned pictures and many interesting varieties of the annual clan.

High Altitude Gardens, P.O. Box 4238, Ketchum, Idaho 83340. A number of annual wildflowers including catchfly, *Silene Armeria.*

C. W. Hosking, Exotic Importer, P.O. Box 500, Hayle, Cornwall, England. Large collection of tropical seeds and the source of *Solanum laciniatum.*

J. L. Hudson, Seedsman, P. O. Box 1058, Redwood City, California 94064. A huge selection of interesting seeds, many of them annuals, from all over the world.

Johnny's Selected Seeds, Albion, Maine 04910. Mostly vegetables but a good section of selected annuals from a fine nursery, now an American institution.

Jung Quality Seeds, Randolph, Wisconsin 53956. Another fine old American seed house with many annual flower selections.

Lafayette Home Nursery, Inc. Lafayette, Illinois 61449. Seeds of prairie plants and native grasses.

LeMarch Seeds International, P.O. Box 566, Dixon, California 95620. Many unusual gourmet vegetable seeds.

Maver Rare Perennials, Route 2, Box 265B, Asheville, North Carolina 28805. A majestic collection of seeds and featuring many, many rare and relatively unknown annuals including grasses.

Earl May Seed & Nursery, Shenandoah, Iowa 51603. One more famous American nursery with a large selection of annual flower seeds.

Moon Mountain Wildflowers, P.O. Box 34, Morro Bay, California 93442. Their catalog includes an entire section of annual wildflowers and features blazing star, *Mentzelia lindleyi.*

Nichol's Herb and Rare Seeds, 1190 N. Pacific Highway, Albany, Oregon 97321. A large selection of special seeds including a number of everlasting annuals.

Olds Seed Company, P.O. Box 7790, 2901 Packers Avenue, Madison, Wisconsin 53707. An old and trusted firm featuring many annuals and unusual vegetable selections.

Geo. W. Park Seed Company, Greenwood, South Carolina 29647. One of the most famous seed companies in America with many unusual varieties of annual flowers.

Pinetree Garden Seeds, New Gloucester, Maine 04260. A fine catalog that includes an entire section devoted to annuals.

Plants of the Southwest, 1812 Second Street, Santa Fe, New Mexico 87501. A charming catalog with many unusual annual wildflowers and grasses.

Clyde Robin Seed Company, P.O. Box 2855, Castro Valley, California 94546. One of the first sources of native American wildflowers, both annuals and perennials. They carry many specialized wildflower mixes.

Shepherd's Garden Seeds, 7389 West Zayante Road, Felton, California 95018. An attractive catalog with much information on fancy vegetables and a good annual flower mix.

R.H. Shumway, Rockford, Illinois 61101. Another American institution in the world of seeds with many varieties of annuals.

Stokes Seed Company, Box 548, Buffalo, New York 14240. A number of annual seeds.

Thompson & Morgan, P.O. Box 100, Farmingdale, New Jersey. One of the oldest of England's seed houses, now with an American office and a catalog with many color pictures and highlighting a vast selection of seeds for annual plants.

Otis Twilley Seed Company, P.O. Box 65, Trevose, Pennsylvania 19047. The last of the American institutions on our list and stocking a number of varieties of annuals.

Woodruff Farms, RD 2, Whitehall, New York 12887. A number of annual flowers including an old-fashioned mix for a beautiful annual bed.

Appendix 6: **Garden and Greenhouse Equipment**

The following firms stock tools, garden gadgets, seed supplies, and many greenhouse items.

Charley's Greenhouse Supplies, 1569 Memorial Highway, Mount Vernon, Washington 98273. A major supplier of greenhouse-related items, including the new bubble insulation.

Clapper's, 1125 Washington Street, West Newton, Massachusetts 02165. Tools, garden furniture, and garden lighting.

Gardener's Supply Co., 128 Intervale Road, Burlington, Vermont 05401. Many interesting and well-made garden tools including the best long-handled trowel and Reemay cloth, perfect for protecting plants against frost.

Gro-tek Supplies, South Berwick, Maine 03908. Greenhouse supplies and sun shades for greenhouse glass.

A.M. Leonard, Inc., 6665 Spiker Road, Piqua, Ohio 45356. A major source for horticultural tools and seed supplies.

Mellinger's, 2310 W. South Range Road, North Lima, Ohio 44452. A large catalog of seeds, supplies, tools, and other horticultural items.

Walt Nicke, Box 433, McLeod Lane, Topsfield, Massachusetts 01983. The original garden supplier with a catalog that's like a supermarket for all kinds of garden equipment featuring many items from England.

Smith & Hawken Tool Company, Inc., 25 Corte Madera, Mill Valley, California 94941. Quality garden tools and watering devices.

Bibliography

Britton, Nathaniel Lord, and Addison Brown. *An Illustrated Flora of the Northern United States and Canada.* 3 vols. 1913. Reprint. New York: Dover, 1970.

Covers just about all the wild plants growing in the United States. Many names have changed but it's still an excellent reference especially for wild annuals.

Crockett, James Underwood. *Annuals.* New York: Time-Life Books, 1971.

One of the best books in the *Time-Life Encyclopedia of Gardening* written by a man who actually gardened in addition to writing excellent books. Fine watercolor illustrations by Allianora Rosse.

Dictionary of Gardening. The Royal Horticultural Society. 4 vols. and supplement. Oxford: Clarendon, 1965.

Next to Hortus Third, these volumes are the most used in my library. Fascinating not only for advice on plants and planting, but for history, too.

Encyclopedia of Organic Gardening. The staff of Organic Gardening Magazine. Emmaus, Pennsylvania: Rodale Press, 1978.

For all the information needed to grow a fine garden of flowers without resorting to artificial chemicals, this is the reference book to use.

Fell, Derek. *Annuals, How to Select, Grow, and Enjoy.* Tuscon, Arizona, 1983.

A great deal about annuals with clear, color photos of the more common varieties.

Hortus Third. New York: Macmillan, 1976.

This is the monumental revision of L. H. Bailey and Ethel Zoe Bailey's original work of nomenclature for the American gardener and horticulturist, overseen by the staff of the L. H. Bailey Hortorium at Cornell University. Very expensive but worth talking your local library into acquiring it, if they haven't already.

Hottes, Alfred C. *A Little Book of Annuals.* New York: A.T. DeLaMare Company, Inc., 1925.

A charming book with timeless information and good garden plans (often used without credits), and an excellent tabular index of plant culture.

Jekyll, Gertrude. *Annuals and Biennials.* London: Country Life, n.d.

The classic English gardener writes about the classic English garden approach to annual flowers. Since climate rarely completely rules the life of an annual, this is a far more valuable book than those on perennials.

Nehrling, Arno and Irene Nehrling. *The Picture Book of Annuals,* 1966. Reprint New York: Arco Publishing Company, Inc., 1977.

Although dealing mainly with the more common annuals, there is a wealth of information and very good black & white photos.

Ortloff, Henry Stuart. *A Garden Bluebook of Annuals and Biennials.* New York: Doubleday, Doran & Company, Inc. 1924.

Another interesting book on annuals written by a landscape architect and containing many bits of information on more unusual types.

Pizzetti, Ippolito, and Henry Cocker. *Flowers: A Guide for Your Garden.* 2 vols. New York: Harry N. Abrams, 1975.

Using the fine color plates from the great eighteenth- and nineteenth-century botanical periodicals for a starting-off point, these books cover both history and culture of a host of garden annuals.

Reilly, Ann. *Park's Success with Seeds.* Greenwood South Carolina: Geo. W. Park Seed Co., Inc., 1978.

Covers a great deal of information on growing both annuals and perennials from seed with color pictures of all the plants described.

Rice, Graham. *A Handbook of Annuals and Bedding Plants.* Portland, Oregon: Timber Press, 1986.

Although Graham Rice writes from an English garden and with an English point of view, this is a valuable book to consult on growing annual plants.

Taylor, Norman, ed. *The Practical Encyclopedia of Gardening.* New York: Garden City Publishing Company, Inc. 1936.

This edition is the book to look for, not the fourth which turned out to be a "cut and paste" job that edited out the marvelous asides that the older edition was famous for. A book for dipping into when you cannot go out to the garden but the muse is sitting on your shoulder.

Taylor's Guide to Annuals. Boston: Houghton Mifflin, 1986.

One of a series of books based on the Taylor *Encyclopedia of Gardening.* It features descriptive color photographs and detailed entries on many unusual annuals. I was pleased to edit the flower descriptions and choose the original list of plants featured.

Vick, Edward C. *Audels Gardeners and Growers Guide,* vol. 4. New York: Theol Audel & Co., 1928.

Timeless information on seeds, hotbeds and coldframes and a number of descriptions of annual plants. Makes one wish for the old days of gardening to return.

Index

'Covent Garden', 12, 70
'Shell Pink', 15

H
Half-hardy annuals, definition of, x
Halpin, Anne, vii
Hardening-off, 31
Hardy annuals, definition of, x
Hare's-tail grass, 181
Hawk's beard, 58
Hawkweed, 109
Heart-pea, 198
Heating cables, 29
Helianthus annuus, 4, 70, **70**
  'Autumn Beauty', 70
  'Italian White', 71, **71**
  'Piccolo', 71
  'Sungold', 70
  'Teddy Bear', **130**
Helichrysum bracteatum, 9, 71, **71**
  'Monstrosum', 71
Heliophila leptophylla, 71, **71**
  linearifolia, 71
  longifolia, 71
Heliotrope, 72
Heliotropium arborescens, 72, **72**
Helipterum Manglesii, 9, 72, **72**
Herb Robert, 163
Heron's bill, 64
Heuchera spp., **134**
  'Purple Palace', 72, **72**
  sanguinea, 3, **134**
Hibiscus, 36
  'Frisbee Hybrid', 73, **73**
  acetosella 'Red Shield', 163, **163**
Hippodamia spp., 23
Holiday peppers, 143
Hollyhocks, 138
Hon Tsai Tai, 154
Honeycombed paper, 28, **28**
Hops, common, 206
  Japanese, 206
Hordeum jubatum, 180, **180**
Horned poppy, 69
Hottes, Alfred C., 3
Humulus japonicus, 13, 206, **207**
  Lupulus, 206, **207**
Hunnemannia fumariifolia, 5, 73, **73**
Husk tomatoes, 97
Hybrid seeds, definition of, xii
Hyoscyamine, 60
Hyoscyamus niger, 73, **73**
Hypoestes phyllostachya, 164, **164**

I
Iberis amara, 74, **74**
  'Empress', 12
  'Giant Hyacinth', 74
  umbellata, 74
Ice plants, 84

Iceland poppy, 92
Iceplant, 131
Icicle plants, 84
Immortelles, 147
Impatience, 74
Impatiens, **122**
  Balsamina, 74, **74**
  glandulifera, 75
  'New Guinea', 75, **75**
  oncidioides, **75**
  roylei, 75
  Wallerana, 75
Indian shot, 156
Insecticides, 22
Ionopsidium acaule, 75, **75**
Ipomoea alba, 8, 208, **208**
  Batatas, 208
  coccinea, 209, **209**
  x *multifida*, 209, **209**
  Nil, 209
    'Scarlet O'Hara', 209
  purpurea, 209
    'Madame Anne', 209
  Quamoclit, 209, **209**
  tricolor, **126**, 210, **210**
Irish lace, 171
Italian red clover, 111
Ivy-leaved geraniums, 94, **94**

J
Japanese beetles, 22
Jekyll, Gertrude, 12
Jewel-of-the-Veldt, 111
Jiffy-7's, 28, **28**
Jimson weed, 60
Job's tears, 178
Johnny-jump-up, 114, **115**
Joseph's-Coat, 1, 152
Juncus bufonias, 181, **181**
Juno's tears, 178

K
Kenilworth ivy, 59
Kiss-me-over-the-garden-gate, 97
Knotweeds, 98
Kochia scoparia, **144**
  Forma *trichophylla*, 164, **165**
    'Acapulco Silver', 164
Kudzu, 216

L
Ladybugs, 23
Lagenaria siceraria, 8, 13, 211, **211**
Lagurus ovatus, 11, 181, **181**
  'Nanus', 181
Lamarckia aurea, 182, **182**
Land, Nancy, vii
Larkspurs, 56
Lathyrus odorata, 212, **212**, 213, **213**
Latin names, see scientific names

Latuca 'Red Sails', 16, 166
  'Ruby', 16, 166
Lavatera trimestris, 76, **76**
  'Mont Blanc', 12, 76
  'Silver Cup', 15, 76, **125**
Layia platyglossa, 76, **76**
Lazy daisy, 43
Lecher, W. S., 173
Legousia Speculum Veneris, 76, 77
Light stimulation, xiii
Limnanthes Douglasii, 77, **77**, **136**
Limonium spp., 9
  Bonduellii, 77
  sinuatum, 77, **77**
  Suworowii, 77
Linanthus dianthiflorus, 78
  dichotomus, 78
  grandiflorus, 78, **78**, **122**
Linaria maroccana, 78, **78**
  'Fairy Bouquet', 78
Linnaeus, 200
Linum grandiflorus, 10, 78, **78**
  'Coccineum', 78
  'Roseum', 78
  'Rubrum', 78
  usitatissimum, 79, **79**
Lisianthus, 66
Little Book of Annuals, 3
Livingston daisy, 84
Loam, definition of, 19
Lobelia erinus, 79, **79**
  'Cambridge Blue', 79
  'Crystal Palace', 79
  'Pumila Snowball', 79
  'Queen Victoria', 79
  'Rosamund', 79
Lobularia maritima, 5, 6, 7, 79, **79**
  'Little Dorrit', 79
  'Rosie O'Day', 79
Lonas annua, 80, **80**
Lonchocarpus spp., 22
Love apple, 170, 171
Love-in-a-mist, 89, 143
Love-in-a-puff, 198
Love-lies-bleeding, 40
Lucrezia Borgia, 73
Luffa aegyptiaca, 214, **214**
Lupinus densiflorus, 80
  Hartwegii, 80
  luteus, 80
  subcarnosus, 80
  texensis, 10, 80, **80**, **135**
Lychnis Coeli-rosa, 81, **81**
  Coronaria, 81
  vaccaria, 112

M
Machaeranthera tanacetifolia, 81, **81**
Macmillan, H. F., 218
Madeira vine, 195
Malabar nightshade, 196